Tales of
NANTUCKET

*Chronicles &
Characters of
America's
Favorite Island*

This work is dedicated to my parents, Lawrence F. Mooney
and Ethel L. Mooney, who are still a part of Nantucket.

Tales of Nantucket
By Robert F. Mooney
Edited by Katherine Becker
Illustrations by Diane Swartz
Book Design by Graphic Arts Consortium

©1990, 2004 by Robert F. Mooney
ISBN 0-9627851-0-5

Library of Congress Catalog Card Number 90-70591
First Printing 1990
Second Printing 1994
Third Printing 1999
Fourth Printing 2004

Tales of NANTUCKET

by Robert F. Mooney

Illustrated by
Diane Swartz

WESCO PUBLISHING
Nantucket Island   MA

ACKNOWLEDGEMENTS

This book is the result of my lifetime interest in the history of Nantucket. Over the years, many people have given me advice and assistance. They include Barbara Andrews, Kathryn Becker, Mimi Beman, Lee Burne, Alcon Chadwick, Adam Craig, Albert F. Egan, Allen Holdgate, Henry Kehlenbeck, Gayl Michael, Mary Miles, Eileen McGrath, Janice O'Mara, and John Newell Welch. The research has principally relied upon the Nantucket Atheneum and the Peter Foulger Museum. I have also had the benefit of the wisdom of Nantucket's greatest historian, Edouard A. Stackpole, who has given me his advice and encouragement over many years.

My special thanks to my graphic artists, Fred and Diane Swartz for their designs and illustrations, which have added much to this work.

To all these people and many others who rendered their assistance, I express my gratitude.

Robert F. Mooney

PREFACE

A WORLD OF DIFFERENCE

These stories are about the island of Nantucket and some of the people who have played a part in its colorful history.

There is something special about life on an island and about the people who live there. They tend to take on the character of the island, with its virtues and faults, as unpredictable as its weather. Even after they are gone, they continue to be part of the island atmosphere.

These people are still here in Nantucket. You cannot see them, but you know they are still with you. You know it as you walk the streets on a wet, chilly night when the fog is full of their memories. You can stand in front of the small office building where the mysterious doctor worked, haunted by his past. You can hike to the lonely hill where another doctor, a century later, disappeared forever. You can step across the wet stones of the lower town square and see where banks were looted, fortunes were lost and dreams were destroyed.

Throughout its history, Nantucket has been an island of independence, with a tradition reflected in its residents. They are often described as independent, proud, stubborn, willful and loyal to traditions. They can be critical of neighbors and cordial to strangers, open and secretive, tolerant and narrow-minded. As the life of the island made them different, so they made the island a different place to live. It was this special perception of the world which created the Nantucket character and developed the difference of island life.

Some of these stories are drawn from the mainstream of history, involving celebrated figures and famous events. Others come from the undercurrents of the island's hidden history. There are mysterious stories of strange people and shocking events which disrupted the community; criminal cases which revealed the darkest side of island life; and heroic tales of islanders who risked their lives to rescue strangers to their shores. From past to present, they tell the story of Nantucket from the island point of view.

That view may be fading with the years, but the memories are worth preserving, reminding us of the Nantucket which often cast a different outlook on the world, but always kept its best stories to itself.

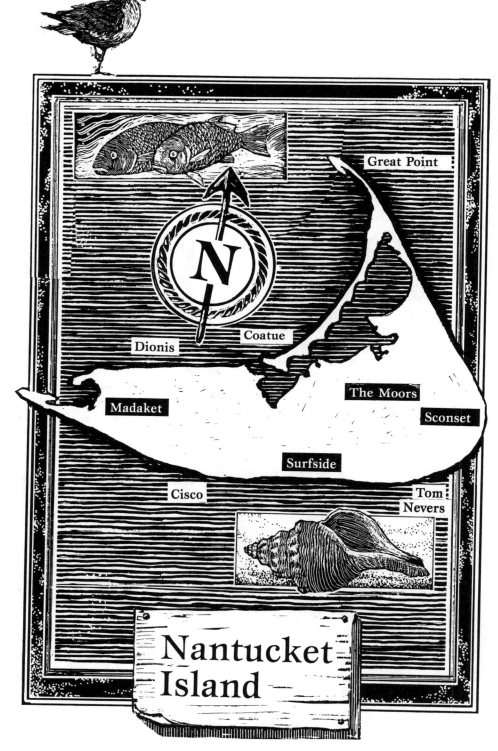

Great Point

Dionis

Coatue

Madaket

The Moors

Sconset

Surfside

Cisco

Tom Nevers

Nantucket Island

CONTENTS

CHAPTER ONE

NANTUCKET'S MYSTERIOUS DOCTOR

In the year 1862, two distinguished gentlemen arrived in Nantucket from New Bedford and announced that they intended to establish a medical office on the island, under the name of Macomber and Franklin. Doctor Macomber was an elderly gentleman and his partner was a handsome young man about thirty years of age, with a trim beard and a distinguished appearance. Although both men were strangers in town, they were welcomed by the small community and their practice flourished. However, Doctor Macomber decided to retire within a year and returned to New Bedford, leaving his younger partner to carry on as a sole practitioner.

A business card was published in the local paper:

"Dr. Franklin, respectfully announces to the people of Nantucket, that he may be found in his office on Broad Street, first door below the Ocean House. Office hours from 8 to 9 morning, and from 1 to 3 afternoons."

The doctor's office was located at 5 Broad Street, in a small wooden building which still exists below the Jared Coffin House as the site of the Nantucket Bookworks. The somewhat unusual office hours were due to the fact the doctor spent most of the day making house calls.

Nantucket's new doctor was known as Augustus E. Franklin, and in the early years he practiced as both a physician and dentist. He was an avid horseman, and soon acquired a handsome pair of horses, which he drove while making house calls. He joined the Masons and the Odd Fellows, invested in local real estate, and became part owner of a drug store on Main Street, known as Pitman and Ellis. He was professionally industrious, was considered the leading physician on the Island and became one of the most successful and popular men

1

in the community.

Despite his popularity, the doctor had few close friends and the townspeople knew little about his background. It was rumored he was worth "about $6000," a sizable sum, and a figure which seemed to recur in his background. During this Civil War era, when the Nantucketers were vitally concerned with the conflict, he was questioned once about life in the southern states, but he quickly changed the subject. Nevertheless, he seemed to fit into Nantucket society perfectly.

Such an attractive man could not go unnoticed by the ladies of Nantucket, and the doctor was much in demand for social engagements. This led to his acquaintance with one of the most eligible young ladies of the Island, the daughter of a successful local businessman. He was greatly attracted to the local beauty, and their courtship proceeded through the usual ritual of public social affairs and family-sponsored parties. She returned his affection and considered herself fortunate to be courted by Nantucket's most attractive and unattached professional man. After they received the formal approval from her father, a date was set for their wedding, which promised to be a great event on the Island social scene.

The doctor had lived on Nantucket about eight years, and had acquired a considerable fortune in local real estate in addition to his successful medical practice. He seemed to be at the peak of his career, with a solid financial background and the prospect of a very promising future. Yet, as the date for his wedding approached, the doctor seemed to grow visibly nervous and ill at ease. He gave no explanation for his condition, but he suddenly sent a message to his young lady saying that the wedding could never take place.

While his fiancee and her family were still reeling from the shock of the broken engagement, the doctor abruptly and without explanation closed his medical practice, sold off his property and left Nantucket, without any indication of his destination or his intentions. To the wonder of the small Nantucket community of 1870, its favorite doctor had suddenly disappeared.

The local newspaper wrote in amazement that Doctor Franklin had departed the Island, "under circumstances that seem to indicate that his departure was a final one." The sudden departure after the rejection of the impending marriage caused a sensation in the town, and the resulting rumors kept Nantucketers in gossip for a full year. One story held that the brother of the young lady had begun to investigate the doctor's background and believed he was operating under a false name and credentials. Another story suggested the strong possibility there had been a previous marriage in his background. There emerged another story which could not be proven on the Island: that the doctor had been told by an informant that his previous wife, whom he believed to be dead, was, in fact, alive. This informant demanded payment to keep the story quiet. In any event, whether to avoid disgrace or blackmail, the doctor decided to break his engagement and leave the Island.

The young lady in question, although shocked by the strange behavior of her betrothed, soon recovered from the blow to her pride. She became quite an object of interest to other men in town, and soon accepted another suitor who made it to the church. She had a happy marriage and raised several children in Nantucket.

Sixteen months after his sudden departure, the doctor just as suddenly returned to Nantucket. The islanders were startled to see his handsome face as he stepped ashore on Steamboat Wharf and began the familiar walk up Broad Street, toward the old office, where his practice had been carried on in the same building by Doctor Livor. He cheerfully announced, "he would be pleased to see the faces of his old friends whom he had so faithfully treated in years preceeding."

But there was a change, and this time the business card read: "Dr. Franklin A. Ellis would respectfully inform his patrons and friends that he has removed his office to the building on Broad Street formerly occupied by him, and recently occupied by Dr. J. Livor, where he will be found ready to attend all cases, by day or night. Office hours from 8 to 9 o'clock morning, and 1 to 2 afternoons."

The people of the town were delighted to see their favorite doctor back at work, but everyone questioned the reason for the change of name. The doctor stated only that "he was now at liberty to use his family name," which was, in fact, Franklin Augustus Ellis. He gave no other explanation for his use of the previous reversed name, nor for his unexplained absence from the Island.

The Doctor's friends and clients on the Island soon returned to him and his professional business increased. He was, if possible, more popular and successful than in his first eight-year career on Nantucket. He was a dedicated and tireless practitioner, making house calls at all hours of the day and night. He gave his time and skill to people from all walks of life, regardless of means, and was known for often buying food for the hungry families he visited.

The doctor's paying clients were many, and he invested his growing fortune with foresight and in the community interest, showing genuine concern for the welfare of the Island. His special interest was in fine horses and farms, which led to his election as President of the Nantucket Agricultural Society. On Main Street, his name was perpetuated on the drug store of Pitman & Ellis. In Sconset, he was a partner in Sunset Heights, one of the earliest developments of the summer cottage colony. In town he was the owner of several acres of prime land near the Cliff. He was a part owner of the Ocean View House, the first hotel in Sconset. He also invested in the optimistic plans of the Nantucket Railroad, another boost to the local economy, destined to promote the real estate ventures in Surfside and Sconset. When President U.S. Grant arrived for the first presidential visit to Nantucket in 1874, the doctor was one of the local dignitaries chosen to greet the presidential entourage.

Despite his success and popularity, the doctor had few close friends on the Island, and his background remained a mystery to most of his neighbors. Although he would not discuss his personal life with his friends, this did not diminish their respect for him. In 1882, Edward K. Godfrey wrote his famous guide book on Nantucket, and dedicated it:

"To Franklin A. Ellis, M.D., for many years my tried and trusted friend in sickness, in health, in prosperity and adversity, I dedicate this little book as a slight testimonial of my regard for him as a man and physician." For twelve more years, the career of the doctor was marked by increasing prosperity and respect in the community. As the rising tide of the summer resort business seemed to lift the spirit of the island community, the increasing fortunes of Doctor Ellis seemed to promise well for his future.

In 1883, things began to change. Although he was still a comparatively young man, the doctor began to show the signs of overwork and fatigue. His friends suggested he take a rest or a vacation from his strenuous practice, which he refused to do. He appeared to lapse into a strange and distracted state of mind, and his robust physical appearance started to decline. Early in 1884, the doctor suddenly closed his medical practice for the second time, and left Nantucket, alone.

A month later, Doctor Franklin A. Ellis was found lying in a Boston hotel room, showing signs of drug addiction. Morphine was the drug of choice in that era, freely available to physicians, and the powerful pain-killing drug had taken its toll. He moved to the Bay State House in Worcester, where he lived until his behavior caused annoyance to the other guests, reportedly making them "decidedly uncomfortable." The doctor made one final move, to his sister's home in Monson, Massachusetts, where he died on May 24, 1884, described in the press as "a victim of the opium habit."

Doctor Ellis was mourned by his friends as a departed and beloved benefactor of Nantucket. At the time of his death, he owned a great deal of valuable real estate, and there was genuine concern about the disposition of this property, together with curiosity about what his will might reveal about his mysterious background. The curious were not satisfied to learn that his will made a single bequest to a local friend, then left the residue of the estate to his legal heirs, according to the laws of Massachusetts. There was no executor named in the will, so Nantucket's only attorney, Allen Coffin, Esquire, was appointed administrator of the estate.

Although it was not realized at the time, the will of Doctor Ellis was to become a source of great tribulation and would lead to the final surprising chapter in the doctor's troubled tale. The will was hardly any will at all, for its disposition of the estate to his "legal heirs," was merely stating what would have happened if no will existed, and, by naming no executor, the doctor left the settlement of his estate to whomever the court might appoint. Perhaps the doctor did this deliberately, but at this stage of his life, his motives were unclear.

Attorney Coffin set about to settle the doctor's affairs. He determined that his legal heirs were his three sisters, the only personal relatives he was able to discover. Therefore, the attorney paid the estate's debts and settled the personal property on the three sisters in equal shares. He then filed his final account, to which the sisters assented. The court allowed his account and the attorney believed his responsibilities were ended.

Allen Coffin was an experienced practitioner and a highly-regarded member of the legal profession. He undoubtedly did the best he could with the settlement of the Ellis estate, for which he was paid $600, but the doctor's tangled affairs were to trouble him and cause future grief. Under Massachusetts law, an administrator who is uncertain of the identity of the heirs of a deceased is obliged to file a petition in the probate court to ascertain them before making distributions of the estate. This was not done by Attorney Coffin before making payment to the Ellis sisters.

The three sisters retained Attorney George H. Newton of Monson, who came to Nantucket to dispose of some of their real estate at public auction. In addition to his office on Broad Street, the doctor owned a home on Ash Lane, a half interest in the Ocean View House and several cottages in Sconset, and 48 acres of land at Miacomet. In the course of one of the real estate auctions, a Nantucketer casually asked the attorney what would be the effect if it were learned that Doctor Ellis had a surviving wife and child. The heirs thought this was a sly attempt to devalue the worth of the property they had inherited, and paid no attention to the inquiry, and proceeded to give warranty deeds to the purchasers.

When Attorney Newton returned home from Nantucket, he received a letter from a man named Ephraim Cleveland of San Francisco, inquiring about the Ellis estate. He was again asked the question, what the effect would be if it was discovered that Doctor Ellis had been married and had a child living. This prompted the attorney to travel to California, where he met with Cleveland in Santa Ana, and learned the astonishing tale of Doctor Ellis.

Franklin A. Ellis had been born in New Salem, Massachusetts, about 1832, and he and Cleveland had travelled south from Worcester to Gaylesville, Alabama in 1859. Cleveland taught writing in the southern town, while Ellis taught school and practiced as a dentist. Both men boarded with a minister named Fleming. They made the acquaintance of a widow named Paty, who had a daughter named Martha Paty, and in the fall of 1860, Franklin Ellis and Martha Paty were married by the Reverend Fleming, with Cleveland standing up for them. In 1861, with the threat of the Civil War growing, Ellis persuaded his mother-in-law to sell her small plantation and few slaves for $15,000 in gold coin and move north.

Franklin Ellis and his wife Martha, together with the widow Paty, moved to Morea, Illinois, where the widow bought a small farm outside of town. This purchase left her with about $6000 in gold, which she concealed in a trunk in the attic of their farmhouse. A few days after their arrival in Morea, Ellis left the house for the purpose of picking up some furniture which was expected at the train depot. He never returned, and was never again seen by his wife and mother-in-law. A few days later, they discovered the trunk in the attic contained only 100 copper cents, a 50-cent piece, and two bricks. The new husband and the $6000 in gold were missing.

Attorney Newton travelled on to Morea, where he learned that after the disappearance of Ellis, his family fell into dire circumstances, and the abandoned wife was forced to struggle to make a living. Furthermore, it was learned that Mrs. Ellis had been in "a delicate condition" when her husband left. She later gave birth to a daughter, named Sarah Anna Ellis. The birth was attended by Doctor Josiah Brown, who gave the attorney an affidavit of the facts. The widow Paty died a year or two later and the young mother and daughter moved away, supposedly to Tennessee, where the mother died about ten years later.

The lawyer now began that thankless task of searching for the lost daughter in the hills of Tennessee. He pressed the search deep into the moonshine country of eastern Tennessee, at some risk, where he was accosted by a gang of local men who were convinced the well-dressed Yankee must be a revenue officer, and threatened him at gunpoint until he explained his mission. He then hit upon the idea of writing a letter to every postmaster in Tennessee, asking for the whereabouts of a certain Sarah Anna Ellis, now about 27 years old.

One morning, in front of a small town post office deep in eastern Tennessee, a local postmaster decided to read Attorney Newton's letter aloud to the illiterate white men loitering outside the post office. As he was doing so, an old man named W.M. Dixon drove up in his wagon and listened. He then announced that he knew the Ellis girl; she was his housekeeper.

Newton arrived to meet the young woman at the Dixon house, and later described her as a "hewer of wood and drawer of water" for the household. She could neither read nor write, but she could remember the story about her father as told to her many years ago by her mother. The lawyer told her she was probably her father's sole heir and he arranged for her to live with a cousin in Alabama where she was taught reading and writing. After being schooled and groomed, Sarah Anna Ellis was brought to Massachusetts, hoping to claim her fortune.

Her attorneys brought two law suits on her behalf. The first was a petition in the Nantucket Probate Court to vacate the account of Allen Coffin as administrator of the estate. The second was a suit in the Supreme Judicial Court against Coffin and the Ellis sisters to recover the money paid them as beneficiaries. In a jury trial held at Taunton, with Justice Oliver Wendell Holmes, Jr., presiding, the jury was asked to answer two special questions:

1. Is the Petitoner, Sarah Ellis, the person described in the residuary clause of the will?

2. Is the Petitioner, Sarah Ellis, the child of Franklin A. Ellis and his wife, Martha Paty?

The jury answered both questions in the affirmative, and Sarah Ellis became an heiress. In Nantucket, the decree of the Probate Court was reversed, the estate was reopened, and the administrator was charged with all the sums he had paid the Ellis sisters as supposed heirs. Attorney Coffin was, therefore, personally liable for the $6000 he had paid the sisters because he had done so without obtaining a judicial determination of the heirs, after proper notice, before distributing the estate. The attorney was now obliged to sue his former clients for $2000 each, which they could not produce because they had spent it. Although they agreed to share the loss, they did not have the means, and the Nantucket attorney had to pay the final settlement from his own pocket.

Coffin was not the only person caught in the legal jam. Several people had bought land in Nantucket from the Ellis sisters. Sarah Ellis' attorneys brought suit against the purchasers of this land, claiming the deeds were void. The purchasers in turn brought suit against the Ellis sisters for delivering fraudulent deeds. It took years to untangle the web of tangled transactions. The estate of Doctor Ellis proved to be as complex as his career.

As the tale unfolded, Nantucket wondered how the kindly Island doctor could have perpetrated such a great injustice upon his pregnant wife and unborn child--a wrong which seemed destined to ruin the lives and fortunes of many innocent people. Many Nantucketers simply refused to believe it. Some felt his medical career was an attempt to atone in later life for the great wrong he had committed in abandoning his family. Others concluded that he had successfully led a double life, and had executed his strange will as a belated attempt to do the right thing.

One thing was certain: Doctor Ellis had many defenders on Nantucket. When the local newspaper, the *Inquirer & Mirror*, published the full story of Attorney Newton's discovery of the lost daughter of Doctor Ellis, it was severely criticized by many of the doctor's friends. In the interest of bringing forth "the right side in this very peculiar case," the *Inquirer & Mirror* felt obliged to publish the details of a private letter to a party in town, from a person whose name was withheld, but who had been " in a position to know whereof he speaks."

This person related that he had read the story of Doctor Ellis in the *Chicago Times*, that he had known the truth since 1870, and had "known it more correctly than it was told in the papers." He knew about Martha Paty but claimed that the child she bore was a son, not a daughter, and that Ellis did not know of the child's existence. He advised that Ephraim Cleveland's story was not to be trusted and that attorney Newton should look up the whole of Cleveland's record. He also hinted darkly that a man named William Drew could tell much more and should be brought forward to testify concerning Doctor Ellis and his legal heirs.

The informant claimed the money theft was misstated; that Ellis had only one thousand dollars of his mother-in-law's money when he left Illinois which he gave to someone he trusted to return to her, and had been assured that this was done. He was therefore not a thief in the usual sense of the word. Some time before the doctor's engagement in Nantucket, he was informed that his wife had died, so he felt free to marry. Shortly before the scheduled wedding, an informer proved to him that Martha was still alive, but promised to keep silent if paid well. The doctor refused the blackmail, broke off the engagement and left town, keeping a foolish silence rather than telling the whole sad story.

According to this story, the doctor had left his estate to his "legal heirs" because of his personal uncertainty about his background and the identity of his heirs. He suspected there might be a living child of his and he wanted to do justice to the child. This was a charitable interpretation of his strange story but these facts were never verified.

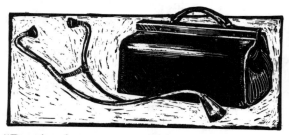

After reciting the various stories concerning the doctor's life, the Nantucket newspaper concluded its obituary of Franklin A. Ellis with these words: "Despite the mystery which hung about him, he had noble traits of character that endeared him to most of mankind."

Many years later, a researcher tried to delve into the medical background of the doctor. There was little professional regulation of the medical profession in those days, and there were many homeopathic practitioners who carried on the basics of general practice with scanty formal training. This research revealed there had never been a graduate of any medical school in the United States named Augustus E. Franklin or Franklin A. Ellis. One must conclude that Nantucket's favorite doctor had enormous talent and considerable skill to practice so successfully for almost twenty years.

The final chapter of the story was left to Allen Coffin, the Nantucket attorney, who selected the monument for the lonely grave in Monson, Massachusetts, and chose the following epitaph which reads like a prophecy:

"God hath his mysteries of grace,
Ways we cannot tell;
He hides them deep, like the secret sleep
Of him He loved so well."

CHAPTER TWO

THE MISSING RECORD

Captain John Gardner arrived on Nantucket in 1672 at the invitation of Tristram Coffin and the other First Purchasers, who needed a master mariner and leader of men to promote the cod-fishing industry on the island. Had they known the full range of his talents, Coffin and his partners would have let Gardner remain in Salem, where his leadership skills had already been noticed in town meetings. He was not only a skillful sailor but also a popular figure in the town, with the makings of a clever politician. Before his long and colorful career was over, John Gardner succeeded in molding the character of Nantucket to his own independent image.

The first settlers of Nantucket were men and women of character and energy, marked by an outstanding spirit of independence. They had no sooner separated themselves from the confines of the Massachusetts Bay Colony than they established their own government on the offshore islands of Martha's Vineyard and Nantucket, seeking to preserve their independence from the mainland. They very quickly showed the world how independent islanders could be.

The First Purchasers, ten white men of wealth and ambition, purchased the island of Nantucket in 1659 from Thomas Mayhew, the powerful Governor of Martha's Vineyard, for the purpose of establishing an agricultural community at sea, free from the political and religious repression of the Massachusetts Bay Colony. In addition to the freedom and financial promise which the island offered, they also saw it as an opportunity to spread Christianity among the Indian inhabitants, a goal which inspired many English colonists.

The leader of the First Purchasers was Tristram Coffin, the First Magistrate of the island, who arrived from Essex County with the first settlers. These ten men each selected a partner to share the financial venture, and these twenty men became the original Proprietors of the Island of Nantucket. Several of the Proprietors were solely mainland investors who never lived on the island. Upon their arrival, the settlers were met by local Indian sachems, who represented the Indian population of about 1500 living on the island. The Indians welcomed the white men and offered no objections to the early plans for colonizing the western end of the island.

At their first organizational meeting, the Proprietors devoted themselves to settling problems of land ownership and developing a civilized manner of dealing with the Indians. In accordance with the directions of their spiritual leaders, the settlers announced they would pay the Indians for each parcel of land they acquired. This was a generous concession by the English, since the current legal doctrine of that day held that all territory inhabited by uncivilized people was owned by the King by right of discovery. To prevent unfair dealing with the natives, it was also agreed that no individual could buy land from the Indians and all purchases would be made by the Proprietorship.

Once the Indian deeds were acquired and paid for, the colony was established around the small harbor at Capaum on the north shore of the island. Here the Proprietors set about surveying and dividing up the land on Nantucket. Except for allotted house lots and common public necessities, the entire area of the island was held in common ownership by the Proprietors, a form of ownership derived from the County of Devon, the ancestral home of many of the settlers. This was also a means of facilitating the development of the sheep-raising industry, since the sheep were allowed to graze at will about the island. The early days of the colony were harmonious but not very prosperous, and the Proprietors began to make plans to bolster the island economy.

It soon became apparent that the island needed more than sheep farmers to develop into a prosperous community. Already there was a need for additional talents, to build the houses, run the mills and build up the fishing industry, as well as practice other necessary trades. Such men were not easy to find in the early colonies, and those who could be found were in demand in other towns. Tristram Coffin and the Proprietors found a method for recruiting these skilled artisans on the mainland, upon the promise of house lots and a half-interest each in the Proprietorship. Thus each man who moved and agreed to live and work on Nantucket was given a home and a one-half vote on matters of government on the island. Fourteen of these "Half-Share Men" were enlisted and came to Nantucket. One of these men was Captain John Gardner, master mariner.

When Gardner arrived, he soon made the acquaintance of Peter Folger, a multi-talented individual known as "the most useful man in Nantucket." Folger had been recruited as a half-share man to run the first mill near the Lily Pond. In addition to his talents, Folger was close friend of Thomas Mayhew, Jr., the son of Governor Mayhew, with whom he learned the Algonquin language and gained the respect of the native Indians, who considered him their best friend among the white men. Folger expanded his activities on the island into mechanics, surveying, teaching, preaching and keeping of the island's first records. As one of the most literate of the settlers, he kept track of the original Indian deeds and maintained the colony records. Soon all the threads of the Nantucket community ran through his busy fingers.

John Gardner was a shrewd judge of men, and he immediately recognized the importance of Peter Folger to his future plans, because Folger had a streak of independence which combined with his natural talents to make him a valuable comrade at the proper time. Gardner saw in the island community the opportunity to exploit the spirit of independence which had inspired the founding of the colony, and he needed Peter Folger and his friends to succeed with his plans.

Presiding over the island of Nantucket was the First Magistrate, Tristram Coffin, who had landed with the first settlers in 1660. Coffin lived in a large house on a hill overlooking Capaum Pond, and he surrounded himself with his sons and relatives like a Biblical patriarch. He and his wife Dionis had eight surviving children; his son James had fourteen children; his son Peter had ten children; and his total grandchildren numbered seventy-five. Tristram expected his large family and his manorial system of land ownership to preserve his plan for the future of Nantucket. His control over the island's affairs was truly formidable.

At this time, the island of Nantucket was nominally subject to the English governor of the colony of New York, and was ruled from the royal governor's mansion located at Fort James on the tip of Manhattan. Since much of the travel between the colonies was by seagoing vessels, it was easier to travel from the offshore islands to New York than to Boston, and the Nantucketers felt closer to New York than to Massachusetts Bay. Furthermore, since the settlers had left the Puritan rule of the Massachusetts Bay Colony to achieve independence, they were more comfortable with the remote and loose authority of the New York government which left them largely undisturbed for many years. The islands of Nantucket and Martha's Vineyard were even allowed to establish their own legislatures and make laws to govern themselves. Each island thus had its own General Court, which was not a law court but a law-making body, consisting of a Chief Magistrate and two assistants for each island. These officials were appointed by the royal governor in Fort James, Francis Lovelace. Governor Lovelace made the annual appointments for the islands and demanded nothing more from his offshore subjects but a token annual tribute of "four barrels of merchantable codfish."

Captain John Gardner was the man who delivered the codfish to Governor Lovelace. Sailing down Long Island Sound on his swift vessel *Endeavor*, Captain Gardner did not miss the opportunity to gain the favor of the royal governor and bring him reports of the state of affairs on the remote island. Gardner soon impressed the governor as a man of action and purpose. Within a year, Captain Gardner was appointed Captain of the Militia on Nantucket and his brother Richard was appointed Chief Magistrate to succeed Tristram Coffin.

An even more startling message arrived from New York's royal governor on the next mail packet boat. John Gardner had convinced the governor that he needed more land near the shore to promote the fishing industry, for working nets and drying codfish. He represented that Coffin and the Proprietors were denying him this land out of spite, to the detriment of the colony. Thus John and

Richard Gardner obtained a royal grant enabling them to purchase land from the Indians to promote their fishing enterprise.

Tristram Coffin and the original Proprietors were furious. They bombarded New York with protests over the Gardner appointments, and they insisted the land grants were invalid as violations of the original charter of settlement and their agreements with the half-share men.

Captain John Gardner and his brother Richard had taken power over a substantial portion of the Nantucket community, by succeeding to offices which the Proprietors would never have granted them. Their additional authority to deal with the Indians brought them into association with Peter Folger, the acknowledged interpreter and friend of the Indians. Although the half-share men were outnumbered and outvoted by the original Proprietors, they had a formidable alliance with the Indian natives which enabled them to assert their rights without interference. John Gardner, the man of action, joined forces with Peter Folger, the man of letters, and Nantucket's revolt of the half-share men was under way.

Two events of greater historical significance now took place upon the mainland, events which reverberated out to the islands and had their impact upon Nantucket. In the summer of 1673, while Governor Lovelace was absent from New York, the Dutch returned in force, seized the island of Manhattan and displaced the British colonial government. This news elated the rebels on Nantucket. Captain John Gardner and his followers knew there was now little likelihood of any interference with their plans to take control of Nantucket. They were in a world of their own.

Following this event, King Philip, the bloodthirsty chief of the Wampanoag Indians, launched an Indian war against the English colonies in Massachusetts and Rhode Island. Frustrated by the incursions of the white settlers, the Indian chief attempted to promote an Indian rebellion to drive them into the sea, and led his warriors in bloody massacres of many towns on the mainland. As a result, many English families sought refuge on Nantucket for the duration of the war, where the natives were known to be friendly. Some of the families who came to the island found themselves in the middle of another conflict, between the Proprietors and the half-share men. They served to tip the balance in the island's political battle.

The British returned in force to retake New York from the Dutch in 1674, and installed a new Governor, Sir Edmund Andros. He had no sooner taken office than he was besieged by Tristram Coffin, who sent a long message to the governor, begging him to settle the problems of Nantucket.

The new governor responded with an order intended to maintain the status quo on the island. He decreed that the proper government was that of the original Proprietors, who had two votes for one of each half-share man. This seemed to be a victory for the forces of Tristram Coffin and they were quick to take advantage of this turn of events. For the first time, they took steps to insure their political advantage.

The Coffin forces had been augmented by the influx of refugees from King Philip's War on the mainland. Among those who moved temporarily to Nantucket was Tristram's son, Peter Coffin, a wealthy landowner and lumber merchant from Dover, New Hampshire. Peter was one of the original Proprietors but had never lived on Nantucket. The question of his voting rights arose in the town meeting: was he an inhabitant entitled to vote or simply another off-island visitor? Tristram ruled and Peter voted.

Seeing the tide turning toward the Coffin faction, several Nantucketers shifted sides. Thomas Macy, a friend of both Tristram Coffin and Peter Folger, decided to cast his lot with the Coffins, and brought his son-in-law, William Worth, with him, which insured the Coffins' control of the island. Tristram now petitioned his friend the governor, and obtained the appointment of Thomas Macy as Chief Magistrate, with Peter Coffin as his assistant. The control of the Coffins seemed secure, and the Proprietors relaxed in the knowledge they had won their battle with the half-share men. They did not reckon with the independent and legalistic minds at work on Nantucket.

The first term of Thomas Macy as Chief Magistrate was due to expire on October 1, 1675, and Nantucket did not nominate any successor. Governor Andros, busy with affairs in New York, did not make any new appointment. The Coffin faction in Nantucket assumed the Chief Magistrate should hold over in office until his successor was appointed and qualified. Thus there was little notice taken when Thomas Macy called a town meeting. John Gardner and Peter Folger were ready with a legal move which brought the underlying conflict to a dramatic confrontation.

As the first order of business at the town meeting, Magistrate Macy called upon Peter Folger, as Clerk of Courts, to turn over the original Town Record Book to the magistrates for their inspection. This seemingly routine matter became the critical turning point in the revolt of the half-share men. The learned and diligent Peter Folger announced he would not produce the book because Thomas Macy was not holding office legally, being neither nominated by the General Court nor appointed by the Governor. A stunned meeting heard the

faithful clerk pronounce the Chief Magistrate to be a usurper in office who could not command the Clerk to do an illegal act. Folger refused to produce the book.

The Town Record Book, which Folger chose to make the issue of his defiance, was more than a minute book of town meetings. It did

contain the records of town affairs and appointments, but it also held the original Indian deeds to the Proprietors, vitally important records to the early colony. Peter Folger, being the great friend of the local Indians, was highly suspicious of the motives of the Proprietors. He had talked about this at length with John Gardner, and he was convinced the Coffin forces intended to alter or expand the land grants of the Indian deeds to benefit the Proprietors. By withholding the record book, Folger was not only defying the Proprietors but benefiting the Indians.

Now the other half-share men and their families joined in the conflict. Captain John Gardner appeared in the General Court to take Folger's side in the controversy, but refused to take off his hat in front of Magistrate Macy. Macy held him in contempt of court and put him on probation. Richard Gardner's wife, a woman of strong mind and sharp tongue, stood up in court and told the Magistrate what she thought of him. She was summoned for contempt but admonished and released, as Magistrate Macy showed admirable restraint in dealing with this redoubtable woman.

Peter Folger's contempt received swift and stern action. In February of 1676, he was thrown into the Nantucket Jail, to commence a 14-month incarceration as Nantucket's most famous political prisoner. Folger was then about 60 years of age. The town jail had not been used for years and had become a pigsty, so the pig had to be evicted upon the arrival of the prisoner. The unheated shanty was soon furnished with a fireplace and chimney by Folger's family to make him comfortable.

The government of Nantucket was now in a curious state. Peter Folger, the Clerk of Courts and keeper of all the records, was in prison and the courts ground to a halt. John Gardner, the Captain of Militia, who controlled all the weapons on the island, was a prisoner at large on probation. Mrs. Richard Gardner, wife of a former Chief Magistrate, was on parole for insubordination. Half the citizens were openly defiant of their officials. Meanwhile, about 1500 restless Indians seemed to be on the verge of open warfare against the white settlers. The Proprietors were deeply worried about the possibility of the Indians joining the half-share men in their rebellion against the authorities.

The eloquent Peter Folger put his time in jail to good use. He composed a long and detailed letter to Governor Edmund Andros in New York, reciting the problems which beset him and his friends on Nantucket. Then he added the description of his prison which has endured for three centuries:

"For want of a Bond away the constable carried me to Prison, a place where never any Englishman was put; and where the Neighbors Hogs had laid but the Night before, and in a bitter cold Frost and deep Snow..."

Folger's friends did not forsake him. His family and their neighbors visited him to bring food and make his cell comfortable. The friendly Indians brought him sweet corn and smoked bluefish. The town jailor became fond of Folger and let him return home on nights when the magistrate was off-island.

The entire island community quickly divided into two factions, with the plight of Peter Folger the symbol of the Proprietors' persecution of the half-share men. Individual families split during the controversy. On Sundays, Chief Magistrate Thomas Macy preached to the faithful from the Town House and half the town gathered to hear him. Across the street, Peter Folger began preaching from the jail house, and the other half of the town turned out to listen to him. Divided by both politics and religion, the islanders saw their government come to a standstill, while the surrounding Indians watched the peculiar performance with rising concern.

Captain John Gardner did not stand idle while a good local fight was brewing. As a successful fishing master, he relied upon his Indian crews to man the boats, and he knew the way to keep his sailors content. He followed the practice of allowing each man a shot of rum to cheer him up before setting sail each morning. This ran Gardner afoul of the famous prohibition law enacted by the first General Court in 1672. This law, which is generally considered to be the first prohibition law in America, forbade anyone from furnishing "wine, liquor or any strong drink" to the Indians, who were perceived to have a weakness in this regard. Magistrate Thomas Macy was an ardent prohibitionist and missionary, who was determined to keep the white man's spirits out of the hands of the Indians.

Macy sent the constable to seize the rum which Gardner was supplying his Indian fishermen, and the constable returned with a half barrel of Gardner's rum. Gardner was summoned into Thomas Macy's court, where he again showed his defiance and refused to recognize the power of the court. Tristram Coffin, who was present in court, stated, "He sat down on a chest where I sat...I spoke to him and told him I was very sorry that he did not behave himself."

Captain John Gardner replied, "I know my business, and it may be that some of those that have meddled with me had better have eaten fire!"

For this action, Gardner was fined and disenfranchised: stricken from the voters' list and deprived of any right to participate in town

21

government. Gardner's response was an appeal to Governor Andros, sent with a long letter complaining about the high-handed actions of Magistrate Macy and his brethren, and threatening the possibility of an Indian uprising on Nantucket, a prospect which brought shudders to the authorities.

Gardner and Folger had now succeeded in their plan to provoke the Proprietors and disrupt their government. Gardner did it by dramatic acts of open defiance and threats; Folger by silence and civil disobedience, for he would not respond to questions about the record book and infuriated the magistrates by his silence.

In New York, Governor Andros finally reached out for a means to bring the Nantucket turmoil to a conclusion. In August of 1677, he ordered a suspension of all cases pending in Nantucket and ordered them referred to him for action. In his letter addressed to "The Magistrates of the Particular and General Court at Nantucket," he decreed that Thomas Macy was to continue as Chief Magistrate but that the sentences handed out to John Gardner and Peter Folger were null and void as "illegal and beyond your authority." This was a clear victory for the half-share men and left Tristram Coffin in a furious state of frustration.

Captain John Gardner continued to rise in Nantucket esteem as the original Proprietors seemed to decline. In 1678, a town meeting voted an apology to both Gardner and Folger, and their disenfranchisement was deemed "utterly void and null," with Tristram Coffin dissenting. Gardner was elected an Assistant Magistrate in 1680. He even made peace with old Tristram Coffin before he died in 1681. Gardner continued in public life and ended his career as Judge of Probate from 1699 to 1706, when he died at the age of 82. Cotton Mather remembered him as being "well acquainted with the Indians, having divers years assisted them in their government by instructing them in the laws of England and deciding difficult cases among them."

Peter Folger left his jail cell and returned to an active life in Nantucket, where he died in 1690. He is today best remembered for his multiple talents and reputation for wisdom, qualities which were inherited by his grandson, Benjamin Franklin, the son of Abiah Folger Franklin. To the end of his days, Folger never returned the missing record book.

Historians have argued over which of the two factions, the Coffin Proprietors or the Gardner Half-Share Men, was in the right in the famous Nantucket political controversy. Coffin and Macy clearly represented the traditional conservative viewpoint, with citizenship based upon property ownership, while Gardner and Folger stood for the more liberal democratic attitude of modern civil rights: one man, one vote. The issue soon became academic, but the bitter battle was long remembered on Nantucket.

With the deaths of Coffin, Folger and Gardner, the last of the early founders and antagonists passed from the scene. The islands of Nantucket and Martha's Vineyard were transferred from New York to the Province of Massachusetts in 1692, by an Act of Parliament, and thus became subject to the firm control of the Massachusetts General Court. Thereafter, all the inhabitants of the island had equal voting rights--so long as they were men. The old Proprietorship faded before the accepted form of the New England town meeting government, although it kept its vitality as a form of property ownership well into the twentieth century.

But what became of Book One of the Nantucket records? Certainly Peter Folger knew where it was hidden, and he considered it important enough to suffer imprisonment to protect it. Probably John Gardner knew where it was, and as a future Magistrate and Judge, he was in a position of authority to insure its preservation. Historians and scholars have searched Nantucket history for three centuries without finding it, and we are left to surmise.

Nantucket's greatest historian, Edouard A. Stackpole, held the opinion the book was gradually reduced to separate pages and quietly introduced into later town records, where the old Indian deeds may now be found. In this manner, the most important documents were preserved without arousing the publicity and controversy which the book itself would have provoked.

A more dramatic possibility involves the continuing conspiracy of John Gardner and Peter Folger. When Folger took the record book, he knew it was not safe on Nantucket, for the magistrates had the power to search every house on the island, so he turned to his great partner, John Gardner, who had both the will and the means to spirit it to safety. Garner also had powerful friends in New York. Thus Gardner could have taken the book from Folger, sailed down Long

Island Sound, and delivered it somewhere in New York for safekeeping. He could then return to Nantucket secure in the knowledge the magistrates would never find it, and Folger could maintain his silence about its location. However, the New York government was then in turmoil, and, probably during the changes in administrations, departures of royal governors, and the subsequent transfer of Nantucket from the jurisdiction, the book was simply lost. History reveals that many original Nantucket documents were later found in the state archives in Albany, leading Nantucketers to the conclusion that the New Yorkers were to blame for anything missing from the island. There remains a strong possibility that the missing record, if it still exists, is probably somewhere in New York, where future scholars may find it some day. Until then, it remains Nantucket's oldest and favorite mystery subject.

CHAPTER THREE

THE NANTUCKET
BANK ROBBERY

When Tristram Coffin and Thomas Macy made the first plans for the settlement of the Island of Nantucket, they dreamed of establishing a peaceful and harmonious community, based upon the sharing of common lands and common endeavors. Tristram Coffin, the patriarch of the Island, who had nine children and seventy-five grandchildren, believed that strong family ties would insure the settlers living together in harmony. As the Island developed, the influence of the Quaker religion, which brought morality and industry into their daily life, seemed to indicate that the dream of a prosperous and harmonious community was coming true.

Thus, for over a century, Nantucket survived without any serious conflict or disharmony. Crime was virtually unknown, shops and homes were left unlocked, and the natives trusted each other. Business was conducted upon trust, without resort to lawyers or courts, because the principles of the Quakers were set against such worldly institutions. As Walter Folger, Jr., the local philosopher, wrote:

"The inhabitants live together like one great family, not in one house, but in friendship. They not only know their nearest neighbors, but each one knows the rest."

By the end of the 18th century, changes began to take place in the island social and political life. The Quakers of Nantucket had become more than a religious sect, for they controlled the wealth, customs and social life of the island. A younger generation of islanders, more progressive and worldly, came to question the rigid rule of the Quaker leaders, who were becoming more self-righteous and despotic in their adherence to the tenets of their "Inner Light." New ideas were spreading in the Age of Enlightenment following the French Revolution, and the influences of the outside world were felt in

Nantucket society. In addition, the political climate of the Island was changing. As Thomas Jefferson broke away from the Federalist Party of Washington and Adams, the ruling Quakers on Nantucket found themselves sympathetic to the Jeffersonian Democrats. The incumbent Federalists, however, held all the political appointments such as postmaster and judgeships, causing them to appear part of the "world's people" to the traditional Quakers who shunned politics. Thus life in Nantucket was serene on the surface, but full of hidden tensions, awaiting only a spark to ignite the social fabric.

The island's isolation, combined with native prejudice and superstition, contributed to the people's fear of the unknown, which was not uncommon in that age. Intelligent people often believed in astrology, soothsayers, and physiognomy, a popular science which held that a person's character could be determined by his facial expressions. On one occasion, a Nantucket father deemed it wise to warn his prospective in-laws: "My daughter, sir, has in her veins some of the blood of all the original settlers of Nantucket, and a queerer lot God never made. So be prepared for anything."

In this climate, due to the increasing demands of the whale oil industry, certain Nantucketers decided to form a bank, called the Nantucket Bank, which was incorporated in 1795. This was one of the first banks in the United States. It was looked upon with suspicion by many islanders, who had never done business at any bank, since they usually relied upon local merchants to extend credit, which was freely done. This bank was largely promoted by the Federalist element in town, consisting of the younger entrepreneurs, the "world's people," but the board of directors included several wealthy and prominent Quakers.

The bank was incorporated with a capital of $40,000, to be paid in installments, a board of twelve directors, and a place of business at the corner of Main and Union Streets on the lower square. It opened for business on June 1, 1795, and prospects looked bright.

Three weeks later, on the morning of June 22, 1795, the cashier of the bank opened the vault, unlocking the final lock on the door, and reached for the heavy chest which contained the coins for the day's operating funds. To his shock, he found it empty. Quickly opening all the other storage chests in the vault, he found all their gold and silver coins gone. The bank had been robbed of $22,000, an enormous sum in that day. It was, also, $8,000 more than the amount the directors had paid on their installments of capital stock.

The cashier was Randall Rice, a native of Rhode Island who had married a Nantucket girl and moved to the Island. He was to become the central figure in the story of the bank robbery. To his friends, who included Joseph Nichols, a merchant with a store next to the bank, he was one of the promising young businessmen of the Island. He was engaged in many real estate ventures and owned a butcher shop, in addition to his banking position. To the Quaker oligarchy, he was considered one of the "world's people" and resented as an outsider.

Rice quickly met with the bank directors, who decided to withhold news of the robbery from the public for a week. This proved to be an unwise decision, for it led to suspicion of their complicity in the robbery of their own bank. Two of the directors, William Coffin, the postmaster, and Albert Gardner, a ship master, had recently formed a partnership to buy whale oil, and it was rumored they had taken the money to finance a scheme to corner the market on whale oil for the year.

The stolen money was contained in several large chests, and consisted of silver dollars, gold British crowns, French coin, and Spanish pistoles. The total loot was very heavy, and could not have been moved without the help of several men working all night. An immediate search of the entire island was carried out, but no trace of the coinage was ever discovered. The only clue found was a dirty handkerchief belonging to Randall Rice, found in the empty vault. Although Rice was the cashier, with every right to be in the vault, this handkerchief made him a prime suspect in the robbery.

About the time Randall Rice was unlocking the vault, a small trading sloop named "*Dolphin*" was slowly slipping out of Nantucket Harbor, in a heavy fog, headed for Long Island Sound. Captain John Clark, Jr., Zeb Withers, and Sam Johnson had come to Nantucket that weekend on a trading cruise. All three came from New Haven, Connecticut, where they had criminal records. The Captain's father, John Clark, Sr., ran a thieves market in New Haven, fencing stolen goods taken from other coastal ports. Nantucket was one of his favorite stops, and in one of his visits, Captain Clark had heard the Nantucketers boasting about their new bank. Concluding that the town which knew little about banks knew less about security, he and his crew decided to attempt the robbery.

After finishing his business ashore, Clark told the public he was returning to New Haven. He then sailed out of the harbor in a thick fog and anchored near Great Point. The next night, the three men returned to town and landed after dark near North Wharf. No one observed them enter the lower square through the unlighted streets. Leaving Johnson to act as a lookout, Captain Clark and Zeb Withers, who was a veteran safecracker, entered the bank building and confronted the vault.

Withers went to work making wax impressions of the locks and whittling pewter spoons into shape as keys. The final lock was a new offset lock from Boston, and gave them some difficulty, but Clark finally forced it and the door was open. All three men then commenced loading the coins into gunny sacks which were carried down to their boat at the wharf. This took several trips, but in the darkness and thick fog, they were undiscovered.

The entire operation took all night, and as dawn arrived, a morning breeze appeared to fill their sail as the *Dolphin* slipped away from Nantucket with her loot. The successful bank robbers returned to New Haven and Captain Clark's proud father, where they enjoyed the fruits of their weekend in Nantucket. Some of the loot was buried along the shores of Long Island Sound, but most of it was spent, and none was ever recovered. Except for some brief time spent in jail by Clark and Withers, the three robbers escaped any conviction or punishment for their crimes.

Meanwhile, Nantucket was in a turmoil. With no real evidence at hand, the Nantucketers resorted to emotion, prejudice, and personal vengeance to produce suspects. Some Quaker officers and stockholders of the bank started to round up their favorite suspects in vigilante style. In those days, criminal prosecutions were often initiated and investigated by private parties, using citizens' arrests and privately-hired prosecutors. The first man they arrested was Randall Rice, and the testimony against him came from one of the island's most prominent citizens. Walter Folger, Senior, was a dedicated physiognomist, and he claimed he could tell a man's character from the look on his face. Folger testified that on the day of the robbery, he passed Randall Rice on Liberty Street, and Rice had "sheared off" to avoid him. Folger concluded that Rice had something to hide, and later that day, upon learning of the bank robbery, he immediately accused Rice.

Joseph Nichols ran the store next to the bank, and was also the part-time Clerk of Courts. He was known as a friend of Rice, and they had been seen talking together the morning the robbery was discovered. Thus Nichols and his son were arrested and held incommunicado by the band of bank directors and stockholders. Joseph Nichols was removed as Clerk of Courts and never reinstated. When a hearing was finally held before a Justice of the Peace, all three men were released for lack of evidence.

In August, the bank president, Joseph Chase, hired an astrologer in Providence to come to Nantucket and solve the crime. He pronounced that four Nantucketers had committed the robbery, a finding which was to have devastating effect upon four innocent men. The astrologer gave descriptions of the culprits, who were identified as William Coffin, the postmaster, Albert Gardner, the ship-master, Samuel Barker, and Jethro Hussey, the Judge of Probate.

In the middle of September, the Massachusetts judicial system got under way, as a Court of Inquiry was convened in Nantucket to hear the evidence against the suspects. This occasion brought the first famous Boston lawyers to the Island, many of whom were nationally distinguished. The presiding justice was Judge James Prescott, Jr., a promising young jurist whose brother had died leading the patriots at Bunker Hill. Many years later, Judge Prescott became the first judge impeached and disbarred in Massachusetts, for bribery, and it was later alleged he had been bribed in the bank robbery case.

The prosecutor hired by the bank directors was Boston's finest trial lawyer, Samuel Dexter, Jr. He was related on his mother's side to the Nantucket Barkers, some of whom he was prosecuting, but the Nantucketers were used to intra-family conflicts and the robbery litigation only served to increase and solidify the hatreds between relatives.

The defendants were represented by Harrison Gray Otis, a great orator and a nationally-known figure in the Federalist Party of Washington and Adams. This clearly indicated the prosecution was turning into a political trial.

The prosecution's case was based upon three supposed eye witnesses, one eavesdropper, and one astrologer. The eye witnesses came from the dregs of the Nantucket waterfront. William Worth had previously testified that he actually saw Randall Rice and Joseph Nichols enter the bank the night of the robbery. Now he confessed that story was a lie, as he had never been near the bank that night. The second witness was demolished because he swore that he had seen William Worth near the bank. The third witness testified she had heard Rice and Nichols say they were afraid Worth had seen them enter the bank. Their perjury was so rank the Court had all three arrested and held for perjury in open court.

The prosecution then produced Peggy Pinkham, the keeper of the boarding house where Attorney Otis was staying. She testified she had listened at a keyhole while Otis was discussing the case with the defendants, and that the defendants had made statements admitting their guilt to him. Nantucketers who had dreamed about the robbery were permitted to testify to the contents of their dreams, and the astrologer gave his opinion as to the guilty parties. Judge Prescott admitted all this evidence in the bizarre judicial proceeding.

At the end of the hearing, Judge Prescott held Randall Rice, Samuel Barker and Judge Jethro Hussey for the Grand Jury. All were held in cash bail of $21,600 each, which Barker and Hussey were able to furnish. Randall Rice was a man of modest means, with a wife and seven children to support. After several months in jail, his brother raised his bail, and Rice was freed to start borrowing money for his defense.

Most Nantucketers had reached the conclusion that the prosecution was so farfetched and the evidence so lacking that the court would soon dismiss the case and exonerate the defendants. But the Quaker oligarchy had powerful friends in Boston, including the formidable Nantucket representative in the General Court, Micajah Coffin. They managed to secure passage of a special law transferring the jurisdiction of this peculiar robbery case from Nantucket to the Supreme Judicial Court in Boston, thus insuring that the defendants would be indicted and tried by Suffolk County juries sitting in Boston, who, it was believed, would be more likely to convict than the Nantucket juries with their personal knowledge of the case.

In September, 1796, the Suffolk County Grand Jury heard over 100 witnesses, defendants and accusers in the bank robbery case. The city jurors were not impressed by any of the evidence, and refused to return any indictments on any charges, including the perjury of the prosecution witnesses. That should have ended the case.

However, the defendants in their turn decided to become the accusers, and commenced a series of law suits demanding satisfaction for slander. Bank director Albert Gardner sued Captain Uriah Swain for calling him a robber, but the jury found against him, awarding costs to Gardner. Fist fights broke out on the Nantucket waterfront between the contending factions. Randall Rice, embittered by his long suffering, brought suit against the eminent physiognomist, Walter Folger, Senior, for slander, in a case brought in Barnstable Court. Many depositions were taken and the cost of pursuing the suit on the mainland was enormous. Rice lost the first trial and the jury assessed him $5,000 in costs. He appealed this decision to a jury trial in Boston before a single justice of the Supreme Judicial Court, and the jury rewarded him with a verdict for Ten Dollars. Folger was so enraged at the result he decided to reopen the bank robbery prosecution, setting the stage for the final act of the human tragedy.

Samuel Dexter remained the paid prosecutor, hired by the bank president and a majority of the directors. Otis retired and was replaced by Fisher Ames, another noted Federalist, as counsel for Randall Rice. Many Nantucketers who had taken opposite sides in the controversy were not on speaking terms with one another. As more people were drawn into the conflict, some islanders left town rather than take sides.

A second Suffolk County Grand Jury met to hear evidence in August, 1797, with Randall Rice, Samuel Barker, and Judge Hussey again accused defendants, plus two bank directors, William Coffin and Albert Gardner. Convinced that the robbery was an inside job, the prosecutors determined that Coffin and Gardner were behind it. Coffin was the postmaster, but also ran a barber and wig-making shop, where the young men of town used to gather to protest the Quaker regime. Gardner was his best friend, and a sea captain with a fast trading sloop, which made him suspect for his motive and means to remove the bank treasure. Fifty-two Nantucket witnesses were mustered by the prosecution and presented to the Grand Jury.

Impressed by the parade of witnesses, the Grand Jury indicted all five defendants in Boston. A jury trial was held a few days later, presided over by Robert Treat Paine, a famous Massachusetts patriot and signer of the Declaration of Independence. Fisher Ames, attorney for Randall Rice, was a congressman with an impressive record as an orator. There was as little evidence against Rice as ever, and none against the other defendants. However, Rice's principal witness was terminally ill on Nantucket and could not appear. Fisher Ames filled the courtroom with four straight hours of his closing address without a recess.

The Boston jury returned with verdicts of Not Guilty for all defendants except Randall Rice, who was found Guilty and remanded to jail under $60,000 bail, awaiting sentence. His brother who had bailed him out the first time, had died, and Rice had no further means. As he remained in jail, all his Nantucket property was foreclosed. His wife was reduced to poverty and his infant son died. Judge Paine, convinced that Rice was innocent, postponed entering sentence, but left him in jail through 1798.

Nantucket sentiment turned strongly in Rice's favor, for it was known that he never possessed or disposed of any such money, and the great weight of coins could not have been moved without help. Nothing could be done because of the Boston jury verdict. A petition of the legislature was denied because of the relentless opposition of Micajah Coffin, a stern old Quaker, who believed all the defendants guilty. Eventually, Randall Rice was persuaded to ask for a governor's pardon, which he had resisted because he had done no crime, and the petition went to the governor. There it was firmly opposed by Samuel Dexter and the prosecuting directors. Finally, in December of 1798, Rice was pardoned by Governor Increase Sumner and released from jail.

For years after the robbery, the persecuted faction of islanders, who knew themselves to be innocent, made great efforts to prove their innocence by finding the real thieves. Wanted notices were sent to all the cities on the east coast, and soon bore fruit. One suspect, Zeb

Withers (alias Weatherly) was found in Philadelphia and arrested, but released for lack of evidence. A Nantucket captain, John Chase, pursued him to New Haven and brought him back in irons to Nantucket for questioning. Chase then sailed to New York and captured John Clark, Jr., and brought him back to Nantucket. Faced with the fury of the Nantucket forces, both suspects confessed and named their third accomplice, Sam Johnson.

The arrests should have settled the mystery of the Nantucket Bank Robbery once and for all. But the vigilante committee of bank directors and stockholders took charge, obsessed with making the off-Island prisoners' confessions conform to the committee's belief that some Nantucketers were involved. When this failed, they were confined to the Nantucket jail under guard of Daniel Kelley. He obtained more detailed confessions of how the three men had looted the bank, without implicating any Nantucketers. After a month in confinement, the prisoners mysteriously escaped from the jail, hid out on the Island,

and slipped away to the mainland. Although this evidence came while the Rice trial was pending, their confessions were suppressed and never brought into court, leading to the general belief that the prosecutors permitted them to get away so their story, which completely exonerated the bank robbery defendants, would never be made public.

This infuriated bank director Albert Gardner, one of the defendants found not guilty, and he was determined to vindicate himself. In his trading sloop, he sailed straight to New York and arrested the heavily armed Zeb Withers at gunpoint on the city streets. Captain Gardner thought it wise to sail him to Boston, where he was lodged in the Boston jail in October, 1797. To everyone's amazement, Withers was locked in a cell next to the convicted bank robber, Randall Rice. When the Boston jury which had convicted Rice learned this fact, it interceded on his behalf. Before anything could be done, Withers escaped again, probably with the help from the influential prosecutors.

Twenty-one years after the Nantucket Bank Robbery, Zeb Withers, in jail in New York for an unrelated crime, told the whole story to a fellow prisoner, William McFate. After Withers died in prison, McFate relayed the story to the prison warden, Alex Coffin, who in turn relayed it to his relative, William Coffin, and Albert Gardner in Nantucket. Coffin and Gardner published a long and accurate account of the Nantucket Bank Robbery, proving that no Nantucketers were involved, but it still failed to convince many of their Quaker enemies on the Island.

The truth came too late for Randall Rice. Returning from his Boston jail cell, he was arrested in Nantucket and jailed for the debts he had accumulated during this trial and confinement. He had to beg the Town Selectmen to enlarge the jail so he could earn a little money to support his family. He was never indemnified for the wrongs done him or the money lost during his trials and confinement. He died a ruined man, a victim of the prejudice and hatred of his persecutors.

The great Nantucket Bank Robbery was a solemn affair, and its aftermath marked a significant turn in the course of Island history. More shocking to the Town than the startling facts of the robbery were the ensuing displays of venom and vindictiveness which swept the Town. Gone forever was the dream of Macy and Coffin for an insular Garden of Eden, sharing common land and common endeavors in harmony with man and nature. Gone was the trust of one's neighbors, the loyalty of one's family and the love of mankind which had founded the settlement. Perhaps the dream would not have endured, but in Nantucket it seemed to have the best chance. Now it was all gone, gone with the years of bitterness and suspicion, gone with the fortunes spent on endless lawsuits, gone with the ruined life of Randall Rice and the dark thoughts which haunted the community for years to come. The dream of Nantucket was gone forever, gone with the winds and tides which carried the sloop *Dolphin* from Nantucket Harbor on one foggy morning in June.

CHAPTER FOUR

THE GREAT SEA BATTLE

The War of 1812 was a deeply distressing conflict for the Island of Nantucket, where its impact was felt upon the economic, political and religious life of the community. It was a war fought close to home, upon the Atlantic Ocean and in the coastal areas where the Nantucketers earned their livelihood. Coming soon after the Revolutionary War, in which the island suffered great hardships while caught in the crossfire between Patriots and Tories, the new war provoked memories of Nantucket's precarious position in any armed conflict. Most of the island's population of 7,000 was engaged in the whaling and fishing business, and all depended upon maritime commerce for the very necessities of life. Early in the year, President James Madison declared an embargo on the coastal ports, which prevented any vessels from leaving port--a crippling blow to an island. Many of the Nantucket whalers were at sea on extended voyages to the South Atlantic and the Pacific Grounds, some unaware of the impending conflict and all in danger of becoming easy prey for the British fleet when war broke out. The island community was primarily controlled by the Society of Friends, who were staunchly opposed to the war, and its Quaker meeting regularly excommunicated members for bearing arms or sailing on armed ships.

Under these circumstances, the attitude of the island turned toward some form a neutrality. Islanders represented to both the national government and the British minister that they were determined to take no active part in this war. By observing a strict neutrality, they hoped to secure to the inhabitants the privilege of maintaining the whaling commerce and to prevent the capture of the whaling fleet still at sea. A committee was sent to meet with a British admiral for this purpose, to no avail, and the federal government paid no attention to the Nantucket proposal. The island of Quakers was stranded between the two great nations as they went to war.

The war was declared on June 18, 1812, and the effect upon the island were immediate. Unemployment, poverty and hardships seemed to be the fate of the island for the future, with the threat of an attack by the British fleet based in Halifax constantly expected to devastate the island. Faced with the oncoming winter, the citizens sent a plea to President James Madison on November 21:

"The island in its detached situation, being beyond the reach of protection from the continent, is exposed to the ravages of an enemy...the peculiar situation of Nantucket has induced us to address you. Experience has taught that the whale fishery, for which this place has ever been famed, cannot be prosecuted while it is exposed to the ravages of war...it seems we have no choice, but that of respectfully soliciting your attention, and that of our government to our alarming condition; requesting also liberty to ask, if in your wisdom any means can be devised to save our fleet of whale ships now in the Southern Ocean...without the risk of capture by the enemy.

"We also beg leave to ask, if any stipulation can consistently be effected with Great Britain, whereby the cod and whale fisheries of both nations may be exempted from the ravages of war."

There was nothing the federal government could or would do about the plight of Nantucket, and all the talk of neutrality only revived memories of the Tory sentiments which had prevailed during the Revolution. The petitions which were sent to Washington with such sincerity during the war caused resentment in later years, when President Andrew Jackson and later administrations in Washington took their retribution on Nantucket by refusing harbor improvements and other federal projects sought by the island.

Although the hardships on the island were great, and the whaling fleet was devastated by the British cruisers, the island was never invaded and was not subjected to the ravages of war in the usual sense. The threat of a British invasion never materialized, although raiders were always close at hand. The greatest loss to the island during the war was the hundreds of Nantucket seamen lost or captured by the Royal Navy, which refused to recognize Nantucket's professed neutrality.

It was not until late in 1814 that the grim reality of war at sea was brought forcefully home to Nantucket, when a bloody sea battle was fought within sight of the island. On October 10, 1814, the American privateer *Prince de Neufchatel* anchored off the south shore of Nantucket near Surfside. The speedy, 17-gun commerce raider had just completed a nine-month cruise in the North Atlantic

which was very successful. She had captured several rich British merchant vessels which were sent into American ports with prize crews on board, and she was bringing with her the latest catch, the 429-ton British merchantman *Douglas*, loaded with rum, sugar and coffee. The necessity of manning the prize ships had depleted the crew of the *Prince*, so she called at Nantucket to enlist more sailors and a Nantucket pilot to take her through the shoals to the port of Boston.

The *Prince de Neufchatel* was an American vessel, built in New York. She was manned by an international crew of 35 seamen from many countries, speaking several languages. She was captained by a Frenchman, one of the most colorful and bellicose characters ever to walk a quarterdeck. His face was dark and ugly, and his body short and squat, which gave him a dwarfish and demonic appearance. Indeed, Captain Jules Ordronaux was described as "a veritable demon in battle", and this was soon proven true.

About 2 p.m., after taking on some seamen and a 35-year old Nantucket pilot, Charles Hilburn, the *Prince* and her prize ship *Douglas* were anchored close to the beach at Surfside. Suddenly, a lookout sighted a warship approaching from the southwest, it was the British frigate *Endymion*, of 38 guns. Seeking to trap the American ship in her perilous position close to shore, the *Endymion* pressed in for the attack, and the *Prince* hastily set sail to the east. Before the frigate's cannon could be brought to bear, a providential Nantucket fog rolled in, and the *Prince* escaped from the trap, with the frigate in pursuit.

The chase proceeded easterly under light winds until the two vessels were about a mile off Madequecham, between Surfside and Tom Nevers Head. About sunset, the lookout sighted five large barges leaving the *Endymion*, loaded with 120 marines and seamen, heavily armed and equipped for boarding and battle. The captain of the *Endymion*, Henry Hope, determined to capture the privateer by direct assault, sent his first lieutenant to lead the attack. The plan was for one boat to attack on each bow, one on each quarter, and one dead astern. Approaching in the darkness with muffled oars, the British boats closed on the *Prince*.

Aboard the privateer, Captain Ordronaux feverishly prepared a warm welcome for the boarding party, vowing that they would never take his ship. He drove his motley crew with relentless fury, slushing down the sides of the ship with grease and tar to prevent boarders, loading his deck guns with musket balls to use as grape-shot, stacking baskets of loaded pistols around the bulwarks, and piling boxes of cannonballs at strategic spots to be hurled through the bottoms of the attacking barges. Amid all this preparation, the captain had to contend with 37 prisoners which he had locked below decks, shouting and pounding to be set free before the battle started. Satisfied that his ship was ready, the fighting Frenchman awaited the British attack.

It came about 9 p.m., when the first boats came within musket shot of the privateer, and the ensuing battle was furious. Boat after boat was repulsed by grapeshot and musket fire. One boat containing 43 men was sunk, with only two saved. Three barges were repulsed with all hands killed or injured. One boat made up the final boarding party, but in desperate hand-to-hand fighting, the attackers were killed or thrown overboard. The entire battle was over in about 35 minutes, and only two of the boats returned to the *Endymion*, carrying 16 men out of the 120 who had left the ship. It was estimated that 100 sailors and marines had been killed or lost, including the first lieutenant who led the expedition. Aboard the *Prince*, six men were killed, including the Nantucket pilot, Charles Hilburn.

Captain Ordronaux, wounded but victorious, had routed the best of the British navy in violent personal combat. It was later said that the noise of the battle could be clear- ly heard in the town of Nantucket, some five  miles away. Nantucket was soon to see the results, for there were many dead to be buried and wounded to be cared for, in the town which hated this war. The *Prince* had only 35 men aboard to start the battle; at the end there were only eight uninjured. In addition, she took as prisoners 30 more British seamen and marines, who had to be kept in the launch astern, since the captain did not dare take more on board.

All the wounded from both sides were landed on Nantucket, some on the south shore and the remainder at Sesachacha, a fishing village north of Sankaty Head. Two British seamen who died of their wounds were buried on the south shore. The surviving British prisoners, after giving their parole - a signed promise not to serve against the United States during the rest of the war - were landed on the island with the wounded. Those who were landed at Sesachacha had to endure an eight-mile journey in wagon carts over the rutted roads to town. One British officer sailed to Tarpaulin Cove in the Elizabeth Islands and returned in a few days with a doctor and medical supplies for the British wounded. Most of the men who arrived in Nantucket town were treated at the waterfront tavern on North Wharf, where local physicians probed for bullets, without benefit of anesthesia, while the native bartender provided the only pain-killer available to the suffering seamen.

Many of the townfolk opened their hearts and homes to the wounded men, depending upon their sympathies in the war, and some men formed enduring friendships on the island. It was later said that two young British midshipmen had such a pleasant time recovering from their wounds at the Defriez home on Fair Street, that they put off their return to duty as long as possible. Years after the battle, they sent annual gifts to the daughters of that family in appreciation for their kindness and hospitality.

The mariners of the nineteenth century were hardy men and they maintained their pride and a sense of grim humor, even after experiencing the terrible ordeal of naval battle and primitive medical care. The Nantucket *Inquirer* later reported that two badly wounded men were landed at Nantucket, one from each side of the combat. One man had his jaw shattered by a musket ball, while the other sustained a wound which required the amputation of his right hand. After they survived the local surgery, they were invited to a Nantucket house for dinner, where they were seen to stick close to one another, although the rest of the party was enjoying a hearty meal. After surveying the other guests who were ignoring their plight, the sailor with one hand, with stern humor, spoke to his broken-jawed companion: "I say, Jack, since you can't grind, nor I carve, and the landlubbers are all tucking the beef under their jackets, what do you say for splicing? If you'll cut the meat for me, I'll chew for you."

An unusual fate pursued the prize ship *Douglas*. She had been unable to engage in the sea battle because she was unarmed, and her prize master sought to avoid further conflict and protect his valuable cargo by sailing her around the easterly shore of Nantucket. While headed north near Squam Head, the master received a report from the shore that warned him of the approach of more British warships coming from the west, and advised that he beach the vessel to save her cargo. This report proved to be a malicious story concocted to obtain the contents of the ship, which was run ashore at Squam. The Nantucketers promptly responded by looting the ship, as every man with a horse and cart headed for Squam to help remove the precious cargo of rum, sugar and coffee. For many islanders, this was the first time in two years of wartime blockade to sample these goods, under the guise of salvage. It was a sad ending for the ship which so many men had suffered and died to save.

Captain Henry Hope of the *Endymion*, having lost 33 men killed, 37 wounded, and 30 prisoners, gave up any further attempt to take the scrappy American privateer. He allowed her to sail away to Boston, apparently conceding that she had earned her right to escape. Later he admitted he had lost more men in the attack on the little privateer than he would expect to lose in a fight with a frigate. Fate would soon tell. Three months after the battle near Nantucket, the *Endymion* was caught  in a running gun fight off New York. In the last battle of the war, the British ship was battered and defeated by Captain Stephen Decatur in the frigate *President*.

Despite the dramatic and historic events which took place about Nantucket in 1814, the great sea battle was only briefly reported on the Island. Nantucket's great historian, Obed Macy, was a devout Quaker, and as a matter of principle was reluctant to write the bloody details of the battle. He stated:

"We forbear to state the particulars of this sanguinary engagement, believing that it would neither please nor edify a large part of our readers,...What we have related is sufficient both as a record of the fact and as an example of the horrors of war...Such a scene, almost under the eye of a large community, one of whose most distinguishing, and, as we think, noblest traits, is a strong aversion to war, could not fail to bring a solemn gloom over their minds."

There remained one more chapter in the saga of the *Prince de Neufchatel*, which added her name to the annals of maritime history. After his return to Boston, Captain Ordronaux, weary from his wounds but wealthy from the prize money he had earned during the war, decided to retire from his career as a privateer. Accordingly, he sold the *Prince* to another sea captain, together with his letter of marque, his hunting license for commerce raiding. Under its new captain, the privateer left Boston Harbor and was damaged in a storm. It was unable to make its usual speed and was captured at sea by a British squadron of three ships, four days after the war ended. The British commander, Sir George Collier, realized he had caught the famous privateer which had eluded and outsailed the British on seventeen occasions. He therefore took his prize back to England where she was taken to the Deptford Dockyard to be refitted for the Royal Navy. During her overhaul, the British craftsmen took detailed drawings of her lines for study and future reference. The *Prince* never joined the navy, however, for an accident in drydock fractured her keel and her sailing days were ended.

The *Prince de Neufchatel* had been built in the New York shipyard of Christian Bergh to a novel design, with a sharp lean hull and lofty masts capable of carrying an extraordinary expanse of sail. These features gave her great speed and endurance in the open ocean, and were just the qualities needed for the coming generation of fast trans-oceanic sailing vessels. The drawings of the *Prince* taken in 1815 remained untouched in Greenwich for almost fifteen years. Then a British captain requested a set of plans for the fastest ship that could be built for the China trade. The forgotten plans were discovered and used to design the first of the British opium clippers, the famous *Red Rover*, which proved enormously successful. These British ships led to the early designs of the American clipper ships of the nineteenth century, the most magnificent sailing ships ever to cross the seas. Thus the tides of marine history which surged from America to England and China and back to America, indicate that the greatest sailing ships ever built may be traced to the proud privateer who fought for her life one foggy night off the shores of Nantucket.

CHAPTER FIVE

THE TRIAL OF
BARKER BURNELL

The curfew bell in the South Tower slowly tolled the 52 strokes which announced the time for all Nantucket to retire for the evening. On this particular June night in 1847, there were many citizens who had good reasons to ignore the curfew as they gathered on Upper Main Street outside the wood-frame building of the Nantucket Court House.

"How long the jury been out, Sheriff?"

"Couple of hours already. Looks like a long night to me."

"What did you think of the trial?"

"I would say it was a mighty fine performance, all around. 'Course you never know how the jury will take it. They certainly got their money's worth from those lawyers."

"I heard they were good, but I could not get inside to hear them. Some folks waited all day for a seat in court."

"Well, we never had such a trial in Nantucket before. Not every day they put a senator on trial."

"Should have been others on trial with him, I say."

"Then we would have needed a bigger court house. This old place will never see another trial like this one. Think what it must have cost for those lawyers to come to Nantucket."

"Lot of money, certainly. But think what Barker has spent already, paying all those debts, losing property in the fire, then losing the boy. I say he has suffered enough."

"We have all suffered lately, brother. I had money in the bank just like the rest of you. Now the bank is gone and the money is gone. Barker is the only one who knows. What did he have to say about it?"

"My friend," said the Sheriff. "We all know the Bank went up in the Great Fire. Senator Burnell had nothing to do with that. Now, as for where did the money go? God only knows!"

THE TRIAL OF BARKER BURNELL

At the height of Nantucket's golden era of prosperity, the name of Barker Burnell stood for wealth and integrity throughout the Island and was respected in the highest levels of government. Barker Burnell, Sr., a wealthy and successful businessman, was elected to the Massachusetts Senate to represent Nantucket in 1825 and in 1838, then elected to serve the district in the United States House of Representatives in 1841, where he served until his death in 1843 at the age of forty-five.

His son, Barker Burnell, Jr., was elected cashier of the strongest commercial bank on the Island, the Manufacturers and Mechanics Bank of Nantucket, in 1841, when he was twenty-two years of age. This bank, which stood on the corner of Main and Federal Streets, was the most important institution on the Island. It was the bank to most of the whaling industry. Burnell was considered a bright young man with a solid family background. He was married to Lydia Crosby and the father of two young children. Following in his father's footsteps, he was elected to the Massachusetts Senate in 1845.

After his election, Burnell resigned as cashier of the bank, but stayed for three weeks assisting the new cashier, Andrew J. Morton. Burnell then sailed to Boston to begin his term in the Senate in January, 1846, after certifying to his successor that the bank was "in very good condition."

The bank had been examined in 1843 and 1844, when it was found that the original capital stock of $100,000 had been depleted by bad loans and the failure of several debtors. On the latter date, the directors were informed the deficiency was about $5768, whereas in truth, the bank was missing about $80,000 of its capital. The amounts due the bank from mainland banks were greatly misrepresented. The accounts were sworn to by the cashier, Barker Burnell, Jr. In March, 1845, the cashier again reported to the directors, indicating the deficiency was made up and the bank was now showing a surplus of $5721. In fact, the capital stock of $100,000 had entirely disappeared, along with an additional $17,000 of depositors' money.

Following the departure of Senator Burnell to Boston, the bank directors obtained a new audit of the books, which revealed the bank was insolvent in the amount of $117,000, a staggering sum in those days. The new cashier, Andrew J. Morton, found to his horror that the cash book was "about ten miles behind-hand," and he was unable to determine the true condition of the bank. The directors sent one of their ablest members, retired whaling Captain David Thain, hurrying to Boston to confront Barker Burnell, Jr.

Captain Thain met with Senator Burnell in Boston on February 12, 1846, and told him the bank was in great difficulty, that the city banks were alleging its accounts to be overdrawn, and that he should return to Nantucket to clear up the situation. Thain suggested Burnell go with him to the City Bank to arrange for acceptance of the Nantucket Bank bills, to which he agreed. While on their way, Burnell said he would stop and get three or four thousand dollars from his account at the North Bank and meet him later. Thain waited a half hour at the City Bank but Burnell did not arrive; instead, he sent $3,000 by messenger for deposit to the Manufacturers and Mechanics Bank account.

That evening, after a Senate Committee meeting, Burnell met with Thain and agreed to return to Nantucket. Thain told him the bank was deficient by a great amount, to which Burnell exclaimed, "God knows, I have not used a dollar of it!" Thain said that he was not accusing Burnell, but the books were in great disorder and for the sake of his family and his own reputation, he should return to the island. Burnell said he would do it but then he suggested Thain return home early next morning, saying he would raise ten or twelve thousand dollars to deposit to the credit of the bank before returning to Nantucket in the afternoon of the next day.

Greatly relieved, Captain Thain assured Burnell he would help him work it out so they could get through this situation without any public disclosure. He then went to New Bedford to await passage for Nantucket where he received a letter from Burnell:

Senate Chamber, Feb. 13th, 1846

My Dear Sir,

Since you left this morning, my mind has been, I assure you, in a pretty bad state. My first course was to go immediately to Nantucket; but connected with that I can see nothing but ruin to myself, or at least disgrace and censure from those with whom I have been intimately associated. And what other course is there for me to pursue? I cannot reflect upon the subject without feeling that my very *existence* is a burden that I cannot bear and what course to pursue I know not.

Every member of the Legislature treats me with all the respect that I could ask or expect. Every citizen of Boston, of any eminence, extends to me the hand of friendship; and added to all this the many friends I have in Nantucket, all conspire to make any stain upon my character the less endurable.

I cannot, I cannot come to Nantucket. The Bank will not suffer a loss from funds that I have made use of.

When this reaches you, I shall be either in eternity (God forgive me for the reflection), or far beyond the sympathy of those who are dear to me at Nantucket.

Death, death. Yes, *any*thing rather than disgrace.

Your Friend,
B. Burnell

Senator Burnell then departed for the city of Washington, where he was well-known in political circles. In mid-February, at Coleman's Hotel, he encountered Jared Coffin, a prosperous whaling merchant who owned the most sumptuous brick house on Nantucket, and together they made the rounds of the capital city. After calling upon the mayor and the War Department, they visited the Capitol to hear a debate on the Oregon Question, and finished with a reception at the White House as guests of President James K. Polk. Following the reception, another Nantucket merchant, Justin Lawrence, arrived at the hotel to persuade Burnell to return to Nantucket. At three in the morning, Burnell was awakened and called to a conference in the hotel parlor.

Justin Lawrence told Burnell the bank was in serious difficulty, then asked if Burnell had not brought a lot of money with him from Boston, $14,000 or $16,000? Burnell said if he had, it was nobody's business. Lawrence persisted in demanding that Burnell return to Nantucket to clear up the affair. Burnell raised his hands and said, "I'll sooner die on this floor than go back to Nantucket with this disgrace hanging over me."

Jared Coffin then offered Burnell a little advice, reminding him of his wife and family, and told him he had nothing to fear in returning to Nantucket where his friends were ready to help him clear up "any little difficulties." He said there was no way to avoid going home; that the road was a pretty straight one and there was no turning to the right or left.

A solemn Barker Burnell returned to Nantucket on February 24. Meeting with Captain Thain, he asked about an anonymous letter from Boston relating to him. Thain said he had destroyed it, as it was of no importance. Burnell worried that someone else must know of this business. Thain asked if anyone else had access to the vault at the bank or whether Burnell had noticed any money missing from the banking house, but Burnell said no.

Captain Thain advised Burnell as a friend not to resist the claims of the directors nor the examination of the bank's affairs. Burnell said the directors need not fear any loss, but he found it "hard to give up everything."

The investigation into the bank's tangled affairs continued. Captain Thain eventually reported an overdraft of $90,000 apparent on the bank's books, which he figured "might be $91,000." The prosperous Main Street brothers, Charles and Henry Coffin, had an overdraft of $50,000, which they settled under protest. The president of the bank himself was overdrawn by $14,000. Captain Thain's own account was overstated by $2,000. The Captain explained he often made deposits in the bank on his way home from the wharf and did not have them entered in his passbook. It was impossible to tell the condition of some bank accounts, as the original entries in many accounts had not been made since January of 1844. The false entries of balances due from mainland banks amounted to about $30,000; and the personal account of Barker Burnell, Jr., Cashier of the Bank, was overstated and overdrawn by $18,000 to $20,000.

Now the investigation focused upon one particular transaction which led to charges against Barker Burnell, Jr. On August 1, 1843, Burnell was in need of $6,000, and not wanting to borrow it from his own bank, he obtained a loan from Sampson & Tappan, a private banking firm in Boston, payable in seven months. In February of 1844, he paid off this loan with a check for $6,000 from the bank, which he signed Barker Burnell, Cashier. He did not charge himself with this payment although it showed as a credit to him on his next bank statement from the City Bank.

During the summer of 1846, complaints were filed against Burnell and he was freed on bail for his appearance before the October session of the Court of Common Pleas. After that court returned indictments charging him with embezzlement, he was imprisoned in the Nantucket Jail until his trial.

During this period, he surrendered $40,000 worth of property to the bank receivers to settle a civil suit against him. While in jail, he suffered the death of his second son from consumption. In June of 1847, a new indictment charged him with unlawfully embezzling and converting to his own use the check for $6,000 signed by him as cashier, which had been used to pay off his loan from Sampson & Tappan. This was the sole issue at his trial--probably the State's strongest case because the bank records were too confused to provide sufficient evidence on the other losses.

The Town of Nantucket now looked forward to its most sensational trial and most exciting spectacle: the criminal trial of a noted citizen, starring several outstanding trial lawyers. The Commonwealth was represented by the able J.H. Clifford of New Bedford, District Attorney for Bristol, Barnstable, Dukes, and Nantucket counties. The Defendant did not disappoint his constituents for he retained the well-known Timothy G. Coffin, a Nantucket native who was once described by Daniel Webster as "my most dangerous opponent." In addition to Coffin, the Senator from Nantucket had at his side the foremost Boston barrister of his day, the formidable figure of Rufus Choate. Choate, whose dynamic statue still dominates the Suffolk County Courthouse in Boston, was a brilliant orator, a former U.S. Senator, and the greatest jury advocate in Massachusetts.

The trial began on June 10, 1847, and a jury of twelve good Nantucket men was quickly seated. The District Attorney rose to deliver an opening address that lasted for more than an hour. There were few time limits on courtroom oratory in those days, and the spectators considered themselves entitled to a full day's rhetoric from the lawyers. Clifford described the general misconduct of Burnell in his management of the bank's business, the various misrepresentations on the books, and then declared him utterly faithless to his trust as cashier of the bank. He described the transaction involving the $6,000 check and how Burnell converted the funds to his own use. All of this he was prepared to prove to the jury.

The first witness for the State, John Williams, the State Bank Commissioner, testified he had examined the bank records in 1843 and found them in good condition, as sworn to by Barker Burnell.

The next witness, Captain David Thain, testified that he had been appointed to examine the bank on behalf of the Board of Directors in 1844. Over vigorous objections from the defense counsel, he was allowed to testify that false entries had been made in the books and about $70,000 had been embezzled between April 8, 1843, and March 30, 1844, when the cashier had again sworn to the good condition of the bank. The Directors first discovered the great losses after Burnell had left the bank on February 8, 1846. Captain Thain then related his pursuit of Burnell to Boston and his conduct when confronted with the facts. Finally, the witness testified about receipt of the fatal letter of February 13th signed by Burnell.

George Sampson of Sampson & Tappan banking house took the stand to testify to the loan made to Barker Burnell in 1843, and its repayment by check of the bank dated February 19, 1844, in the amount of $6,000 signed by Barker Burnell, Cashier. He also testified he had done business with Burnell for several years from 1841 to 1846, that his credit was always good, and Burnell expressed no desire to keep the transaction secret.

Now the defense counsel, Timothy Coffin, rose to cross-examine Captain David Thain. Coffin had made an intensive study of the bank's affairs for several months before the trial, and his preparation had probably given him more insight into the state of the Nantucket bank than was possessed by any of its officers. He then waded into Captain Thain to test his knowledge of the matter.

The Captain testified he made out the amount of the bank's deficiency to be about $91,000 but the books were in such bad condition he "Came as near as he could." It was impossible to tell the condition of some accounts, but $91,000 was not too far out of the way. However, if the true figure was $104,000 in overdrafts, well, then he must have made some mistake in his work.

Thain admitted that Burnell had settled $40,000 on the bank receivers to settle their civil claim against him. Thain was one of the receivers and had agreed to release the cashier and his bondsmen for this payment because his colleagues, gentlemen learned in the law, advised it. He was one of the largest depositors and shareholders in the bank.

When the deficiency was discovered, he ordered the cashier to call for the payment of all outstanding loans due the bank, but no such notice was sent him. Eventually, the bank asked for payment and he paid his note soon after, but felt he had been ill-used. He was the one who had advised Burnell to settle the claim of the Directors because the books were in such confusion, not because of any enmity toward Burnell.

Andrew Morton, the last cashier of the bank, testified that he took office without making any examination of the bank assets and swore to the good condition of the bank because he had confidence in Burnell, who stayed to assist him for several weeks. He knew that many of the accounts were not fully entered on the books, and the cash book was "about ten miles behind-hand." He admitted on cross-examination, however, that Burnell had agreed to pay him for writing up the books, for with the books in the condition he found them, no person could tell the true condition of the bank, and "there was a cart-load of passbooks not written up." Timothy Coffin's cross-examination of Morton gave the Nantucket jury a colorful picture of the state of the Island's favorite bank.

The next witness was the imposing figure of Jared Coffin, who related the story of his meeting with Barker Burnell in Washington and their activities in the capital city; the conferences with Justin Lawrence and their efforts to persuade Burnell to return to Nantucket in February of 1846, to which the Senator exclaimed, "I'll sooner die on this floor than go back to Nantucket with this disgrace hanging over me."

Two more witnesses testified to various false entries in the bank records concerning erroneous statements of the amounts due the Nantucket bank from mainland institutions, and again traced the record of the $6,000 check. The court sat until seven o'clock in the evening, when the government rested its case.

Nantucket courts put in a full day's work in the nineteenth century, for the trial resumed at 8:30 the next morning with every juryman in his seat. Timothy G. Coffin rose to make the opening statement for the defense. He began by expressing a strong sense of embarrassment due to the relations between the Defendant, the community, and himself. (They were, indeed, close...for the jury contained three Coffins.) He reminded the jury to confine itself to the specific charge of stealing a piece of paper from the bank and converting this check to his own use. Most important, the Defendant was charged with intentional fraud, not with negligence, or oversight, or forgetfulness. On this specific charge, all the mistakes and alterations in the bank records had no effect; the jury must be satisfied that Burnell intended to commit fraud when he took that check.

Timothy Coffin related to the Nantucket jury the story of the career of Barker Burnell; he was a man of means, he did not need funds, he had money in various banks, his credit was unbounded, and, if he were to steal that check, he would be certain of conviction. The entire conduct of the Defendant was certainly intended to screen himself from charges of neglect, not criminal fraud. Look at the condition of Barker Burnell, his education, his property, his friends. Where was the motive to commit this crime? Why, at the time this check was mishandled, Burnell had $19,000 of his own money, $22,000 from his wife, $18,000 from his father, $14,000 from his business partnership, and was owed $30,000 in Nantucket and $8,000 in Boston. The careful Captain Thain had found overdrafts amounting to $91,000, but where was the Bank President who had overdrawn $50,000? Where were the other Directors whose accounts were overdrawn? Why were they not here to protect the Defendant? Why were they not here to say, "We took the $91,000?" The District Attorney objected, and Coffin left the questions hanging.

Coffin resumed his speech with a question about the alterations in the bank records; when were they made and who made them? There was testimony that miles of books were not written up, and there were no entries in cartloads of passbooks. Yet all the books were turned over to Mr. Morton to write up, which would surely reveal any felony if there were any. That letter of Burnell to Captain Thain was no evidence of fraud; the Defendant had not admitted guilt but only delay. What would this jury say of a shipmaster who had lost his way and suffered the loss of his ship? Would he then be charged with piracy?

The first witness for the defense was Abraham Wing, a business partner of Burnell since 1843 in the whale oil business. He testified they did about $100,000 per year, and Burnell had about $14,000 in his account at the time of the problem with the check.

He knew Burnell's credit was always good and he often had offers of loans, but was never under any pressure for money. Wing was also a Director of the bank, which had doubled its business after the Pacific Bank difficulty of 1843, and knew that Burnell had no help as Cashier, but was expected to do all the book entries himself. Burnell had told him that he would rather do the work of a clerk himself if they would pay him the salary. In the summer of 1845, Burnell owned one-fourth of the whale ship *Ganges*, worth about $30,000, offered to furnish the captain of the *Orion* with a ship, and had $10,000 available to loan for twelve months. No reputation was better than Burnell's until this bank business.

William Mitchell, Cashier of the Pacific Bank, testified that Burnell occasionally used his private funds to pay balances due the Pacific Bank from the Manufacturers and Mechanics Bank. Without book entries, it would be difficult for a cashier to know the standing of the accounts, and he might be liable to overdrafts.

Justin Lawrence told the jury he was asked to go to Washington by Burnell's friend, Tappan, and went to a lawyer for legal advice, who recommended he persuade Burnell to return. Burnell greeted him cordially and said, "If anybody says I have taken the funds of that bank, it is false." He tried to get Burnell to turn over the sum of $14,000 to him, but Burnell said he had no money of consequence. He hesitated about returning to Nantucket, said Burnell, until Captain Thain had arranged matters, and said the idea of being charged with dishonesty was more than he could stand.

Matthew Crosby testified he was connected to Burnell by marriage, for which he had paid Burnell $23,000 as the marriage portion of his wife. He had purchased Burnell's share of the ship *Navigator*, but Burnell told him to keep the funds as he did not need the money. He narrated to the jury that Burnell had interest in ten whale ships amounting to $325,000. Burnell also owned a house and farm in 'Sconset worth about $1,500 and that his father had a house on Ray's Court worth about $20,000.

The case for the defense lasted from 8:30 a.m. to 3:30 p.m. on a warm Saturday, with two hours to lunch. When Coffin rested, he had shown that Barker Burnell was a young man of good reputation with abundant financial resources, but was over-worked and careless in his bookkeeping at the bank. He had also displayed an impressive list of character witnesses from the highest level of the Nantucket business community. He had scarcely mentioned the subject of the $6,000 check, and, most important, he had kept Barker Burnell sitting silently at the counsel table without taking the witness stand.

Monday morning dawned with a great crowd assembled outside the Nantucket courthouse, which stood near Monument Square on Main Street. When the doors opened, there was a rush for seats to hear the summation of the great Rufus Choate. Although the trial preparation of Timothy Coffin and his handling of the witnesses had been skillful, the local crowd was looking forward to hearing the great Choate at his best, and they strained to hear every word. Rufus Choate spoke for four hours.

"What a charge! Is it judicially and morally certain that Barker Burnell, on February 14, 1844, took this check of $6,000 with the felonious intent to steal and never replace the money? This man, this young man, almost a boy, with such multiplicity of business, with over-occupation enough to crush anyone, alone in the Bank, suffered the money to waste. He found himself in arrears, astounded at the evaporation of the funds, and in some instances, made false statements; but, did he ever form the conscious intent never to replace it? How different this case has developed from that you have discussed in your streets, on the decks of your ships, and in your bar rooms, if you have any. As cashier of the Bank, he was required to devote all his skill and attention to the bank, and for this he has been held responsible to the last dollar. He has made ample restitution: in the payment of $43,000, in the long days in jail, gladdened by the affection of his wife but saddened by the death of his child. We say the money has been lost by a series of neglect; the government says he stole it.

"Barker Burnell was placed in charge of this Bank at the age of 22, when no man on this Island had a more stainless reputation, no man under less temptation to fall from his bright prospects. He started fine, bright, and stainless...one of the jewels of the Island. Born in prosperity, married to a worthy wife, one who does not desert him today. Now, they claim this young man with ample fortune, above temptation, within a year and a half steals $100,000 or $125,000. Is that probable, is it reasonable? Or, have we all looked for guilt and crime where there was only neglect? During all these months, he was with you, never off the Island more than ten days. Did he not win your approval so that you sent him to represent you in the Senate of the Commonwealth? Here is the solution: he was alone; the Directors gave him no aid at the bank; and he neglected his trust. He was living in a community eminent for its energy and enterprise all over the world. So he bought oil and ships; that is no evidence of embarrassment. One things alone was neglected...the entire bookkeeping. Entries were not made, checks were crowded into pigeon holes, no posting of the books after August of 1844. We have the stupendous fact that for two years no man could tell the condition of that bank within $200,000. What would you think of a master of a ship lost in the fog for one hundred days with no dead reckoning? Ten thousand mistakes concurred, and all against the bank. The President of the bank, an honest man by name and reputation, had overdrawn his account $50,000; hundreds of others, as honest as he, had overdrawn their accounts twice over. The solutions are before you: is it theft or neglect? Gentlemen, if that man there should come back to you from the shadow of a living grave, spare yourselves the regret of having convicted him on insufficient evidence!"

Choate paid tribute to the masterly trial work of his brother Coffin in marshalling the evidence and proceeded to nail down the critical facts for the jury. "When Barker Burnell drew that check, he furnished three or four witnesses of his act, and in the pressure of his business, he forgot to charge it, although he had funds in the bank and right to draw on them. The act did not excite the suspicion of Mr. Williams or Simpson & Tappan, all high and honorable gentlemen. Weighed down with domestic grief, with eleven ships at sea, and $200,000 worth of business and half the farms on Nantucket, he received the account of the bank from Boston on April 1st and filed it away. There is no proof the bank lost $6,000; no proof he did not replace it; no proof it was not part of the general overdrafts of $91,000. He can only be convicted for the money he did take. If a man is indicted for stealing a horse in Nantucket, and it is shown he stole a horse in New Bedford, that does not prove he stole one in Nantucket. The government has failed to show that Burnell stole any money. Mr. Burnell had a foolish ambition and he declined the offer of a clerk. He did half his business and neglected the other half; he was there in the morning when the checks poured in, but did not post them in the afternoon. Is not this stupendous neglect sufficient to account for this phenomena?

"One other piece of evidence needs discussion. It is said that Burnell's flight gives evidence of his guilt. But when he wrote that letter to Captain Thain, he was in agony over the confusion in the bank. Thain found him calm and cooperative. 'I have taken nothing,' said Burnell. 'God knows where the money is.' Yes, Burnell went away to Washington, dallying awhile with the gilded scene, but his heart was in Nantucket. I thank God that it was his own heart that prompted his return.

"Consider, finally, the openness of the transaction. He drew the check and signed his own name, telling the world he was taking the funds of the bank. Does he run away? No, his funds were in the bank, there was $10,000 in his account at the time the government says he was stealing $6,000! Burnell was buying ships and oil, evidence that he intended to stay here. Did he flee to Jersey City or Mexico? If he took the $100,000 the bank is missing, how did he spend it? Do you believe he could take $100,000 and spend it on this Island without being known? Here? Where everybody knows what everybody else knows? Where did he spend it? He has property worth $94,780. He has paid the receivers of the bank $44,000. Where is the theft?

"Think of his agony as he looks out from the gloomy prison walls on the funeral procession of his child, as he thinks of his wife, and his mother. Gentlemen, you are to try this case on your oaths, and unless it is morally and judicially certain that he meant to take that money and intended never to return it, you are bound to acquit him. I do not believe he embezzled a dollar, certainly not that $6,000. He is a mere boy compared with you...send him forward ready to take a stand, less in haste to get rich, a sadder but wiser man."

District Attorney J.H. Clifford of New Bedford rose to sum up for the prosecution, delivering a speech lasting two and three-quarter hours. He began by complementing the great Rufus Choate on his eloquence and intellect. "There is scarcely a conceivable state of facts upon which he would not be able to make a plausible explanation. Indeed, if this Defendant were to rise from his seat and strike a victim dead upon the floor of this courtroom, right before the jury, his able counsel might succeed in procuring his acquittal."

He then recapitulated the prosecution's case, solemnly stating that the Defendant's intention to return the money at some more convenient time did not detract from the fact that he actually converted the bank's money to his own use. "If he converted that money to his own use and concealed the fact from his employers, that is fraudulent conversion. We cannot look into his motives. God alone can read the human heart. If he defrauded the bank to help personal friends, or to obtain popularity, that is no different from using it to buy meat and drink, or houses and lands. If he cannot be convicted on the evidence we have presented, it would be difficult, if not impossible, to convict him even though he had taken all the capital stock of this bank.

"The effect of all his alterations on the bank's books was to make the bank appear sixty or seventy thousand dollars better than it really was, and to cover up the gross misconduct of the cashier. Who made these alterations? Who had any motive to make them but Burnell? He made them all. Why, if innocent of fraud, did he write that note to Captain Thain? Why did he not return to Nantucket? He said he had to retire to collect his spirits...but where? To the festivities of Washington city!"

The prosecutor finally turned to the evidence of Burnell's good character. "In a case like this, it is worth less than nothing, for no man can rob a bank if he does not bear a good character. True, he has made restitution to the receivers, but..."

District Attorney Clifford now hammered home the final argument.

"Has he paid the Commonwealth for the wrong he had done? She demands something higher than money...she will not permit the wealthy to buy immunity from crime. Is the law which punishes the man who steals a loaf of bread not strong enough to punish he who steals one hundred thousand dollars? One final consideration: Some of you men have sons growing up who will hear of this case. One of these boys may someday be exposed to strong temptation and the last restraining consideration may be the fear of punishment. But, if your son remembers that Barker Burnell, though guilty of a great crime, was acquitted by a jury that included his father, this may turn the scale and work the ruin of your son!"

It was a powerful and emotional appeal to the Nantucket jury. The judge followed with a charge on the law which lasted about an hour. The jury retired at 6:40 p.m., and remained out all night.

The Court reconvened at 7:30 a.m. after a night of deliberation. The foreman announced the verdict: Not Guilty. The Defendant Burnell was remanded to custody as there remained seven other indictments against him pending in the Court. His bail was reduced to $10,000, which was produced to obtain his release. The remaining charges were dismissed at the October, 1847, term of the Court, and Barker Burnell returned to public life.

Barker Burnell departed from Nantucket with his wife and remaining child, and they eventually settled in Chile, where he died a forgotten man in 1861. Today there remains no memory of the famous family on the Island but for the name of Burnell Street, which led to the family farm in 'Sconset. The Manufacturers' and Mechanics' Bank itself was destroyed in the Great Fire which swept through the Town in July, 1846.

The trial of Barker Burnell left behind it more mysteries than it solved. What became of the capital stock of $100,000 which disappeared from the bank? Why did Burnell borrow $6,000 and risk prosecution when he appeared to have abundant wealth? Did he use the money for himself or for another party? Why were not the Directors of the bank prosecuted for the missing money? The celebrated trial ended the case, but left the lasting question: Where did the money go? God only knows!

CHAPTER SIX

THE WRECK OF
THE BRITISH QUEEN

On the cold winter morning of December 18, 1851, the town of Nantucket was awakened by a familiar cry from the watchman in the tower of the South Church on Orange Street.

"Ship in distress! She's a full-master with distress flags a-flying! Big shipwreck off Muskeget!"

For most of the people of Nantucket Island, the news of another ship wrecked along the shore was a grim reminder of their perilous position in the Atlantic Ocean, because the shoals of Nantucket had claimed many ships over the years. During the nineteenth century, all vessels bound for New York and most coastwise traffic were forced to skirt the shoals around Nantucket, where dangerous breakers revealed shallow waters and shifting sand bars. In an era before modern navigational equipment and wireless radio, the safety of the ship depended upon celestial navigation and skillful seamanship.

Following the decline of the Island as a whaling port after the Great Fire of 1846, the waterfront of Nantucket was reduced to a scene of abandoned wharves and empty warehouses, with only a few small ships remaining as reminders of the great old days. Most of the former whalemen were now elderly citizens, spending their days chatting with old friends, playing endless games of checkers and cribbage, dreaming of the past. There still existed a small band of Nantucketers who followed the sea and made their reputations among the dangerous elements which surrounded the Island.

The ablest of these veteran skippers was Captain David G. Patterson, a native of Chatham, whose ship-handling ability had earned him great respect from the Nantucket shipowners. When the Gold Rush of 1849 drew many fortune hunters to California, David Patterson skippered a 50-foot sloop from Nantucket around Cape Horn to California -- a truly remarkable achievement. Returning to find Nantucket marine business in decline, he remained alert to the possibilities of the salvage business as a lucrative sideline for the skillful pilot.

The Island was accustomed to salvage operations and the news from the tower brought a hum of life to the sleepy waterfront. Aside from natural feelings of humanity to rescue the passengers and crew in distress, Nantucketers were alert to the potential of a valuable salvage operation, as the prospect of a "full-masted ship" presented a tempting prize to those enterprising and fortunate enough to salvage its cargo. The usual award was one-half of the value of the ship and cargo saved from the sea. There was no monetary award for saving lives.

The prospect was not brightened by the fury of the December gale which remained unabated. Winter struck early in December of 1851, when freezing weather and high winds had set ice floes surging through Nantucket Sound. The northwest winds were still howling into the harbor and the ice and tides were running against any rescue attempt. Throughout the day of the eighteenth, no vessel was able to leave port. Furthermore, the stricken ship, visible through the long glass from the tower, was caught in a dangerous channel between Nantucket and Martha's Vineyard, a full twelve miles from Nantucket Harbor.

The *British Queen* was an old, full-masted sailing ship, pressed into service to transport the flood of Irish emigrants bound for America to escape the Great Famine of 1846-1851. During those years, a deadly disease destroyed the potato crop which was the staple food of the Irish peasants, one-half of whom depended upon it for their sole sustenance. With the failure of the potato, famine and disease swept the country, and one million people died during the famine years.

There was no help forthcoming from the British government, which believed that government should do nothing to interfere with the natural forces of supply and demand. One of these forces was the English demand for Irish produce, and even during the depths of the famine, Ireland continued to export food to Britain. Ironically, the *British Queen* herself, during the summer of 1851, carried a cargo of 688 barrels of wheat and 450 barrels of oats from Limerick to Glasgow.

For many of the surviving Irish, there was only one hope for escape from their misery: emigration to America. Within six years, over two million left their native land. The conditions aboard the emigrant ships were often as miserable and dangerous as those in Ireland, but millions were willing to take their chances on the journey across the Atlantic. Most of them walked the long miles from their cottages to the port cities, carrying their few possessions in a single bag, and paying five pounds for a berth in the steerage of the ship. They were also obliged to purchase their own food for the voyage, a trip that normally took four or five weeks.

On the morning of October 22, 1851, the *British Queen* cast off from the port of Dublin, carrying 226 Irish immigrants bound for New York, with Captain Thomas Conway in command.

The favored vessel available to make the rescue attempt was the paddle-wheel steamer *Telegraph*, which served as the Island's steamboat service to the mainland and occasionally engaged in the rescue business. She was captained by George Russell and the company also employed Captain Thomas Gardner as professional wreck master. The *Telegraph* was moored at Nantucket's Straight Wharf, but her 8-foot draft prevented her leaving harbor until high tide, and her paddle wheels were in danger of becoming disabled by the ice if she ventured into the shoals near the wreck.

On the evening of the eighteenth, a small group of men met in the brick building of Joseph Macy, the leading merchant and shipowner of the Island, to plan the rescue. It was agreed that an attempt must be made to reach the ship, for she would not last long under the pounding of the wind and seas. Macy had at the wharf two schooners, the *Hamilton*, with Thomas Bearse in command and Captain David Patterson, a half owner, as pilot and wreck master, and the smaller schooner *Game Cock*, with his brother, Captain William Patterson, in command. All these men were personal friends, but often professional rivals. Together they devised a plan of rescue for the *British Queen*. Since the *Telegraph* could not approach the wreck, she would tow the two schooners out of the harbor ice and over the bar and let them get in close to make the rescue. Nothing could be done until the next day, while the passengers of the wrecked ship huddled in darkness and terror, praying for deliverance.

The morning of Friday, December 19, saw the *Telegraph* building up steam at the wharf, while the crews of the *Hamilton* and *Game Cock* prepared for sea. The news of the wreck had spread beyond the waterfront and several churches and charitable organizations had been alerted to the situation, while public halls were made ready to receive any survivors who might be brought ashore. The efforts of the Islanders were all private and voluntary, for there was no Coast Guard, no Red Cross and no public help to be had.

The departure of the rescue ships depended upon high water over Nantucket bar, the troublesome sand bar which blocked the entrance to the harbor before the construction of the jetties. High tide came at 1:00 in the afternoon when there was nine feet of water over the bar. The *Hamilton* drew eight feet and the *Game Cock* drew seven. At the last minute, Captain David Patterson declined the tow and his *Hamilton* remained at the wharf. He gave no explanation, and the situation did not permit time for discussion. Promptly at noon, the *Telegraph* got underway, paddles churning through the ice floes and towing the *Game Cock* around Brant Point and out to sea. Once over the bar, the *Game Cock* set here sails and plunged through the wind and seas to the west. In the early afternoon, she reached a point a half mile from the wreck where she dropped her anchor to survey the situation. The *Telegraph* followed and anchored three quarters of a mile from the wreck.

Aboard the *British Queen*, 226 passengers had endured a night of terror as eleven feet of water drove them out of the steerage decks to the freezing darkness of the main deck. Half frozen and suffering from lack of food and water, they learned that two passengers had died during the night, a grim foreshadowing of what was yet to come. Praying and moaning, they huddled on the main deck and clung to each other, while beneath their feet the old ship slipped slowly toward the icy waves.

Captain Thomas Conway, muffled in his greatcoat, stood at the rail, sweeping the ocean with his long glass. The ship had experienced a terrible voyage, eight weeks from Dublin and still far from New York, with head winds all the way. Conway himself was suffering from illness which prevented him from doing the navigation, and the ship had found itself south of Nantucket, then driven into the dangerous Muskeget Channel, where she had grounded in a snowstorm, north of Muskeget. Unable to free the ship, Conway ordered the foremast and mizzenmast chopped away to prevent the ship from wrenching herself apart, and set the distress signals atop the mainmast. There was not much more he could do but gaze toward the low-lying Island on the horizon and pray for help.

The *Hamilton*, with Captain David Patterson aboard, left Nantucket Harbor a half hour after the *Telegraph* and *Game Cock*, but by skillful sailing, soon reached the wreck and anchored. Captain Russell hurriedly conferred with Patterson, and they rowed to the *Game Cock*, where Captain Thomas Gardner shouted: "Whose boat is that?" Russell informed him it was David Patterson's.

"Why, I left him at the wharf!" said Captain Gardner.

"Well, he's here now," called Captain Russell, "and you'd better invite him to join us!"

Patterson's independent action undoubtedly irritated the other captains, but in the emergency, they were glad to have him aboard. The two wreckers now combined their crews in the boats and set off toward the wreck, knowing that time and tide were running against them.

Captain George Russell took the steering oar of the ship's boat with Captain David Patterson on board and started to approach the starboard side of the *British Queen*. Half way to the wreck, some low breakers showed their white teeth and Gardner said, "Captain Patterson, you'd better take the steering oar --   you are more acquainted with these breakers than I."

With Patterson at the helm, the boat passed through the breakers and into the heavy current sweeping between the *Game Cock* and the wreck. Patterson then swung the boat toward a sea ladder hanging from the ship, handed the oar to his mate, and leaped onto the ladder. He then worked his way aft to meet Captain Conway, who was in shock and despair, able only to say that he carried no cargo and his ship was not insured. Captain Gardner then climbed aboard and announced he was the agent for the steamboat and ready to save the passengers. He then signalled the *Game Cock* to lay alongside, and the frightened passengers began climbing down to the deck of the schooner. It was a perilous procedure, for the smaller boat could not get close aboard, and the surging sea would first lift her high above the rail of the wreck, then drop her into the trough below the ship's counter.

When about sixty passengers had been transferred, Captain Gardner shouted that the *Game Cock* could take no more, as she was striking bottom. By the time he could take the schooner to the *Telegraph* and return, the tide would turn and make seas too rough for further rescue in this manner. Captain Patterson knew that if he brought the *Hamilton* in to rescue the remaining passengers, he would not only endanger his ship but would leave the salvage of the wreck and its gear to Captain Gardner and the *Game Cock*.

Captain Conway of the *British Queen* said, "We have no cargo and the ship is a total loss. All I want is to get my passengers to safety. The water has been up over the lower deck all night, and they are in horrid condition."

"We get nothing for saving lives, " said Captain Patterson, "but be assured, my schooner will save your people."

Patterson then brought the schooner *Hamilton* alongside as soon as the *Game Cock* got underway. The *British Queen* was now headed north and listed heavily to starboard, with the waves smashing against her stern. The *Hamilton* approached her bow, dropped an anchor, and payed out her anchor cable until she lay across her bow, then slowly worked down her starboard side. Clinging to the wreck with mooring lines, the *Hamilton* was heaved high above the ship with each rising wave, then smashed down on the shoal.

Meanwhile the passengers were jumping or being thrown from the wreck to the schooner, where they were hustled below and wrapped in blankets. As the day darkened and the tide turned, every one of the passengers was rescued without the loss of a single person. When all were aboard, Captain Conway and David Patterson climbed aboard the *Hamilton* and she got underway for Nantucket Harbor.

Shortly after five o'clock, the *Telegraph* and the *Hamilton* reached Straight Wharf, where a large crowd waited in the cold and dark to take charge of the immigrants. Their appearance presented one of the saddest sights the Island had ever seen, for in addition to the peril and horror they had endured, they had lost all personal possessions and arrived with only the clothes on their backs. Most of their clothing had to be exchanged or burned to prevent disease, but the local citizens donated food, clothing and bedding to them. The unfortunates were housed in Pantheon Hall, two fire houses, and Temperance Hall on Federal Street, now the site of Saint Mary's Church. Captain Conway was lodged in the Ocean House to recover from his illness, and the British Consul, William Barney, made arrangements for the crew of the ship. Many women and children were taken into private homes in town. The gratitude of the Irish immigrants was readily apparent, and for several days Nantucketers were stopped on the streets to hear "May God Almighty bless you," from those grateful people.

On Christmas Day, 1851, the old reliable steamer *Telegraph* embarked from Nantucket with most of the immigrants on the first leg of their final voyage to New York. Several of them elected to stay on Nantucket, unwilling to risk another sea voyage, content to remain on the only piece of America they ever saw. One such couple was Robert C. Mooney, age 29, and his 21-year-old bride, Julia (Donegan), who had been married in Ireland shortly before embarking on the *British Queen*. After their experience on the sea, they never went near the water, and settled down as farmers on Nantucket, raising a family of seven children.

The old *British Queen* broke up on the shoals and was sold as she lay for $290. There was little to salvage and no money to be made by the heroic Nantucketers who had risked their lives to save a shipload of strangers from a foreign land. The only remnant of the ship was her quarterboard, which floated ashore and was presented to Robert Mooney as a reminder of his fateful arrival on Nantucket. He kept this last vestige of the ship to the end of his long life, and it has since been preserved by his descendents.

From The *Mirror*, Nantucket, Mass., December 27, 1851;

"We, the shipwrecked passengers of the ill-fated ship, *British Queen* of Dublin, deem it our bounden duty to return our most heartfelt and sincere thanks for the cordial and human reception we have received from the hospitable citizens and inhabitants of the Island of Nantucket. To those brave and humane men who came to our rescue when all hope had died within ourselves -- we are at a loss to express our gratitude. To the citizens and inhabitants of the Island of Nantucket at large, we feel a debt of gratitude which will only be forgotten when life ceases to exist. To you, human and Christian men, we may well express the language of the Patriarch of old, and say, 'When our ears heard you, then we blessed you; when our eyes saw you, they gave witness unto you; because you delivered the poor that cried, the fatherless and they that had none to help them. The blessings of those that were ready to perish came upon you, for you caused the widows' hearts to sing for joy.

"Your reward will surely come at the great day when, before assembled worlds, the great Disposer of events will allot to each and all his final sentence in His own words: 'Come ye blessed children of my father, inherit the kingdom prepared for you from the foundation of the world; for we were hungered and ye gave us meat, we were thirsty and ye gave us drink, we were strangers and ye took us in, naked and ye clothed us.'

"And now, preservers of our lives, permit us in conclusion to commit you to the care and keeping of Almighty God. May He watch over you and yours; may He increase your store a hundred fold, and may there be no lack or falling off among you.

"Signed, on behalf of all the passengers,

-- Nelson T. Johnston"

Robert C. Mooney and his wife Julia settled in Nantucket to become tenant farmers, managing the fine farm of Frederick C. Sanford at Beechwood, where they produced the best butter on the Island. They eventually came to own several farms along the Polpis Road and a home on Pleasant Street. When they arrived in Nantucket, the only possession they carried from Ireland was the family stone crucifix, but they never dwelled upon the bitter memories of the old country. Robert was anxious to forget the past, and when he was naturalized in Nantucket in 1855, he stoutly denied allegiance to any foreign powers or princes, "...especially to Victoria, Queen of Great Britain and Ireland." There was only one *British Queen* in his life, and he proudly displayed the quarterboard of the old ship which had carried him to Nantucket.

Julia died in 1893, never once leaving Nantucket. When Robert was 80 in 1901, he was "persuaded" by his sons to travel to the mainland to visit the Brockton Fair, a great event in his life, and his single view of the America for which he had crossed the Atlantic fifty years before. He died in Nantucket at the age of 86 in 1908, perfectly content with his Island home, survived by seven children, twelve grandchildren and nine great-grandchildren. Robert and his wife were devoted to their faith, and are today memorialized by a stained glass window in Saint Mary's Church, built in 1896 on the site where the survivors of the British Queen spent their first nights in America.

In the words of Arthur Elwell Jenks, writing in the *Inquirer & Mirror*:

"I cannot withhold my offering of respect in memory of the late Robert C. Mooney. His name when spoken reflected sterling character; he was a good citizen; as a husband and father, kind and affectionate to the end. Although not in the public eye and much apart from the daily walks of his fellow-countrymen, the good influence of his genial disposition was felt by anyone whom he met, and his speech was flavored with a ready wit that was a heritage from his nationality."

CHAPTER SEVEN

MURDER ON NANTUCKET

The pivotal year of 1860 saw many changes taking place in the way of life on Nantucket. The whaling industry had vanished since the Great Fire of 1846 had destroyed the center of the town, and the last whaler had left port for the whaling grounds, never to return. The stately homes on Main Street and Orange Street stood as proud reminders of a bygone era, but many houses were empty. The population had declined from 9,700 in 1840 to 6,000 in 1860, and would soon be half of that figure. As the old whalemen died off and the young men left for the promised lands in the west, the town itself seemed to drift into the past, with many of its houses occupied by elderly women.

In a small house on Silver Street, a neighborhood of modest homes built by the Nantucket mariners of early years, lived Phebe Fuller, an elderly widow who kept a small store in the front room of her home. She had lived a quiet and solitary life, which was soon to end in violence and tragedy. On the evening of November 22, 1860, a neighbor found her front door open at 9 o'clock and, fearing she was ill, entered the shop. Finding the shop empty and dark, she continued into the living room where, by the glow of a whale oil lamp, she saw the body of Phebe Fuller sprawled in a pool of blood.

Captain Nathaniel Fitzgerald, a retired mariner, answered the neighbor's call for help, picked up Mrs. Fuller, and carried her to a couch. Dr. John H. Sherman arrived soon after and found her alive but unconscious from a severe head injury and loss of blood. Her head had been badly battered, her right ear was split, and her nose was fractured. Her right arm was bloody and bruised from defensive wounds as she sought to avoid the attack. A large amount of blood had splattered the floor and walls of the living room.

Nantucket had no police force in those days, only a fire watch in the evening hours and a county sheriff for formal occasions. The actual investigation of the crime, therefore, was turned over to Alfred Macy, Chairman of the Board of Selectmen, with Captain Fitzgerald helping him out. The first object they seized was the murder weapon, a whalebone "fid," a heavy, tapered instrument used on board ship to work rope and untangle lines, like a marlin-spike. The fid was covered with blood.

The little cash drawer in the Fuller store was found half open, but contained so little money it was impossible to determine whether anything had been taken. The first reports of the crime stated the drawer had been rifled in a robbery attempt, but this proved untrue. In the absence of a motive or a suspect, the authorities were baffled by the senseless assault on the old woman.

Meanwhile, Phebe Fuller lingered close to death. On November 25, she told Doctor Sherman she would never recover as she had received a mortal injury. Later that day she told Captain Fitzgerald, "I cannot live. Let no one follow me to the grave; I am principled against it."

Captain Fitzgerald pressed closer. "Tell me, you must tell me, who did this dreadful thing to you?"

Slowly, painfully, Phebe Fuller spoke. "Patience...Patience Cooper...she came in to pay her bill...then I saw an evil smile on her face and...she struck me..." Her voice faded as she lapsed into a coma.

The town authorities now had a suspect, and they immediately sent Sheriff Frederick H. Chase to arrest Patience Cooper at her little house on lower Pleasant Street, only a few blocks from the Fuller home.

The town now seethed with excitement at the startling violence of the crime and the naming of such an unlikely suspect. Patience Cooper was a black woman who lived in the respectable colony of Nantucket people of color in a district known as "Guinea" (from the original home of the whalemen recruited from Africa). A quiet and hard-working woman of 50, Patience was a church-going member of the community and as unlikely a suspect as Phebe Fuller was a victim. The local authorities were certain they had their woman, based upon the statement of Mrs. Fuller. Other townspeople thought they were rushing to judgment in a hasty attempt to take action without full investigation.

Phebe Fuller lingered in her coma until December 12, when she died from her injuries. Patience Cooper was charged with murder and incarcerated in the Old Jail on Vestal Street under the watchful eyes of Sheriff Chase. The charge of murder did not allow the defendant a release on bail, and the authorities postponed her trial in an attempt to obtain a confession from the prisoner, but she steadfastly maintained her innocence. Finally, her case was called for trial in the Nantucket Superior Court before Justice Lincoln Flagg Brigham.

The capital charge against Patience Cooper required the assistance of able trial counsel, and although Nantucket was not blessed with many lawyers in 1860, one man of talent and ability came to her defense. Edward M. Gardner, a Nantucketer of some education but little legal training, had begun his career as a school teacher on Nantucket and was later admitted to the Bar. He reached the peak of the Nantucket legal profession in 1858 when he was appointed Judge of the Probate Court, where he served 14 years. Since this was a part-time position, Gardner could practice in other courts, and he felt obliged to offer his services to Patience Cooper. The record indicated that the country lawyer, handling the biggest case of his career, did a good job for his client.

The District Attorney presented the evidence of Doctor Sherman and Captain Fitzgerald about the discovery of Phebe Fuller and the bloody scene of the attack. Selectman Macy testified about a search and examination of Patience Cooper's home, which revealed no bloodstained evidence. The defendant maintained her innocence throughout the trial and sought to prove she was elsewhere on the night of the assault, as well as introduce evidence that the Selectmen had assured her that they were satisfied as to her innocence. The jury was impressed with the dying declaration of Mrs. Fuller to Captain Fitzgerald that Patience Cooper committed the deed, although this was the only incriminating evidence against her. This statement was contested by the defendant's attorney vigorously as critically dependent upon the accuracy and state of mind of the elderly woman.

Counsel Gardner now sought to prove by several witnesses who knew Phebe Fuller well and would testify that she was often in the habit of mistaking persons for others whom they did not resemble, that her mind was often confused and her memory weak. The judge ruled this evidence inadmissible.

The Nantucket jury found Patience guilty and her attorney claimed an appeal based upon the questions of law on the evidentiary rulings.

In November of 1862, the Supreme Judicial Court heard the appeal of Patience Cooper in Boston, and ordered a new trial be held. The court upheld the admission of the statement identifying Patience Cooper as a dying declaration...made under a sense of impending death. But the testimony of the witnesses that Mrs. Fuller often made mistakes in identifying people was crucial and should have been admitted. The great question in the case was the identity of the assailant, and on this issue, the defendant was entitled to every consideration.

Thus the case was returned to Nantucket for a retrial the next year before Justice Henry Vose. The stalwart Edward Gardner again handled the defense, but the trial proved to be much shorter without the evidentiary questions which occupied the earlier trial. Again, the jury heard Captain Nathaniel Fitzgerald repeat the dying declaration of Phebe Fuller, and, again, the jury returned a verdict of guilty.

Judge Vose then pronounced the sentence. "Patience Cooper, the jury having found you guilty of the crime charged, I sentence you to serve ten years in the House of Correction."

The sentence of the court surprised the townfolk and satisfied no one. If truly guilty of the murder, Patience had received a light sentence for a horrible crime, one which usually called for at least a life sentence. If innocent, she should have been freed. Many people believed there was serious doubt in the minds of both the jury and the prosecutors as to her guilt, and the sentence reflected some sort of compromise by the court.

Patience Cooper resumed her lonely incarceration as the only inmate of the old House of Correction which stood on Vestal Street next to the Old Jail, which was built in 1805 and is still standing. The House of Correction was used for petty criminals, debtors, and prisoners who did not require the maximum security of the jail. Patience was lodged in a first floor cell at the east end of the building with a cot, washstand, and a few belongings. A nearby stove was tended by the jailor and a yard, surrounded by a high board fence, was available for exercise.

As she had always been a hard-working and active woman, the dreary prison routine weighed heavily upon Patience. She was allowed freedom to exercise in the yard every day, where the neighbors often heard her singing a hymn in her beautiful voice which she had often raised in the congregation of the Colored Baptist Church. Many local citizens took pity upon her plight and brought her gifts and handicrafts. In order to keep busy, she was permitted by the jailor to take in laundry and perform sewing jobs for the neighbors, earning money which the jailor saved for her future needs. One day she told him, "I am glad to have the money put aside. I want to know that I will be buried proper...that's all I want it for."

From the day of her arrest, through two trials and one appeal, Patience said little about the case except to maintain her innocence. Even after the guilty verdict and the ten-year sentence, she refused to change her attitude or discuss the crime. This led many to conclude she was either an innocent victim or an accessory covering up for the true murderer.

Now her case attracted more attention. Several summer visitors to Nantucket heard about her and took an interest in her. The nation was in the midst of the Civil War, a conflict which deeply involved the Nantucket community for the citizens were ardent in their support of the Union cause. The island strongly supported the Abolitionist Movement and cheered the Emancipation Proclamation which freed the slaves. To many people, the incarceration of this black woman at this point in history seemed grossly improper. Yet the law had spoken, and nothing could be done to commute her sentence unless she made a full confession of guilt and showed a sincere promise of reformation. It thus appeared that Patience Cooper was doomed to ten years in jail unless she broke her silence.

There now entered a dark, mysterious stranger known as Mark Salom, described by the reports as a "wealthy summer resident from Boston." He took it upon himself to befriend Patience Cooper and began visiting her regularly. Gradually, he persuaded her to talk about the murder, and one day he announced to the Sheriff that Patience was ready to talk. In the presence of three witnesses, Mr. Salom went to her cell and interviewed her, but on this occasion she placed her hand on the Bible and denied all knowledge of the crime. Then she added her belief that sooner or later her sentence would be commuted. Salom explained to her that any leniency would require a certificate of good conduct, evidence of sincere repentance, and a full and free confession of guilt. She thought this over and asked him to return the next day.

It was on Sunday, May 12, 1865, that Mr. Salom obtained the famous and long-sought confession of Patience Cooper. Written by him and dictated in the presence of Captain Oliver Cushman, her confession answered his questions in full, and the results were printed the next week in the *Inquirer & Mirror* to satisfy the doubts of the public. Mr. Salom began by asking the direct question, "Are you not guilty of the murder of Mrs. Fuller?"

She replied, "I confess that I did do it."

Patience then related that she went to the Fuller shop in the early evening to discuss a bill which she owed of about eight dollars, although Mrs. Fuller was not pressing her for payment; in fact, "...she was always good to me and frequently said not to hurry about paying it."

Suddenly, Patience related, Mrs. Fuller became agitated, and "...flew into a great passion and said she would never trust no more niggers!"

At hearing this, Patience said she picked up a "piece of board" about two feet long which was lying on the store counter, and struck Mrs. Fuller on the side of the head, saying, "I cannot tell how many times...if she was so wounded as the evidence said, I must have struck her several times for there was no one else to do it."

"Why did you do this?"

"I was very much provoked. I never heard any person make such use of such bad language as she did that night. I did it because she was so impudent and saucy to me."

Patience said she left Mrs. Fuller leaning on the counter, then went straight home through Silver Street and Pleasant Street past the Colored Baptist Church. Once home, she felt "awfully sorry" about the attack, and sat down and did some sewing. No, she stated, she had no need to wash her hands because, "...there was no blood on them. Not a single drop."

Now Mr. Salom pursued the final questions. "Why did you deny it?"

"Because I thought and had been told it would be best for me. I do now confess to ease my mind and acknowledge the justice of the sentence for I am guilty of the murder. I am sorry I killed her. I am sorry I brought disgrace upon my family."

"Had you any accomplice in this murder?"

"None," she said. "No one should be accused of this but me, as I did it and I alone."

The *Inquirer & Mirror* congratulated Mr. Salom and gave him great credit for the ingenuity he displayed in obtaining the confession, "thus removing all doubts of the innocence of the prisoner." But doubts remained, and many questioned the contents of the confession as well as its motivation. The prisoner had stated she attacked the victim in the store and left her standing at the counter; yet, all the evidence placed the victim and the bloody fid on the floor of the living room. The scene of the attack was spattered with blood, yet the attacker claimed to be spotless. Many reached the conclusion that the confession was given only to obtain a shorter sentence. Others persisted in thinking that Patience was shielding another guilty party. The actions of the two women, as related by Patience, were inconsistent with their previous modes of behavior, and the overall contents of the confession seemed pre-arranged.

Responding to this criticism, Mr. Salom wrote a letter to the *Inquirer & Mirror* on June 17, stating his curious role in the matter. "I do not now nor never did believe that the circumstances she narrated were anything but falsehoods. I gave the confession to the public for what it was worth. It certainly goes to show that she did commit the murder...but it does not, in my opinion, warrant the recommending of such a woman as a fit subject for executive clemency."

With these parting words, the last friends of Patience Cooper drifted away and the public lost interest in her case. She finished her lonely stay at the House of Correction in poor health, returned to her little home on Lower Pleasant Street, and finally moved to Our Island Home, where she died on October 29, 1885. She left behind her no family and no memory of her life, except for the many unanswered questions which surround the aloof and mysterious figure of Patience Cooper.

CHAPTER EIGHT

CHARLES O'CONOR
IN NANTUCKET

There was great interest in the large Victorian mansion under construction at Sherburne Heights on the North Cliff of Nantucket during the summer of 1881, for this was the first of the great summer homes built on the island. The owner of this house was also a subject of intense curiosity, for he was the first of the notable summer visitors to retire to Nantucket, thus launching a movement which has continued to the present time. The memory of his days on Nantucket has become legend.

One summer day, the dock-hands and wagon drivers on the Nantucket wharf observed with approval as the schooner *Onward* arrived from New York and made fast to the wharf. One young hand greeted the captain as he stepped ashore on the dock.

"Welcome ashore, Captain. Any cargo to be handled?"

"Aye, there is. And a heavier load you lads never hefted. We are going to need all the wagons and strong backs we can get."

"We have the men, Captain, but where do you want it hauled?"

"This entire cargo is consigned to the residence of Charles O'Conor, Esquire, at Sherburne Heights."

"Oh, we know where that is, Captain, but what is it we deliver?"

"Books, my friend. Law books. Over 18,000 of them."

"I say that is a mighty lot of books, Captain. But Squire O'Conor is almost 80 years old. I wonder how he will ever have time to read all those books?"

The Captain smiled. "From what I know, Charles O'Conor has already read those books. I would say he just wants them for company on this Island."

Charles O'Conor was born in New York in 1804, the son of Irish patriots who immigrated to America to find religious and political freedom following the Act of Union with Great Britain. His father, Thomas O'Conor, was born in Dublin and became a noted Irish patriot and scholar. The son attended only six months of formal schooling, but received his most important education from his father, who taught him the traditions of Irish and American history, foreign languages and the classics. From this background, he emerged with a first-rate intellect and brilliant legal mind.

Despite the father's wisdom, his son, living in an era when Irish Catholics were victims of prejudice and discrimination in New York, seemed doomed to obscurity and poverty. Young Charles soon realized the poor Irish needed their own legal advocates if they were to secure the benefits of American justice. He began the study of law as an apprentice in law offices, where he worked all day and studied by night. Studying all night, he developed a prodigious memory, and it was said he read the entire set of Blackstone's *Commentaries* not once, but twice. He always attributed his success to industry, not talent. As a tribute to his ability, he was admitted to the New York Bar at the age of twenty, and, although the rules required three years' service as an attorney before attaining the more privileged rank of counsellor, he achieved that distinction in three months.

At the New York Bar, O'Conor rapidly gained an immense reputation as a legal scholar, and became involved in almost every important case in the New York courts. His preparation was meticulous, his style was elegant, his elocution was graceful, and his arguments were persuasive. William Evarts called him the most accomplished lawyer in the learning of the profession, and John K. Porter ranked him with the greatest lawyers the country had ever produced. Throughout his career, he personified the highest qualities of integrity and character, honesty and dedication to the public interest. One judge once remarked of him: "I have often heard him state the case of his adversary with greater clearness and force than the adversary was able to state it himself."

The turbulent political times of the century drew the eminent attorney into the public affairs of the day. He served as U.S. Attorney for New York and was often mentioned for Attorney General of the United States, a post he declined. He was a member of the State Constitutional Convention of 1846, and represented his friend and colleague, Governor Samuel J. Tilden, before the Electoral Commission to resolve the great presidential election contest between Tilden and Hayes in 1876. In the year 1872, Charles O'Conor was nominated by a splinter group of the Democratic Party known as the American Party or "Straight-Out Democrats" to run for the presidency against Horace Greeley and U.S. Grant. O'Conor made no campaign, but received 29,489 votes, together with the honor of becoming the first Catholic to run for president.

Despite his involvement in American political life, Charles O'Conor always maintained a lively interest in the land of his ancestors. On his only trip abroad, he visited Ireland and commented bitterly on conditions after the Great Famine. His family came from the O'Conors of Roscommon, and he traced his ancestors back to Roderick, the last King of All Ireland in 1200 A.D. Following his research, he changed his family name from the common form of "O'Connor" to the ancient form using one "n" and thereafter explained the change by saying, "Did you ever know an Irishman who could make both n's meet?"

O'Conor's fame as a lawyer is based upon two great causes which stand as milestones in American political history. After the Civil war, he served as counsel to Jefferson Davis, former president of the Confederate States, who was arrested and imprisoned in Fortress Monroe in Virginia on charges of treason. Davis was a graduate of West Point and a former Secretary of War, who had taken the oath of loyalty to the United States. He realized full well that only a courageous lawyer would undertake his defense in the face of popular sentiment in a country which was seeking revenge for the assassination of President Lincoln. Charles O'Conor, a lifelong Democrat, had been partial to the cause of the South during the war, and he wanted very much to try the Davis case on the merits, but it never came to trial. O'Conor undertook the defense of Davis and based his defense on the Fourteenth Amendment to the Constitution, one provision of which barred any Confederate official from holding any Federal office. This was one of the post-Civil War amendments designed to be the final nail in the coffin of the Confederacy. O'Conor took his argument before Chief Justice Salmon P. Chase of the Supreme Court and successfully argued that Davis had been fully and finally punished by the Constitution itself. The Government attorneys found technical difficulties with every other charge against him, and Davis was never brought to trial. When he was released on bail in 1867, both Charles O'Conor and Horace Greeley were sureties on his bond.

In the 1870's the political corruption in New York City became a scandal of monumental proportions. Masterminded by William Marcy "Boss" Tweed and his powerful cronies, the wholesale thievery of the Tweed Ring involved scores of politicians and millions of public dollars. At the heart of the corruption sat the judiciary of the city, most of whose members had been appointed by Tweed and were easily reached to protect his interests. The most notorious of the Tweed judges was George Barnard, who often presided with his feet on the bench and a brandy bottle in hand. It was in this atmosphere that New York Governor Samuel J. Tilden conceived the brilliant stroke of enlisting the venerable Charles O'Conor to lend his great legal talent and moral prestige to the cause of political reform. O'Conor was appointed Special Assistant Attorney General and he began by indicting Boss Tweed on 120 counts before the Grand Jury.

The strange course of New York justice in the Tweed era was illustrated by the events following the charges against Tweed, who was then a state senator. He was arrested by his close friend, Sheriff Matthew Brennan, and lodged for the night in the Metropolitan Hotel, which Tweed owned. The next day he applied for bail and was denied by one judge. He immediately sought out Judge Barnard, who was presiding in the new County Court House, which Tweed had built, sitting in a judge's chair behind which hung a life size portrait of Tweed himself. Charles O'Conor argued against any bail, but the judge ignored him and set bail at $5,000, which Tweed paid immediately. His trial was then postponed several times as his lawyers pleaded for more time for trial preparation. Finally, Judge Noah Davis ruled, "Considering the brevity of human life, this rate of preparation would postpone this trial to the next generation."

Senator Tweed was wealthy enough to employ no less than seven of the leading lawyers of the day, including David Dudley Field, John Graham, and the young Elihu Root. O'Conor and his staff tried the case for several months, but the jury disagreed, and a new trial was ordered. The public was convinced Tweed had bribed some jurors. At the second trial, the state used detectives to gather information about the jurors, and Tweed's agents hired detectives to watch the state detectives. After a brief trial, at which Tweed did not testify, the jury returned a verdict of guilty on 102 counts. Judge Davis sentenced him to twelve years in prison and to pay a fine of $12,500. Tweed was taken to the Tombs prison to await the results of his appeal. When he registered at the jail, he gave his occupation as "statesman."

Charles O'Conor was not through with the Tweed Ring, and he now launched the famous "Six-Million Dollar Suit," to recover the spoils for the benefit of the people of New York. The claims involved many separate suits and lasted over several years. O'Conor's accomplishments brought him national fame for the brilliance of his legal strategy and the relentless pursuit of the guilty parties. At this point, his health began to fail from the exertions of his labors, and he became gravely ill. Many feared the aging barrister was close to death, and some newspapers printed obituaries which he lived to read. By sheer determination and the power of his will, O'Conor carried his crusade to its conclusion. Many of the Tweed ring managed to flee and conceal their wealth in Canada or Europe, so full recovery was very unlikely. At one point, O'Conor was in favor of releasing Boss Tweed on condition that he testify to all he knew about everyone connected with the frauds, but this was just what the politicians of the city and state did not want to happen. Weary of his battles, O'Conor completed his work for the prosecution in the following memorable scene.

On the last day of the final trial, Charles O'Conor, aged 72 and in frail health, rose from a sickbed to speak, and one witness wrote: "I saw the tall form of Charles O'Conor, pale, emaciated, and feeble-looking, with the collar of his greatcoat raised about his neck, slowly and painfully walking toward the bench. Almost every man in the Courtroom rose to his feet, but maintained a respectful silence."

O'Conor won his last victory in the courtroom in the civil verdict against Tweed, but the wily politician waited only long enough to carry out his final illegal escapade. In December of 1875, Boss Tweed managed to finance an escape from the New York jail which reportedly cost him $60,000. After a dramatic trip across the Hudson River by rowboat, he hid in New Jersey until he heard the results of the civil suit against him. Once he knew that all was lost, he fled by ship to Cuba, from which he caught another ship to Spain. Upon landing in Spain, he was recognized by authorities who based their identification upon the famous Thomas Nast caricatures of Tweed which had gained international circulation, and was arrested and imprisoned. The U.S. Navy sent the cruiser *Franklin* to bring him back to New York. While serving time in the Ludlow Street Jail, which he had helped build, Tweed died in 1878. O'Conor had won his last battle as "the people's lawyer."

Rich in honors, but poor in health, Charles O'Conor decided to retire from the forum. He had married in 1854, but he and his wife had no children. Now widowed and childless, he vacationed on Nantucket Island in 1880, where he stayed at the Ocean House and looked about the island carefully. Nantucketers were growing used to the seasonal influx of summer visitors, but it came as a great surprise when this famous man made the startling public announcement that he intended to make Nantucket his permanent home. This was done with deliberation and planning, and the climate of the island was the deciding factor.

Travellers during the nineteenth century were continually seeking healthy retreats, and the cool and clear air of Nantucket seemed a welcome relief from the heat and pungent aromas of New York in summertime. Convinced that he needed a change of climate, O'Conor wrote his friend, Frederick C. Sanford, that his summer in Nantucket had given him so much vigor he knew he had found "the finest and most healthful spot on the Atlantic Coast."

Charles O'Conor was considered to have enjoyed the finest professional income of any lawyer in New York, where he owned a town house valued at $400,000 and eleven acres of land at Washington Heights. At the age of 78, he set out to build a Nantucket home which suited his means and his desires. He became the first purchaser in the new development at Sherburne Heights, where the Coffin brothers had laid out homesites on the Cliff overlooking

Nantucket Sound. Selecting a site eighty feet above sea level, O'Conor commenced construction of a large Victorian style mansion, with a huge veranda and spectacular views in all directions. The wooden walls were lined with brick for warmth, and the marble for the fireplaces was imported from Italy. The *Inquirer & Mirror* reported weekly on the progress of the construction, while the town marvelled at the elegance of the mansion rising from the highest point on the Cliff.

It was not the great house, however, which the lawyer considered his most valued possession, but the library which he had amassed over a lifetime. The newspaper reported O'Conor had chartered the schooner *Onward* to transport his personal library to Nantucket. This was reputedly the greatest private law library in the United States, consisting of over 18,000 volumes, containing a comprehensive collection of Irish law books and over ninety leather-bound volumes of O'Conor's greatest cases. It also contained his legal opinions and annotations upon every subject in the law. In order to house this library, a separate brick building was constructed near the gate of his homestead, connected to the house by an extension of the veranda.

O'Conor treasured his library as it represented the labor of his lifetime. A friend once remarked, "*Harpers* would give you $100,000 for that library."

O'Conor exclaimed, "A hundred thousand dollars! Do you know that I would rather be stripped of everything else that I have and begin naked again rather than to part with that library?"

On Nantucket, O'Conor lived with a staff of four domestic servants and a housekeeper. He hired a young Nantucket teacher, Emma Folger, as his secretary. His one rule for the household was to maintain a strict silence to all the world as to his habits and affairs. He would employ only those he could trust. One of these was a Nantucket lad named George Hamblin who discovered a fire in the basement, and by his prompt action saved the house from destruction. O'Conor was so grateful he gave him $300 on the spot and promised to employ him for the rest of his life.

The people of Nantucket looked with awe on the great man who had chosen to live among them, but he was not an easy man to approach, maintaining a cool and aristocratic attitude toward the public. The natives looked forward to meeting the tall man with the fine Irish face and fringe of white beard, wearing his familiar rusty black suit and carrying his polished cane on his long walks about the town. They soon found that, although O'Conor was fond of the island and its people, he was personally aloof. Nantucket at that time had only one lawyer, and, in the words of Edward Underhill, "...For years his morning prayers and nightly vigils have been that the Lord would vouchsafe another lawyer for the island. When Mr. Charles O'Conor came from New York and took up his residence in Town, a ray of hope illumined the darkness of the horizon which encircled the solitary lawyer. But as soon as it was announced that the distinguished jurist had come to escape clients, and not to get them, the Bar subsided into a hopeless gloom."

In his own crusty way, Charles O'Conor could be warm and generous with his few close friends, men as diverse as Frederick C. Sanford, president of the Pacific National Bank, and the Reverend J.E. Crawford, the popular black preacher who also ran a barber shop and served as his personal barber and confidant. When Crawford refused to charge him more than ten cents for a shave, O'Conor would quickly give him a ten dollar bill and depart. He never forgot a favor and always remembered his early benefactors. Sixty years after a man lent him $300 to buy his first law books, he repaid the favor by hiring the man's granddaughter as his housekeeper and leaving her one-third of the residue of his estate. He always insisted that his charities remain private matters. On one occasion, he laid a ten dollar bill on the plate at the local Catholic church, and a week later, the priest made the mistake of mentioning his generosity. O'Conor gruffly said, "They will get no more from me!" And they did not.

One must wonder what this solitary man in the black suit was thinking about during his last years on Nantucket, as he spent his time brooding over the great law library, strolling the cobblestone streets, and pacing the veranda of his mansion with its endless view of the sea and sky. He left no record of his latter years and few people were aware of his innermost thoughts. He did entertain old friends who visited Nantucket and was considered a liberal host, who provided generous meals and vintage wines to his guests, while he merely picked at his food and took a single sip of wine. He had the finest home in Nantucket, but no family and few friends to appreciate it. He seemed content to spend his retirement from the world in his own way, becoming, in his own words, "a recluse on Nantucket." After all the years of publicity and controversy, Charles O'Conor had finally found peace, in the "quiet and more congenial climate" of his chosen home.

To the end of his days, O'Conor was interested in the prosperity of the island, and it was rumored he quietly distributed money around Nantucket, but the true extent of his charity was covered by his vow of secrecy. In April of 1884, the Town of Nantucket was surprised to receive an anonymous donation from a private citizen in the amount of $7,000--sufficient to pay off the entire debt of the Town. The gift was accompanied by a strong admonition that the townspeople never again burden themselves with that root of all evil, public debt.

Charles O'Conor died in his home on May 12, 1884, and only after his death did the Town learn the name of its benefactor. The local paper expressed the public gratitude, praised the man and his career, and reprinted in full his handwritten will, which was filed in Nantucket Probate Court. In accordance with his will, his great law library was returned to New York and donated to the New York Law Institute. His funeral was held in Saint Patrick's Cathedral in New York, attended by the governor, the mayor and many jurists. In respect to his memory, all civil courts in the city adjourned for the day, and the New York Supreme Court honored him as "the embodiment of the qualities, mental and moral, which should enter into and constitute the character of a great jurist and advocate."

Charles O'Conor's mansion remained for eighty years as a familiar landmark atop the Cliff on the north shore of Nantucket. It was later acquired and occupied by Ambassador Breckinridge Long, a noted diplomat during the administration of President Franklin D. Roosevelt, and maintained by his family. Finally, the old mansion was demolished in 1962 and replaced by a modern summer home. The brick building which housed the great library was removed, brick by brick, and is no more than a memory. The sole memorial on Nantucket to the man who rose from poverty, devoted his life to public service, and made his last public act a gift to his adopted home of Nantucket, is his fine portrait by Matthew Brady in the Peter Foulger Museum of the Nantucket Historical Association.

CHAPTER NINE

CHADWICK'S FOLLY

On January 1, 1885, Albert G. Brock assistant cashier of the Pacific National Bank of Nantucket, detected puzzling figures in the account of the bank and hastened to inform the president, Frederick C. Sanford. The directors were called together and the books of the bank were audited. They indicated that the cashier, William H. Chadwick, had overdrawn his personal account by a small amount, but Chadwick's explanation of other discrepancies in the books did not satisfy the directors, and he was asked to resign.

The resignation of the bank cashier soon became public knowledge and the town was swept with rumors and anxiety about the condition of the bank. Honorable Joseph Mitchell, together with fellow directors Whitney and Calder, publicly stated their confidence in the soundness of the bank, based upon their personal examination of the books. The public, wondering about the visible signs of Chadwick's recent activities, had its doubts.

William H. Chadwick, at 38, had been cashier of the Pacific National Bank for six years. He was a genial and popular local figure, possessed of many friends and enjoyed the confidence of the community. His father, William S. Chadwick, was a man of hard-earned wealth, and his mother came from a long line of Nantucket Coffins. For the past few years, the bank cashier had been a principal figure in extensive real estate operations on the island which had aroused local curiosity. There was nothing wrong with a local banker dabbling in real estate, but the size of his personal expenditures had caused the directors to become uneasy and to keep a daily watch upon his personal transactions. Despite this vigilance, shortages in the accounts had crept in, forcing them to conclude the bank had become the victim of deliberate swindling. The amount missing was estimated at $10,000 to $15,000, a huge amount for the local bank at that time.

Local rumors held that many people had been victimized by the bank cashier, but the *Inquirer & Mirror* calmly suppressed their names, adding, "it appears to be the old, old story, and comment is unnecessary. No arrest has been made."

The object of Chadwick's attentions in recent years had been a choice parcel of real estate on the eastern end of Nantucket known as Squam Head. There, on an estate of 50 acres, he had commenced extensive building operations on a high bluff overlooking the Atlantic Ocean. The project included an immense brick stable and a giant dwelling house, three stories high and topped with an enormous cupola, visible for miles around. The town could only wonder about how Chadwick was building this on his bank salary, but it was generally believed that he was operating on behalf of "parties abroad." This seemed to lessen the local anxiety while leaving the mystery of who was behind the project. Local gossip traded opinions that it was to become a summer hotel, a country club, or even a gambling casino for the yachting crowd from Newport and New York.

These were the years when Nantucket had just started to realize the potential of the tourist economy, and grandiose construction was the symbol of the era. Charles O'Conor, the retired lawyer, had finished his mansion on the Cliff, complete with Italian marble fireplaces and his 18,000 book law library. The Hotel Nantucket had been constructed on Brant Point, sprawling 260 feet in length. The Riverside Hotel had been floated down the Providence river and rebuilt at Surfside, while other projects were planned for building on the barren shores of Coatue and Tuckernuck. Anything was possible on Nantucket in those years, but the Chadwick estate at remote Squam Head was destined to outbuild and outlast them all.

Chadwick assembled his estate at Squam Head over years at an estimated cost of $100,000. The lumber for the project was shipped to Nantucket on schooners, then hauled over the rutted roads by teams of horses to the eastern headland, where teams of craftsmen were engaged in the construction. The bricks for the great stable were salvaged from the Citizens Bank on Main Street, which was torn down in 1884. Hundreds of islanders made the long trek to the site to witness the great production. Uppermost in everyone's mind was the cost of the project, and where all the money was coming from.

The Pacific National Bank, founded in 1804, was the leading commercial bank on the island, with a capital of $100,000 and a surplus of $35,000. Its president, Frederick C. Sanford, was an outstanding citizen of the island, noted for his integrity and philanthropy. The Pacific National Bank had been founded in the days when most of the islander's money was earned in the Pacific Ocean, and the name had endured while several other banks had failed.

Nantucket banks had a curious history in the early years of commerce on the island. The first chartered bank, the Nantucket Bank, opened for business in 1795, and within three weeks was looted of its entire cash assets, leading to the dissolution of the bank and the bitter controversy over the Nantucket Bank Robbery. There followed the Quaker-inspired Phoenix Bank which was chartered in 1812 and failed in 1825. This was immediately succeeded by the Manufacturers and Mechanics Bank, started in 1825, which collapsed in the wake of the Barker Burnell scandal of 1845, and was destroyed in the Great Fire of 1846. A second Nantucket Bank was chartered in 1831 but never started business. This was followed by the Citizens Bank in a brick building on Main Street, which ceased business after the Great Fire. In 1834, the Nantucket Institution for Savings was incorporated, and somehow survived, along with the Pacific National Bank, as the two Nantucket banks for the past century and a half. It is no wonder that a visitor to Nantucket remarked in 1847: "A strange fatality seems to have attended all their banking operations and their losses by such institutions have been serious."

The Nantucketers of 1885 were familiar with the history of bank robbery and embezzlement, which caused them to harbor deep suspicions of the leading citizens who ran the local bank. Many claimed the directors had gone out of their way to cover up for the cashier and keep the public in the dark. Wild stories of shortages and swindling swept the town and concerned depositors marched up the steps of the bank on Main Street to demand their deposits in hard currency. The directors continued to repeat their assurances that the bank was still in good condition. Cashier Chadwick had strong forces on his side, for the family was respected and his father was known to be wealthy. As the weeks passed, it seemed that Chadwick might be able to survive further legal difficulty. Conditions did not improve, however, when the state Bank Examiner, Colonel Needham, arrived on the island to examine the books of the bank.

On January 30, a letter was circulated in Nantucket by J.B. Tibbets, of Troy, New York, a summer resident who owned many acres near the Chadwick property in Squam. Tibbets publicly announced his willingness to put up all his land in Nantucket, consisting of some 400 acres with building and improvements, as security for all of Chadwick's debts on Nantucket. He offered to pledge his property provided "a certain party in town" would pay off all these debts beyond Chadwick's personal assets of $12,500. Tibbets also offered to raise the sum required, himself, to pay these debts, if the "certain party" mentioned would offer his own property as security for the payment. He placed these propositions in the hands of Doctor J.S. Sanborn of Nantucket to show to anyone who was supportive of Chadwick, and they were printed in the *Mirror* in April. Tibbets' letter added that it was to be understood he was not motivated by any desire to shield Chadwick from the consequences of his misdeeds, if any, but, rather from a hope of saving him through these means for "a higher end than he was hitherto set for himself in dealing with Mammon."

This interesting letter indicated that the writer knew a great deal about the Chadwick property and the extent of the debts involved. The curious reference to "a certain party in town" may have been an effort to provoke a response from other parties who were morally or legally obliged to come to Chadwick's rescue, or may have been suggested to put to rest the public rumor that Chadwick was an agent for "parties abroad." As a friend and neighbor, Tibbets was in a good position to know more of the truth than had come to light at that time and the names of any other parties who might be involved. The effort did not succeed and events took a turn for the worse for William H. Chadwick.

In April, 1885, a federal marshal came to Nantucket and arrested former Cashier Chadwick and transported him to Boston on the Saturday afternoon steamer. He was charged with embezzlement and alterations of the books of the Pacific National Bank, and held on $10,000 bail. Unable to raise the bail, he was committed to the East Cambridge Jail.

The arrest of the local cashier caused a sensation in the town, where it was widely believed he could have avoided criminal charges upon his promise to make good his debts to the bank and many island creditors. The *Inquirer and Mirror* commented: "...it had come to the general opinion that the unfortunate man would escape arrest on a criminal charge, and there was speculation as to who instigated the arrest."

The defendant was now forced to appear in a federal court in

Boston, which had jurisdiction because the Pacific National Bank was a federally-chartered institution. This effectively removed him from trial in the state court in Nantucket, where a local jury might have reflected the sentiment expressed by the local newspaper. It, also, avoided the embarrassment which a local trial might have caused for certain parties in town.

Chadwick's problems were now increased by his many creditors on the island who reached in desperation for his assets. Within a month, multiple attachments were placed on his property in Squam, and dozens of civil actions were filed against him in local courts. The massive estate at Squam Head was almost complete, but the empty mansion was nothing but a monument to guilt and greed, and was soon given the enduring name of "Chadwick's Folly."

Unable to raise his bail money and swarming with creditors, William H. Chadwick pleaded guilty without a trial to charges of embezzlement and making false entries in the books of the bank. Judge Colt in the federal court sentenced him to five years in jail, but permitted him to serve it in the Nantucket jail. He was then brought home by the U.S. Marshal and lodged in the jail on Vestal Street to await the many civil trials.

Four civil cases involving the Pacific National Bank and William H. Chadwick were finally heard before the Supreme Judicial Court sitting in Taunton in April, 1886, with Justice Oliver Wendell Holmes, Jr., presiding. Captain William T. Swain was sued by the bank on a note, requested by Cashier Chadwick, given to cover Swain's overdrafts at the bank. Swain counterclaimed that the bank was guilty of fraud and conspiracy for covering up Chadwick's actions which had caused the overdrafts. Chadwick was, at the time, heavily indebted to Swain for lumber used in the Squam Head property, and promised to take care of the debt by paying off Swain's notes at the bank. Chadwick had, actually, paid off most of Swain's note but in the meantime Swain brought suit and attached Chadwick's land at Squam. When Swain received his bank passbook and found several items omitted and underlined, he sued the bank to find out what was going on.

The trials in Taunton brought out much of the local feeling about the confusion in the bank and the sentiment about Cashier Chadwick.

It was shown that the bank took a note for $8,000 from Chadwick to cover his deficiencies, but only after Chadwick had paid the father of Albert G. Brock, the present cashier, his personal debt of $1,800 in cash. Swain claimed the bank notes were part of a scheme to relieve Chadwick of any criminal responsibility. The Honorable Frederick C. Sanford, President of the bank, took the stand to deny this allegation. He said that Chadwick admitted owing the bank about $10,000, at which point Sanford gave his own note to the bank to cover the shortage until Chadwick made it good, which he promised to do within a few days. He stated that, although he knew Chadwick had done very wrong, he could not bear the thought of his being "cast adrift with the stain of criminal prosecution." Moreover, he was moved by thoughts of Chadwick's invalid wife, his small children, and his aged parents, and the knowledge that the situation might provoke a run on the bank which would prove disastrous. During the portion of his testimony about Chadwick and his family, Sanford was visibly emotional and on the verge of tears.

William H. Chadwick took the stand to testify that he had worked for the bank about ten years. He testified about various entries made in Captain Swain's account which were made to cover overdrafts, for the benefit of the bank examiners. These entries were made without notice to Swain. He also freely admitted he had taken about $12,400 and for this was now serving his sentence in the Nantucket Jail.

Chadwick was strongly pressed by counsel to tell the court where the money went:

"Don't you remember any other parties to whom a portion of that money went?"

"No, sir, I have no one else to name."

"Did you not keep a memorandum of your transaction?"

"Yes, sir."

"Where is it?"

"Destroyed."

"Why did you destroy it?"

"Because it was a record of my private business with parties who did not care to be known."

The results of the cases are not as important as this testimony. In fact, the Taunton jury threw out all the plaintiffs and sent the Nantucketers home to straighten out their own affairs. But William H. Chadwick, facing five years in jail and the loss of all his property and reputation, would never mention the names of those "parties abroad" who had brought him to ruin.

Chadwick returned to his lonely jail cell where he served until his release on good behavior. His father eventually put up the money to satisfy the claims of the Pacific National Bank, but his creditors did not fare as well. The old estate could not shake the curse of Chadwick's Folly nor the mystery of the man who built it.

As the only occupant of the Nantucket Jail, Chadwick was allowed to live in comparative comfort and privilege. His family, who lived nearby on Lily Street, were permitted to furnish his jail cell with rugs and a rocking chair. He soon had a generous supply of books and weekly newspapers to keep him busy. He also worked on handicrafts and weaving Nantucket lightship baskets. Years later, one of his daughters delivered a lightship basket to a neighbor with the admonition, "This was made by Pa in jail. Don't tell anyone."

The Chadwick family was always convinced that William was the victim who took the blame for the acts of others. Embarrassed by the fate of their ancestor, the Chadwicks refused to discuss the matter for many years.

The great empty house at Squam Head stood brooding over the desolate landscape for several years. Like many of the grandiose schemes of the real estate boosters, Chadwick's dream of development was wildly out of contact with reality and doomed to failure. In addition, this property could never overcome the name of "Chadwick's Folly." The estate was sold at auction in 1894, and subsequent owners parcelled it out into various waterfront and waterview lots.

The huge old mansion was gradually dismantled; the great cupola on the roof was large enough to become a summer cottage on the land. The last remnants of the estate were levelled in 1956 and modern homes now stand on the site of the local cashier's dreams.

William H. Chadwick did not live to see the fate of his great dream. A broken and lonely man, he died in Nantucket on April 1, 1893, at the age of 46. To his dying day, he would never discuss his problems nor name the associates who had led him into his schemes and left him to bear the full burden of his folly. The Town of Nantucket did not forget him, however, for upon his death he was recorded by the Town Clerk with the occupation: Bank Cashier.

CHAPTER TEN

WHO STOLE SURFSIDE?

The sandy shore land south of the Town of Nantucket was originally designated by the Proprietors as the South Pasture, but it proved to be so bare and windswept that even the hardy sheep of Nantucket abandoned it. The thin soil did not support any farms and this land remained open and undeveloped for two centuries. As the Nantucketers began to use it for beach parties and summer excursions in the 1870's, these hundreds of shore acres, bounded by the pounding surf, acquired the popular name of "Surfside."

Most of this land was owned by the old Proprietorship, and in the course of time it fell into the hands of the Coffin family. By the legal device of exchanging their sheep commons interests in other sections of the island, the brothers Charles and Henry Coffin gradually acquired good legal title to over 1200 acres of this land with its imposing sweep of sand and sea. In 1873, they announced the incorporation of the Nantucket Surfside Land Company, with an authorized capital of two hundred thousand dollars.

The Coffin brothers of Nantucket were the most respected businessmen on the island. Sons of Zenas Coffin, who had made his fortune in ships and whale oil, they were grandsons of Micajah Coffin, the leading statesman of his day, and direct descendents of the partiarch, Tristram Coffin, the founder of the Coffin clan in America. The brothers were the best and brightest representatives of the Golden Age of Nantucket. Charles G. Coffin, born in 1801, built an impressive brick mansion at 78 Main Street, while Henry Coffin, born in 1807, constructed a similar mansion across the way at 75 Main Street. Together they shared in the Coffin domination of the island's destiny through most of the nineteenth century.

When Zenas Coffin died, he was the owner of a fleet of seven whaleships, which his sons continued to operate while adding several new vessels. One of these ships, which they named *Charles & Henry*, sailed into the South Seas in 1843, carrying a young deck hand named Herman Melville on the only whaling voyage of his life. The Coffin brothers maintained the whaling fleet so long as it was profitable, but circumstances dictated its decline within a short span of years. Nantucket was struck by the Great Fire of 1846, followed by the Gold Rush of 1849, and the discovery of petroleum in 1854, which foretold the end of the market for whale oil. The Coffin brothers gradually sold off the ships and turned their attention to other island business.

Operating from a Boston office at 174 State Street, which was managed by Henry's son, Charles F. Coffin, the Nantucket Surfside Land Company produced a grandiose plan of over one hundred acres of Surfside. This 1873 plan was imaginatively laid out into 480 lots, with curved avenues and beach pavilions, centered on a bandstand by the sea. The land was located in an area bounded by Weeweeder Pond on the west and Nobadeer Pond on the east. It was to be served by extensions of Atlantic Avenue and Lover's Lane, and by a broad but completely fictitious avenue running along the shore.

The great plan of 1873 never amounted to anything. As one historian wrote: "The imagination of the buyers was not as vivid as that of the sellers." Before the first lot was sold at Surfside, a new phenomenon appeared on the Nantucket horizon.

In 1879, it was announced that Nantucket was about to have its first railroad. Promoted by the energetic Philip H. Folger, a former Nantucket resident then living in Boston, the Nantucket Railroad was started as a tourist attraction. It used second-hand narrow gauge equipment and the level topography of the island to promote the transport of visitors from Steamboat Wharf to the outer reaches of the island. After some early proposals to circle the island with railroad tracks, it was decided to run the line south to Surfside and then east to Siasconset, but Surfside came first. A large wooden depot building was constructed in Surfside, the tracks were laid in record time, and on July 4, 1881, the first train ran to Surfside.

The engine of the first Nantucket train carried the famous name of Dionis, selected by Charles F. Coffin, to honor the name of the wife of Tristram Coffin, mother of his nine children and matriarch of the Coffin clan. The first passengers to arrive at Surfside pronounced the railroad a great success, and complained only that the ride was not long enough. Many of these Nantucketers had never before ridden a train. Unfortunately, there was nothing for them to see at Surfside but the depot, which served as the social center for the imaginary village. However, the prospects for Surfside looked bright on that Fourth of July.

The summer of 1881 also witnessed the greatest social event ever scheduled on Nantucket, the Coffin Reunion to honor the 200th anniversary of the death of Tristram Coffin. This was the favorite promotion of Allen Coffin, Nantucket's only lawyer, who was so full of good will and optimism that he once ran for Governor of Massachusetts on the Prohibition ticket. Allen Coffin proposed inviting a thousand Coffins from the mainland to gather in Nantucket to honor Tristram, enjoy the old home town, and hopefully invest in some real estate.

The Coffin Reunion was held on August 16-18, 1881, with over 500 Coffins in attendance, and the first session of the reunion was held at Surfside. Transported over the moors by the sturdy engine Dionis, the Coffins lined up on the shore to take part in the historic reunion photograph. They were treated to a shore dinner at the depot, now known as the Pavilion, followed by band music and speeches. The featured oration was given by Judge Tristram Coffin of Poughkeepsie, New York, a noted author and historian of the family. Before the reunion was over, the old judge was so overcome by sentiment that he purchased the old Jethro Coffin House on Sunset Hill to be preserved as a permanent memorial to the family.

The Coffin Reunion was proclaimed a great success. The Nantucket Railroad had proven itself efficient and popular, transporting over 30,000 passengers during the summer of 1881. All the visiting Coffins had enjoyed themselves thoroughly. There was only one problem: none of them had bought any land at Surfside. The island's only lawyer was in despair.

The Surfside Land Company responded with a new promotion for the next season. A revised plan of Surfside was drawn up, and the curved avenues were replaced with a grid pattern of streets and avenues which accommodated the village to the layout of the railroad. The plan also featured a large public building which was to become the Surfside Hotel. The company opened a real estate office in the railroad depot and the first sixty house lots were sold, each one 50 by 100 feet in size. The end of the 1882 season was highlighted by the visit of President Chester Arthur to Nantucket, and the presidential excursion featured a trip on the Nantucket Railroad to visit "the prospective city by the sea."

The new plan of 1882 called for another cottage city, with hundreds of summer cottages to be built on the lots which covered the plain of Surfside. The new village was bounded on the west and south by the railroad line. Its centerpiece was to be the grand hotel to be erected at the junction of the new Atlantic Avenue running from Pleasant Street in town and the imaginary Atlantic Avenue along the bank of the south shore. By the end of the year, the promoters claimed that 300 lots had been sold, but no cottages appeared. There was, however, some serious construction underway on the foundations of the great hotel which fronted the proposed development.

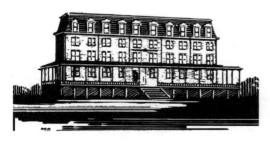

The Surfside Hotel was a large, four-story, wooden building with a mansard roof. It was built to accommodate fifty-four rooms on three floors, together with a kitchen, dining room, and reception room. Surrounding the entire building was a large piazza ten feet wide. The hotel had originally been built in Riverside, Rhode Island, where it was purchased, dismantled, and shipped to Nantucket by schooner in 1883. With strenuous effort, it was reassembled, outfitted, and opened for business on July 4, 1883.

As soon as the grand hotel had been completed at Surfside, the ambitious Nantucket Railroad began extending its tracks to Sconset. The year 1884 featured the opening of the Sconset line as the main tourist attraction on the island. This was great news for Sconset but a bad omen for Surfside.

The allure of Sconset as the village of the future drew many potential buyers away from Surfside. The erosion of the beach near Surfside required the railroad tracks to be moved several feet inland each year, and the additional expense of the longer run to Sconset started to drain the railroad. The increasing popularity of Sconset combined with a series of natural disasters, and while Sconset was developing its tennis courts, golf course, and tourist accommodations, Surfside was swept by annual storms which seemed to emphasize its fragile situation. The heavy gales of autumn tore into the shoreline and inundated the railroad tracks. First the Surfside Hotel, then the Nantucket Railroad announced they were in financial difficulties.

In 1887, the Surfside Land Company failed to meet its mortgage payments, and 900 acres of its waterfront land were auctioned off to Jacob McCrellis of Denver for $2.80 per acre. Under new ownership, the Surfside Hotel was renovated and the new electric power lines were installed along the sandy roads of Surfside to attract patrons. None of these improvements could compete with the attractions of Sconset, and by 1889 the hotel and the surrounding lots were again sold off to Seth Doane of Boston.

Under new Boston management, the Surfside Land Company advertised in the Boston papers, "a limited number of choice shore lots," for sale at reasonable prices, without success. These prices ranged from $100 per lot (20 feet by 100 feet) near the shore, down to $20 per lot inland. By the end of the season, the company's tireless real estate agent, Almon T. Mowry, made the ultimate pitch to the public. He offered to give away lots in Surfside to those who would contract for a house to be built "on very liberal terms."

The Boston promoters fared no better than the Nantucketers, and now it was time for the New Yorkers to try their luck in Surfside. In 1890 a syndicate of New York investors took over the Surfside Land Company and the Nantucket Railroad. Their names were Francis C. O'Reilly, John Firth, Thomas H. Spaulding and Daniel McKeever. They were mainland investors inspired by the optimism of the era, for the charms of Sconset had spread the popularity of Nantucket to the metropolitan area. Their first move was the sale of the hotel and real estate to William Gwynn, of Cohoes, New York, who promised to revive the hotel with fifty new rooms, trapeze entertainments and pigeon shoots. The promises were prophetic, for the winds of autumn soon blew the trapeze artists into oblivion, and the only pigeons to fall in Surfside were the financial backers of the venture. The heavy storms of that season swept away the remains of the railroad depot and shorted out the electric lines. Within a year, Attorney Allen Coffin became trustee for the creditors of the Surfside Hotel. His dream of a city by the sea in 1881 had turned into a nightmare, but like the resourceful lawyer that he was, he made the best of a bad situation.

The year 1894 marked the end of the Surfside Railroad. A new railroad was organized to run a direct route from town to Sconset, parallel to the Old South Road. The old location of the railroad at Surfside fell into decay in the bleak landscape, now marked only by the rutted roads and abandoned signs of the cottage city which never existed. The town of Nantucket advertised the few lots which had been purchased, and tried to sell them at a tax sale. No buyers came forth.

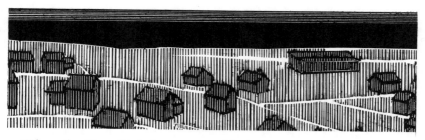

When the New York investors sold off their investment, no bank would consider lending money on Nantucket land, so the sale was financed by a loan from Francis C. O'Reilly, of Orange, New Jersey, who secured the loan with a blanket mortgage on all the real estate in Surfside.

Francis C. O'Reilly, generally known as Frank O'Reilly, was the man whose name became involved with Surfside for most of the twentieth century. He was a self-made man who made most of his fortune in construction projects, including canals and public works in New York and New Jersey. He had a wife and four children in New Jersey but he kept his business affairs closely-guarded between himself and his partners. Little was known about him or his syndicate in Nantucket, where the islanders waited to learn the next plans for Surfside.

One day in 1890, O'Reilly and seven other men arrived on the steamer *Island Home* and drove out to Surfside to look over their new property. They announced the hotel would be all fixed up and open for the coming season, and retained a local contractor to grade the streets of Surfside. Then they hired the tugboat *Nellie* to carry them back to New Bedford.

While O'Reilly was on the dock, some local character noticed the tall, broad-shouldered man with the handlebar moustache, and started spreading the word that the great John L. Sullivan was on Nantucket. The Boston Strong Boy was the heavyweight champion and the most popular athlete in the country. It was rumored that Sullivan had come to Nantucket for the fishing, and O'Reilly's friends obliged by referring to him as "John." When the *Nellie* reached New Bedford, a large crowd had gathered to give three cheers for Sullivan, which Frank O'Reilly acknowledged with a warm greeting and a broad Irish smile.

The New York syndicate developed differences within a few years, and various real estate transactions were carried on between the partners and with outside investors. Some of these business deals were tortuous and complicated, and during the course of the next decade, the record title to Surfside became confused. Charges of chicanery and breach of trust were levelled at some persons, but none of these involved Frank O'Reilly. It was his fate to pick up the pieces of Surfside and the syndicate was finished. What O'Reilly planned to do with the real estate is unknown, for he died in 1901 without even telling his family what should be done with his large holdings in Nantucket.

With the death of Frank O'Reilly, his name became attached to Surfside for a half century and the annual tax bills were sent to his family by the Nantucket assessors. Relying upon the wisdom of their ancestor, the family paid the Nantucket taxes on his investment for fifty years. By 1953, several O'Reilly heirs lost interest in the project and refused to pay any more taxes on this land which they referred to as "O'Reilly's Folly."

Over the course of years, the single ownership of Frank O'Reilly had devolved upon his heirs and now the problems of multiple ownership became acute. O'Reilly left all his property to his widow, and upon her death it went to three of her children, named George O'Reilly, Ralph O'Reilly and Eleanor O'Reilly MacMahon. Only the MacMahon family was in a position to bear the costs of ownership, and the problem descended to Eleanor's son, Myles MacMahon, who continued to receive and pay the Nantucket tax bills. When these bills on land of unknown quantity and uncertain value continued to mount, the family decided in the late 1950's to abandon Surfside.

Eventually the Town of Nantucket took an interest in the Surfside Lands and petitioned the Massachusetts Land Court to foreclose its claim for unpaid taxes. Because there was a total lack of surveys and definite current deeds, the true extent of the land was still unknown, but it was "supposed to contain 600 acres." The actual area was later found to be closer to 1400 acres. The MacMahon family was notified to the court petition but took no interest, and the Town was awarded a default judgment in 1964, by the Land Court. Whether this judgment gave the Town good title is very problematical, because at that time there were at least nine owners and the notice of the suit went only to the MacMahon family address. In the years before the environmental revolution, the interest of the Town was solely the recovery of its tax revenue, and it never had any serious plans for owning hundreds of acres of undeveloped and unmarketable land.

At this point, there came into the picture a Boston real estate investor named William J. Braun, who was originally interested in buying some of the O'Reilly land in Surfside. He finally gained the attention of Myles MacMahon, who agreed to meet with him and discuss the situation. A meeting was arranged in May of 1965 at the Harvard Club in Boston, attended by Braun, MacMahon and their attorneys. At this fateful meeting they agreed to form a joint venture and become partners in the business of clearing the title and marketing the O'Reilly land in Surfside.

Within a year, the MacMahon-Braun forces were successful in petitioning the Land Court to vacate the previous decree and redeem the Surfside property, upon payment of many years' back taxes, penalties and costs to the Town of Nantucket.

This put the tax problems to rest. But it did not solve the larger question: Who owned Surfside? Solution to this puzzle would involve a massive title search to find the missing heirs of Francis C. O'Reilly, an engineering survey of the extensive Surfside lands, and obtaining a court decree to settle the title and determine the proper owners. The extensive legal procedure and the accompanying court hearing took over ten years to complete, involved more than a dozen lawyers on behalf of the parties, and covered a decade of great changes in Nantucket.

The greatest of these changes came from the pressure of popularity and development upon the island. The rebuilding of the waterfront and the downtown shopping area in the 1960's was accompanied by the development of a modern airport and greatly improved transportation services to the island by air and sea. The year-round population increased steadily from 3600 to over 7500 and the number of summer visitors multiplied each year. This produced a demand for more homes on the island and a steep increase in real estate values. As the island gained in popularity and accessibility, the appeal of a home in Nantucket increased. National prosperity, improved transportation and commercial publicity boosted Nantucket into prominence as a desirable summer resort which was within the reach of millions of people on the east coast. Most of these people wanted to be near the water, and nothing was nearer than Surfside.

As the island witnessed its first large-scale modern real estate developments, many residents were surprised to learn that the open spaces they always took for granted were, in fact, privately owned and destined for private homes. A powerful environmental movement swept the island, and several hastily organized groups tried to prevent further development in the name of conservation. The Town of Nantucket adopted its first zoning bylaw in 1972. In the same year, a bill was filed in Congress by Senator Edward M. Kennedy, which would declare much of the island, including Surfside, "forever wild," under a far-reaching scheme of federal land control. It seemed the fate of Surfside would never be settled as various forces contested its destiny.

After ten years of research and frustration, the modern heirs of Francis C. O'Reilly were finally identified and located. They were proven to be nine individuals, living from Massachusetts to Mexico, and they were beneficiaries of an estate which most of them had never seen or heard about. The beneficiaries agreed to retain Boston attorney Edward C. Mendler, Jr., a real estate expert in the firm of Nutter, McClennan & Fish, and placed the management of the real estate in the hands of three trustees under the name of Surfside Realty Trust.

When the new owners of Surfside made known their plans to develop and market their land, many islanders complained about the proposed development of these open spaces which had, until lately, been considered "owners unknown." Dark thoughts and wild accusations were rumored about the island: How had this happened? Was this not public land? Who had stolen Surfside?

The true owners of the Surfside lands were, in fact, proven by recorded deeds and probate records dating back to the original Francis O'Reilly, and the title was affirmed by several title insurance companies and the Massachusetts Land Court. Except for the shoreline eroded by the sea, Surfside was still intact and in the hands of its rightful owners.

The long years of delay and frustration were forgotten. The seemingly-endless legal proceedings had proven providential, for the value of Surfside land had risen enormously, as prices for houselots doubled and tripled, year after year. The Town of Nantucket recovered all its back taxes and now had vastly more valuable land on the tax rolls. The Town itself obtained twenty acres of land for a modern sanitation plant and another twenty-five acres for public beach land.

The new development at Surfside was vastly different from anything envisioned by the promoters of the nineteen century. The ancient ideas of cottage colonies on tiny lots were forgotten and the new Surfside offered two and three-acre lots, featuring extensive homesteads on modern roads, with most of the open space preserved in its natural state. Surfside had not been stolen. It had been discovered, a century later, and was now fulfilling its promise. The land once known as O'Reilly's Folly had turned out to be Frank O'Reilly's best investment, thanks to the Luck of the Irish.

CHAPTER ELEVEN

JOHN BROWN'S BOOTY

There were few men in Nantucket more popular than genial John Brown, who had been elected to more public offices than any man in the history of the town. Born in Nantucket in 1840, Brown was a Civil War veteran, a member of several social clubs, and a likeable character in the Town, where he had served as Town Clerk for twelve years. He proved so popular in 1888 that he won re-election unanimously, winning all the votes cast in the annual election—a rare feat even in a small town.

The Town recognized Brown's talents by appointing him to several town positions. He was also the tax collector, the clerk of courts, the county clerk, clerk of the registrars of voters, and assistant register of deeds. He never complained as the various jobs with their small salaries were thrust upon him. Brown was a jack-of-all-trades, operating a real estate business, helping people with their business affairs, and, although he was not a lawyer, drafting legal documents. He even helped widows and orphans collect their pensions.

Brown carried on all his businesses from a small office in the Town Building on Union Street. His business card in the *Inquirer & Mirror* read: "JOHN F. BROWN, Real Estate and General Business Agent. All persons contemplating the purchase or sale of real estate in Nantucket will find it very much to their advantage to call on me. Money to loan in sums from $100 to $5000 on real estate, household furniture, stocks, bonds and all kinds of collateral securities. Legal documents of every description carefully and correctly drawn up. Come and see me and learn all about it."

After John Brown's unanimous re-election, his future seemed secure, but there were clouds on the horizon. The County Commissioners made a report to the Town Meeting of 1888, the substance of which was that a number of errors had been discovered in bills that had been approved for payment. The Registrars of Voters made a similar complaint that one of their bills had been tampered with. The Town Meeting voted to investigate the matter.

The moderator appointed a committee of three men to investigate these matters and report back: they were Daniel C. Brayton, Herbert S. Sweet, and Thaddeus C. Defriez. The chairman of the committee was the Judge of Probate for Nantucket County, and Judge Defriez also happened to be a retired whaling master who stood for authority and integrity in the community.

Within a month, the Defriez Committee held fourteen meetings, heard dozens of witnesses, and issued its report to the local newspaper. In the small world of Nantucket public affairs, the impact of this report shook the entire structure of government.

Nantucket is both a county and a town, as well as an island. Massachusetts is divided into fourteen counties, each formed of several townships making a distinct geographical area, except for Nantucket, where, because of its insular location, the Town and County are one and the same. Therefore, the Selectmen of the Town are also the Commissioners of the County. The Town Clerk is elected to maintain the town records, among his many other duties, while the Clerk of Courts is a county officer, and by virtue of his office also the County Clerk and Clerk of the County Commissioners.

The report of the Defriez Committee charged, in substance, that the popular Town Clerk was a rogue, a fraud, and probably a thief. There was evidence that over the past five years, John Brown had pursued a practice of altering and adding to county bills in various amounts and pocketing the additional money. He also submitted double bills which were paid by both the town and county. He had raised figures on bills and forged receipts as a matter of routine. Because the County Commissioners met only once per month, when all bills were presented for payment, the board passed a vote authorizing the Chairman to approve bills between the regular meetings, to expedite payment to local merchants and workmen who disliked waiting a month for payment. Once the Chairman approved a bill, an order was attached which authorized payment as directed by the Clerk. When the local bills included small items amounting to a few dollars. Brown had the treasurer issue a check for the total amount payable to "Bearer." He then distributed the proper payments to the local contractors and kept the balance.

As County Clerk and Clerk of Courts, Brown was also responsible for the supplies of the court system purchased from Boston suppliers. In these cases, his practice was to double the bills or duplicate bills from such Boston firms as Little, Brown & Co. and Thomas Groom & Co., obtain approval for both bills, pay the genuine bill, and keep the duplicate payment. The system worked well until he began to submit bills on ordinary letter paper and sign his own receipts with the company names.

One year when his public salary of $600 proved insufficient for his needs, John Brown presented the County Commissioners with a bill for additional services in the amount of $57. One of the commissioners objected, stating the matter was covered by his salary, so Brown wrote the state comptroller of county accounts, asking for his approval if it was all right. "If not," he wrote, "I would only be glad to know it, and make amends for wrong-doing." The comptroller informed him it was not a proper bill, and if he did not refund it, the board should take it out of his salary. Brown told the investigators he had forgotten about this. One of the conclusions of the Defriez Committee was that, throughout their investigation, "Mr. Brown has evinced a woeful lack of memory, and if in the deductions we have drawn from the evidence before us, any injustice has been done him, it has been through his inability or indisposition to explain when called upon."

On April 21, the Board of Selectmen reported their findings to a Special Town Meeting which packed the old Town Hall on Orange Street. The report, read by Selectman Arthur H. Gardner, was listened to by the members, who sat in silence as it detailed the many peculations of the Town Clerk; many seemed indifferent to the tally of small sums pilfered by Brown over the years.

The public showed no emotion until the Selectmen presented the final and most dramatic charge: John Brown had even stolen from the Dog Fund! The Town Clerk was responsible by law for collecting the annual license fees for all dogs in town, for which he was entitled to retain a fee of 20 cents per dog. Brown had no record of the dogs taxed in 1886 and 1887, so it was impossible to tell exactly how many dogs had been licensed and what fees had been collected. Brown showed he had accounted for 43 male dogs and 4 female dogs in 1887, a figure which the Selectmen found totally inadequate. The only solution was to hold a new census of the Nantucket dog population, which the Selectmen conducted personally and thoroughly. This revealed that 101 male and 15 female dogs were licensed in the town, plus 9 male and 3 female dogs owned by summer visitors, "and presumed to have been licensed." This tale of the Nantucket dog population convinced the public and moved the Town Meeting to action.

In conclusion, the Selectmen tallied the various accounts, counted up the Dog Fund, and found that John Brown had taken the town for a provable total of $460.81. This sum is trivial by modern standards, but it loomed large to the townsfolk of 1888. Furthermore, it was generally accepted that other money had disappeared over the past five years which could not be proven. The report solemnly concluded that the Town had been victimized by a pattern of bogus bills and false charges, and found "the self-apparent fact that for years money has been constantly filched from the town in small and varying amounts which aggregate hundreds of dollars."

Undaunted by the evidence and counting upon his popularity with the voters, John Brown appeared before the Special Town Meeting and was granted permission to present his case in an address that was remarkable for its frank approach to the situation. Addressing the "Moderator and Gentlemen of the Town Meeting," Brown stated: "On the 14th of February 1876, you made me the Clerk of your town. How much I appreciated the honor thus bestowed, I never shall be able to tell. That I performed the duties devolving upon me as clerk in a manner satisfactory to you has been fully demonstrated by your conferring upon me that honor each successive year since. During the first seven years I was not only Town Clerk but virtually the collector of taxes, making all the bills and receipting for and receiving a large amount of the money...

"Until 1883, or five years ago, everything went along very smoothly, but on that day I was appointed Clerk of the Courts for Nantucket County, and then the trouble commenced. As clerk of the county I became clerk of the county commissioners, and on the 3rd day of July the same year my appointment as Assistant Register of Deeds was confirmed by the Superior Court sitting in this county. One year later, May 29, 1884, by an act of the legislature the board of registrars of voters was established and by virtue of my office as Town Clerk I became clerk of this board. Thus you see that I hold the position of Town Clerk, County Clerk, Clerk of the Courts, Clerk of the County Commissioners, Clerk of the Board of Registrars and Assistant Register of Deeds.

"In fact, I have controlled this town, aided and supported by the Selectmen or County Commissioners, who have approved all bills that I ever received any amount on...

"Gentlemen of the town of Nantucket, if I had been so disposed with the chances I have had, I could have stolen your whole treasury; and with the name I now have in town as a dark-dyed villain, it is certainly very strange that I didn't, and I can only congratulate you on the safety of the larger part of the funds...

"Now what I want, gentlemen, is a chance to report my side of the case, a chance to look over the books and papers and compare them with one another, and I know I can greatly modify the charges made against me. And then I will get down and out of the way of those who have destroyed my peace and happiness."

John Brown's plea fell on deaf ears, for the meeting had its collective mind made up. His motion to continue the matter was lost in an overwhelming vote. He was excused from the meeting, and Allen Coffin, Esquire, was chosen as Town Clerk protem. The meeting proceeded to the substantive part of its deliberations, and voted to remove John F. Brown from the offices of Town Clerk and Clerk of Courts, and to authorize the Selectmen, on behalf of the town, to bring a criminal action for embezzlement of town and county funds against John F. Brown.

In what can only be described as a Nantucket judicial procedure, a warrant was issued from the court for the arrest of John Brown, with instructions given the sheriff not to serve it unless Brown attempted to leave the island. The next day, Brown went to the steamer, but was notified of the state of affairs, and returned home.

John Brown soon got his trip to the mainland at government expense. The next day, United States Deputy Marshall MacDonald arrived with another warrant for Brown to appear in federal court in Boston. The street talk in Nantucket said it was something to do with pension money, an important matter among the townspeople.

Nantucket in 1888 had many widows and orphans as a result of the Civil War, when the town had sent so many volunteers to serve the Union cause that it won recognition as the Banner Town of the Commonwealth. The casualties among the Nantucketers had been high, and the government honored its war dead with pensions for the widows and orphans. Many of these people needed help with the official forms and they naturally turned to the readily available Town Clerk, who was himself a veteran and always willing to help those in need.

A trial was held in Boston before Judge Nelson and a jury in the United States District Court. On the first count, John Brown was charged with making a false pension voucher with fraudulent intent.

It appeared that John F. Brown was entitled to a U.S. pension under the name of Franklin J. Brown, but he followed a strange method to collect it. First, Franklin J. Brown appeared as applicant for the pension before John F. Brown as notary public. Then John F. Brown swore to an affidavit that the said Franklin J. Brown was personally known to him, and, finally, John F. Brown, as justice of the peace, swore that Franklin J. Brown was the person named in the voucher as the person entitled to draw the pension. Therefore, Franklin J. Brown, who was entitled to the pension, was innocent of any crime; but John F. Brown, who helped him obtain it, was charged with a serious federal crime by trying to make the government believe they were two different people.

John Brown was fortunate to have the services of a Boston attorney named Henry W. Chaplin, who asked the Court the simple question: "What did he gain by this act?" The prosecutor answered that the question of gain was not material. Attorney Chaplin said that the defendant had the right to collect the pension and there was no intent to defraud anyone. Judge Nelson agreed with him and ordered a verdict of not guilty.

Brown was then put on trial on another pension matter, which involved money collected from government pensions on behalf of Mary Spencer and the minor children of William Orpin. They charged that Brown had illegally withheld $240 from the pension money he had collected for the widow. This case went to the jury, which deliberated all night. They returned on Saturday morning to report a disagreement: the jury stood seven for conviction and five for acquittal. Judge Nelson had heard enough about John Brown for one week, so he ordered a mistrial and sent Brown home.

John Brown's luck ran out, however, when he faced a jury in Nantucket Superior Court, where he had once served as Clerk. In July of 1888, after hearing an overwhelming body of evidence against him, the Nantucket jury convicted him on 22 of 24 counts of forgery and embezzlement. His sentence was stayed pending his appeal, and Brown proved to be a very appealing defendant.

In what the local newspaper referred to as "a practical illustration of the perversion of so-called justice," John Brown pursued two appeals to the Massachusetts Supreme Judicial Court and a petition to the United States Supreme Court. He asked the court to set aside his conviction on constitutional grounds because he had not had an impartial trial by jury. This claim was based on the fact that the Town Meeting of Nantucket had appointed the Selectmen a committee to prosecute him; that the same Selectmen then made up the jury list and selected the juries that indicted and then convicted him; that all the jurors who convicted him were also present at the Town Meeting which voted for his prosecution; and therefore, that he had been tried by a jury that had already decided his guilt.

Whatever the merits of Brown's appeal to the lawyers of the twentieth century, it did not appeal to the Supreme Court, which affirmed his conviction in 1892. The *Nantucket Journal* proudly headlined the news: "Nantucket Courts Good Enough."

Throughout the lengthy appeal procedure, public sentiment swung back to John Brown in many circles. The District Attorney who finally moved to sentence him stated that it was a painful duty, inasmuch as the prisoner had been a personal friend of his and had done him many favors in the past. The newspaper agreed: "Anyone who, officially or otherwise, has ever sustained intimate relations with Mr. Brown, can readily understand this feeling, for whatever may have been his faults, he was affable and accommodating to all in his official relations."

Brown was sentenced to serve two-and-one-half years in the New Bedford House of Correction. He served part of this time, then was released on good behavior and returned to Nantucket, where he died in 1897.

John Brown left a legacy of petty larceny and a reputation as a likeable rogue in public office. He also left a name and a popularity with the public which was handed down to one of his namesakes. A century later, everyone knew the familiar figure whose weather-beaten face decorated many postcards and newspaper stories as Nantucket's "waterfront philosopher." Wilson H. Brown, who became even more notorious than his predecessor, will always be remembered as Nantucket's favorite "Brownie."

CHAPTER TWELVE

THE LAWS OF SCONSET

The village of Siasconset stands on the easternmost end of the Island of Nantucket, and is always called Sconset by the natives. The original Indian name meant "Near the Great Bone," but there were so many bleached whale bones about the shore of the island, we now have no indication of where this bone was located or whence it has gone. Being the outermost point of the island, Sconset has always held a fascination for Islanders and visitors, so no visit to the island is complete without a trip to Sconset. The modern state highway takes a few minutes over seven miles of road, or about an hour on the state bicycle path. In the nineteenth century, the trip to Sconset was made over a random pattern of rutted roads, winding over moors and hills, until the traveler topped the rise at Bean Hill and sighted the village by the sea. When he first saw the shining sea, he knew he had arrived at Land's End, where it was "3000 miles to Spain." In reality, the eastern tip of Maine lies farther to the east, and the island of St. Croix claims the distinction of being the most easterly point of the United States. Yet when one gazes out into the endless Atlantic Ocean from the bluff at Sconset, it is easy to conclude that this is the outermost limit of America.

The earliest houses of Sconset date back to the seventeenth century, when they were fabricated as fishing shanties from scrap lumber and driftwood, or moved to Sconset from other sites on the island. They soon became summer homes of a highly individualistic character with no two alike. Their first inhabitants enjoyed the isolation from the business and social life of the Town of Nantucket, and preferred it that way. As a result, the village of Sconset developed some of the most colorful and independent characters who ever lived on the island.

Over a long span of years, Sconset became the place where many

Nantucket mariners came after retirement from the sea, as the peaceful village offered a welcome change from the whaling life. The pace was a little slower and the cost of living was a little lower. Nantucketers with spacious homes in town often kept a summer place in Sconset, where they lived a more informal life. The village gradually acquired a reputation for old-time simplicity, a place for genuine, unpretentious people.

> The song, the jest, the smile serene,
> Amuse the friend that haunts it;
> Here old Simplicity is seen,
> In ancient dress at Sconset.

The Laws of Sconset were plain and simple, for they were based upon common sense, honesty and fair dealings in society. As the early Nantucketers were frank to admit their failings, the island accepted them without dispute, so long as their dealings were plain and open. The laws were set down for posterity in a lengthy piece of poetry attributed to a Congregational minister, the Reverend Leonard, writing under the *nom de plume* "Philo Simplicitas," over a century ago. Their moral continues to apply and to influence the lives of many Sconset natives. One year, two local carpenters won a bid to build the wooden bridge across the gully in Sconset, for which the Town appropriated $300. They finished the job for $299.99, and returned one cent to the town treasury.

In the early 1870's, Sconset continued to slumber, with its few rental cottages being let to occasional seasonal visitors for $75 per summer. There was no post office before 1872 and no store until 1883. It was still the summer resort of the Nantucketers, "the Newport of the Nantucketoise." Then its charms were discovered and promoted.

By the 1880's there were two summer hotels operating in the village, the Atlantic House on Main Street and the Ocean View House on Ocean Avenue. The clientele consisted largely of visitors from New York, for the city was unbearably hot in the summertime and air-conditioning was nonexistent. An increasingly prosperous population began to seek summer resorts to escape the heat and unhealthy conditions of the big city. The famous New York attorney, Charles O'Conor, first visited Nantucket in the summer of 1880, and pronounced: "In my opinion Nantucket has no equal as a cool and healthy summer resort, and I shall probably make it my permanent home."

Among the visitors to Sconset that year was a man named Edward F. Underhill, who had just retired from his position as chief stenographer of the New York Surrogate's Court. Possessed of personal wealth and a shrewd business judgment, Underhill soon became a tireless promoter of Sconset and the first successful developer in the island's history. He immediately recognized the charm of Sconset in its simplicity and quaint architecture, based upon the style of the ancient fishermen's shacks on the northerly side of the village. He saw the appeal these cottages would have for the city-bound visitors, and commenced his activities with an appeal to the New Yorkers seeking a healthy climate and peaceful surroundings.

The first thing Underhill did was buy up several acres of land on the south side of the village, where he laid out simple streets named after his daughters, Lily and Evelyn. These were designed as tiny old lanes, covered with crushed shells. House lots were laid out and plans were filed showing the new cottage colony, which he called the Underhill Cottages. Before any cottages could be built, however, it was necessary to find a builder, and there was none in Sconset.

It seemed there was a man in the village named Asa Jones, who used to be a carpenter in town, but had retired due to the lack of business on the island. He was so discouraged that he sold off his tools and moved out to Sconset to go fishing. He had not built a house for twenty years when he was approached to build the first of the Underhill cottages. The owner wanted a traditional cottage, built in the style of the Sconset fishermen's shanties. Jones found some tools and went back to work. Then Underhill wanted another cottage, and another. By the time he ran out of lots, Edward F. Underhill had built over twenty houses, and moved several more, and Asa Jones was the busiest man in Sconset.

Edward F. Underhill's greatest talent, however, was as a publicist, and he soon became known as the first publicity agent for Sconset and for the charms of Nantucket Island. His background included a stint on the staff of the New York *Tribune* before his court career. He became a one-man Chamber of Commerce, sending Sconset copy all over the eastern United States, writing letters to correspondents in the major cities, and publishing books, brochures and pamphlets giving all the pertinent data about Sconset. He located the village and the Island of Nantucket in the minds of the vacationing public for the first time.

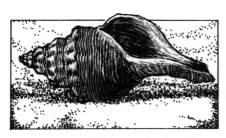

When persons wrote Underhill for information, they received a hefty package extolling the virtues of the village, including maps of the island, exterior views of the cottages, floor plans showing the number and size of rooms, and lyric descriptions of the nearby beach. One pamphlet even listed the names of previous tenants by city and state. To promote the quaintness of the seaside village, he also sent out press releases in nautical language signed by a fictional Cap'n Shubael. His advertisements for his furnished seaside cottages had something for everyone:

> Cool and quiet by night and by day, SCONSET is a haven of rest for brain workers and tired out business men, and is a natural sanitarium for those suffering from nervous exhaustion, hay fever or malaria. It is a paradise for children. The most restful climate for invalids and convalescents. Influenced by the tonic properties of the ocean air, extinct appetites are born again and manifest aggressive activity. It is not unusual for an invalid to gain 25 to 40 pounds during

the season.

NANTUCKET is the island of long lives. More than half of its people live from 70 to 100 years. The average duration of life is 64 years, nearly double that in any other part of the world. SCONSET is its most wholesome spot.

Picturesque cottages with six to nine rooms fully furnished are to let there at from $90 to $175 for the season.

Underhill was also a public-spirited businessman, who spoke up for public improvements, including a sewage system for the village, better boat service, and the extension of the Nantucket Railroad to Sconset. He reminded the islanders that, before the arrival of the tourists, "the wage of unskilled labor was then ten cents an hour; now it is fifteen cents and men are hard to get at that. The compensation of skilled workmen has increased correspondingly, and with the demand for their services, such as the island has not known since the decline of its principal industry. If the prosperity of the island has not come from the summer visitors, to what is it due?"

Although some old-timers in Sconset grumbled about the new construction and sudden influx of strangers in the sleepy village, there was little disruption of the traditional way of life. One old native woman exclaimed: "Seems as if all the seekers on this earth have turned round toward Sconset! And questions—sakes! They ask till they drive me wild!" Despite the skeptics, the Underwood cottages proved immensely popular with the tenants, who enjoyed the simple life they offered, and remarkably good investments for their owner.

To the modern visitor, the Underhill cottages retain much of their charm. Although some have been greatly changed by additions over the past century, many of the cottages remain as they were meant to be, snug structures, simple and economical as the old fishermen's houses they emulated, covered with rambling roses in the summer. Considered by many the most charming houses in

Sconset, they could not be duplicated in the modern age, because their construction defies almost every rule of the modern building codes: they are too low, too cramped, too unsafe for habitation, lacking proper foundations and safety features. Yet they have endured for more than a century, like Sconset itself.

> This court guards well our dearest rights,
> And when the county owns it,
> Lawyers will starve with all their wits,
> And curse the laws of Sconset.

Along with the Underhill development, other far-sighted men were making plans for Sconset. Doctor Franklin Ellis and Charles Robinson laid out the lots on the south bluff known as "Sunset Heights," and William H. Flagg planned an extensive development running toward Sankaty Head. The popular Nantucket Railroad, which first reached Sconset in 1884, proved a great stimulus to the village economy by making travel from Town swift and more or less reliable. The first golf course was laid out in Sconset and in 1900 the Siasconset Casino was erected, providing a social and athletic center for the village inhabitants.

About the turn of the century, Sconset began to attract a new and colorful quantity of summer visitors, the first actors and actresses from the New York theater who formed the original Actors' Colony. The city was hot and unpleasant during the summer, and consequently the theaters of Broadway normally closed for three months. Everyone with the means to travel was seeking a cool seaside resort, and although Nantucket Island was 200 miles away, there was a convenient and pleasant mode of travel from New York. The large and comfortable steamers of the Fall River Line were then in their glory, running from the dock at the tip of Manhattan. The travelers could enjoy a luxurious dinner and comfortable stateroom as the liner steamed through Long Island Sound, landing at Fall River in the early morning. They could then transfer to the train for the short trip to the dock in New Bedford, where the train met the Nantucket steamboat at the wharf. Once aboard the steamer, it was a mere five-hour cruise under sunny skies to the wharf at Nantucket, where most of the Town gathered to view the arrival of the tourists. From the Steamboat Wharf, the Nantucket Railroad departed for the eight-mile trip to Sconset with some of the passengers. The majority of the travelers, however, made the journey in horse-drawn carriages from the local livery stables to the village by the sea, some families using their favorite driver to meet them each year.

One of the first of the New York actors to make the trip was the colorful George Fawcett, who enjoyed himself in the luxury of the boatrides from New York and New Bedford, which only cost him six dollars, but grumbled about paying "some local pirate" the sum of four dollars for the wagon ride to Sconset.

Once the actors and actresses arrived in Sconset, they thoroughly enjoyed themselves, living in any style they pleased, some in simplicity and some in opulence, but all having a grand time on the island. The social scene gradually changed from the beach to the Casino, where the thespians annually produced their own versions of comedy and melodrama to entertain the community. This was the age when the movies were still in the silent era, and the true stars were those of the Broadway stage. At one time, over fifty members of the Lamb's Club could be counted in Sconset. Their numbers included George Fawcett, Robert Hilliard, Harry Woodruff, DeWolf Hopper, Isabel Irving and Lillian Russell. Later arrivals included Digby Bell, Nanette Comstock, Frank Gillmore, and the ever-popular Robert Benchley. They played, they partied and they performed summer after summer in Sconset. While the Nantucket Railroad was running, there was a custom of greeting and sending off friends with the famous "Sconset Cheer." The colony looked forward to its annual production of the "Sconset Follies" at the Casino. When the men finished playing golf at the Old Sconset Golf Club on the Coffin Farm, they continued the game right up the road to the putting green on the lawn of the Ocean View House.

The Actors' Colony flourished through the 1920's and then declined, like its members, with time and changes in the economy. The rise of the movie industry was the end for many of the New York stage performers, and the coming of the Depression lowered the curtain on their summer celebrations. Some of the stalwarts stayed on and were replaced by other family members in later years. Writers like George Frazier, John Cheever and James Reid Parker spent summers in Sconset, and John Steinbeck lived there for one season. It is probably no coincidence that the famous novel, *The Lost Weekend*, was written in Sconset.

Amid all the celebrities, Sconset did not change. Local families with names dating back several generations still kept up the homes and businesses, winter and summer. There were always enough Coffins, Egans, Eldridges, Folgers and Holdgates to keep Sconset going. Enough children lived in Sconset year-round to merit a small one-room school, where the first four grades were taught by one teacher. When the Sconset children finally came to town to attend the fifth grade, they were total strangers to their Nantucket classmates, who had never seen them before. One of the standard schoolboy jokes pictured the Sconset student always walking in circles while reading a book, since the only light in Sconset came from the rotating beacon of Sankaty Light.

As Edward Underhill suggested, may citizens of Sconset lived to ripe old age, often surviving all the contemporaries of their youth. They attributed this to their hardy background. One of these was Jesse H. Eldridge, who died in 1935 while still serving as the summer police officer in Sconset. As a young man, he had been a member of the famous Coast Guard crew at the Coskata Station, which had gone out to make one of the most famous rescue attempts in the history of Nantucket. When Eldridge was the only man left of the crew 43 years later, he credited his survival to the fact that he was the only Sconseter, the rest being Nantucketers.

It was the night of January 20, 1892, when the schooner *H.P.*

Kirkham with a crew of seven men, struck the Rose and Crown Shoal, 15 miles east of Great Point. A bitter northerly wind, carrying sleet and snow, was howling across the winter sea. The Keeper of Sankaty Lighthouse, Joseph Remsen, spotted the ship's masts and distress signals, and called the Coskata Station for help. The man in charge at Coskata was the famous Captain Walter Chase, a giant of a man and a fearless mariner. Despite the distance involved and the savage weather conditions, Skipper Chase immediately launched a lifeboat with a crew of six men to row out to the wreck on the shoals.

After 15 miles of rowing, his lifeboat reached the wreck, to find the schooner's crew clinging to the icy rigging as the ship broke up beneath them. By masterful boat handling, the rescuers got heaving lines over to the wreck and successfully dragged each of the frozen sailors into the rescue boat. One hour after they backed away from the wreck, the *Kirkham* slid under the waves. Skipper Chase and his men then bent their backs to the more difficult task of rowing their heavy burden of helpless survivors back to the island, which was out of sight of the boat. This took far longer to accomplish, as Skipper Chase had to wait for the change of tides and skillfully maneuver the boat across the rips and shoals to reach safety. With the entire population of Sconset gathered on the beach, Skipper Chase and his crew brought in their boat with the seven survivors of the wreck, and landed them on the beach. They had been rowing continuously for over 30 hours, largely out of sight of land, and they had been given up for dead.

Once word of the miraculous rescue was sent abroad, Skipper Chase and his crew received the highest civilian award the federal government could bestow. An act of Congress recognized their famous rescue, and the Secretary of the Treasury issued an official commendation, awarding them medals for heroism, courage and seamanship. These awards were presented during a ceremony held a year later in the Unitarian Church, and each man treasured the medal that Congress had voted him for heroic action on the high seas. To the end of his days, Jesse Eldridge was proud to be a member of the famous Gold Medal Crew.

On that winter morning when Skipper Chase and his men arrived on Sconset Beach, they were immediately taken into the nearby homes to be warmed and fed with bowls of hot chowder. Somebody later asked Skipper Chase if the men on the beach had cheered them when they landed.

"No," said Skipper Chase. "They just helped us get the boat up the beach, then gave us something to eat and shelter—cheer in that shape, you know. After all, what did they have to say? They were all boatmen and understood."

> Fresh from the wave they take the cod,
> To feast the soul that wants it;
> Its air is pure, its water good,
> Its name is Siasconset.

Sconset understood and Sconset survived, but some people in Sconset were shaken when the newspapers confirmed the startling fact: there were liberals in Sconset. An advertisement for the Sconset School of Opinion was published in 1922, announcing that a summer school of liberal opinion would be held in Sconset, featuring a number of educators, publicists and writers of a liberal turn of mind. The topic for the season was "The World We Live In," which included The American Mind, The Political and Economic State, and Our International Relations. The advertised speakers included Roger Baldwin, Director of the American Civil Liberties Union, and Norman Thomas, leader of the Socialist Party. Clearly, this was something new on the Sconset scene.

The School of Opinion was the creation of Professor Frederick C. Howe, a summer resident of long standing and the owner of several properties in Sconset. Finding Sconset the ideal place to relax with his friends and contemplate the problems of the world, he purchased a large cottage on the edge of the village overlooking the moors, which he named the "Tavern on the Moors." Here he conceived of his summer school as a successor to Emerson's School of Philosophy at Concord, a gathering place for scholars and intellectuals, with the public invited to participate and learn in congenial surroundings.

Fred Howe was a man of international reputation, who came to Nantucket after a colorful career as a lawyer, economist and political reformer. He practiced law in Pennsylvania and Ohio, lectured on law and government as a college professor in Cleveland and Wisconsin, and served on President Wilson's staff of experts at the Versailles Peace Conference. *The New York Times* later summarized his career:

> A perennial reformer and champion of liberal causes,

both lost and realized, ranging from Henry George's single tax and the LaFollette Presidential campaign of 1924, to the New Deal, Mr. Howe began his career in the reform movement of the early 1900's in Cleveland. The climax came in the early days of the first Roosevelt administration when Mr. Howe, then consumers' counsel in the Agricultural Adjustment Administration, was one of the earliest and most criticized members of the "Brain Trust."

During the 1920's, Fred Howe brought to Sconset many educators, scientists, and writers to lecture at the School of Opinion. The morning and evening sessions were open to the public and the enrollment at the school reached 125 during the first year. Among the early lecturers were Carl Van Doren, Harry W. Overstreet, Harlow Shapley, Gutzon Borglum, Robert Benchley, and Sinclair Lewis. The chief difference between these lectures and classroom lectures, wrote one commentator, was that both students and professors seemed to be having a good time. Perhaps that was because the lectures were followed by afternoons of swimming, tennis and golf, plus long walks across the moors.

It did not take long for such a collection of intellectuals to stir up controversy in town. Although Sconset liked Fred Howe, it suspected his friends of having a "pinkish tinge" and the Tavern on the Moors of harboring "Commies on the Moors." A lively controversy sprang up when Anne Paddock Ford delivered a long letter announcing "the time is ripe for rousing the American people to a grave and imminent danger." She denounced "the unhealthy-minded Americans, who under the guise of advanced thought and freedom of discussion, are poisoning the sources of education and inspiration for our youths." The solution suggested was, "The time to kill it, is before it gets under way."

A public meeting was held to denounce the School of Opinion, where Ford declared that the Sconset School was a hotbed of revolutionary propaganda. More controversy erupted when, in addition to the lectures, the School added weekly dances and Miss Anita Zahn with the Duncan School of Dancing and Body Development. The School's enrollment grew to 250 registrants, many of them from Nantucket. The critics of the school were answered by Amy S. Jennings and Marion Trairs, who wrote: "All those who have attended the sessions of the school know how utterly unwarranted such assertions are. It is a kind of Woods Hole for teachers and students in the fields of philosophy. There have been no propaganda lectures[and] all points of view were welcomed as throwing more light on the subject."

While the controversy simmered, the School of Opinion continued and prospered. Fred Howe imported professors from Europe, members of Parliament, and internationally known figures to lecture and enjoy the summer in Nantucket. While William Jennings Bryan and Clarence Darrow were battling over the theory of evolution in Tennessee, Howe had Professor E.G. Conklin of Princeton lecturing on biology and evolution, Everett Dean Martin speaking on popular psychology, and Harry W. Overstreet of New York expounding on modern education. As Fred Howe explained it, "When all America is watching the Scopes trial in Tennessee on the question of evolution and the origin of man, the discussion of man himself, how he came to be, what are the influences that made him what he is, why he acts as he acts, and is what he is, is extremely timely."

The School of Opinion in later years featured Robert M. Lovett, Mortimer Adler, and Will Durant among its speakers, and its curriculum expanded into science, literature, drama and foreign affairs. A distinguished list of guests lent their names and support to the Tavern on the Moors, and the early criticism of the School was tempered by public acceptance of Fred Howe and his friends. They may have been a threat to the established social order of the 1920's, but they were no threat to Sconset.

Although the Nantucket of that era was a conservative Republican community, the strange people with the liberal ideas which came from the Tavern on the Moors did not disturb Sconset. The village was content to live and let live. Fred Howe was no threat to his neighbors, but he was often a problem to his creditors, because his real estate ventures were far ahead of his time on the island. As the Depression years took their toll on the summer visitors, few could afford the luxury of the summer school and the School of Opinion closed. Fred Howe was busy with the tasks of the New Deal, and had less time to devote to Sconset. Meanwhile, his financial affairs became overextended, and one by one his Sconset properties were sold off or taken over by the bank. The last to go was the Tavern on the Moors, and with it went an exciting era in Sconset history.

Fred Howe died in 1940. He was a reformer to the end of his life, and, although he could never reform his favorite village of Sconset, he left it with many happy memories of a man and his dreams of the future.

> Thrice happy vill, extend thy reign
> Till every nation own it;
> Thus shall the world its glory gain
> Beneath thy laws, O Sconset!

During the years of World War II, Nantucket Island was an outpost in the Battle of the Atlantic. The beaches of the island were patrolled by Coast Guardsmen with guard dogs, all exterior lights were blacked out across the island, and the residents were warned to be on the lookout for Nazi spies on the coast. Early in the war, the Nazis had landed spies on the beach at Long Island, and it could happen here. Every night there were calls to the local police station and civil defense headquarters reporting mysterious lights flashing along the shore, strange noises in the dark, and suspicious characters spotted about the island. No place was more nervous than Sconset, where everyone realized how easily an enemy spy could land on the beach. However, none was ever found, and the island considered itself lucky when the war ended in 1945.

On a hot July afternoon in 1946, a well-dressed gentleman carrying a briefcase stepped off the Nantucket steamer and strode rapidly up Steamboat Wharf toward Main Street. He stopped briefly to ask directions from a local taxi driver, then crossed the cobblestones to the red brick building on Washington Street which was headquarters for the Nantucket Police Department. The curious cab driver and several benchwarmers on Main Street watched him with interest.

"Government business," said the driver. "Looks like a G-man to me. Going to see the Chief.."

The Nantucket Police Department consisted of five patrolmen, a sergeant and a chief, operating out of a one-room office in the Old Town Building on Washington Street. The station held one large desk for the chief, a telephone and six wooden chairs. Adjacent to the office was a jail room which contained two sturdy cells with heavy wooden doors and strap iron bars on the windows. Outside the building, on Washington Street, was parked the first police vehicle the town ever owned, a 1940 Chevrolet sedan which had survived the war and looked it.

Seated behind the desk in the station was the Chief of Police, Lawrence F. Mooney, Jr., who was to serve 39 years on the local force. A cheerful, heavy-set man who ran the department with his own combination of native humor and common sense, the Chief prided himself on knowing everybody on Nantucket. On this summer afternoon, he was smoking his pipe and listening to the Red Sox game on the radio, when the stranger entered.

"Good afternoon, Chief, My name is Homer Wilbur, and I am a special agent with the FBI in Boston." He showed his identification and took a seat near the desk.

"Glad to meet you," said the Chief. "What brings you to Nantucket?"

"We have a report of an escaped prisoner of war living on Nantucket," said the agent. "A member of the German Army who was interned at Fort Devens. His name is Fred Kammerdiner."

"Don't know him," said the Chief. "Nobody on Nantucket by that name. Got anything else on him?"

"Yes, we have. He is probably going by an assumed name, but we have a picture of him right here. He has a heavy German accent. We have a tip he might be with a girl friend, name of Anna Hamilton. She has a house in the village of Siasconset..."

"Sconset," said the Chief. "I just don't get out there very much. I have to take care of the station. But you just wait a minute and I'll go get Wendell." The Chief rose and put on his chief's cap. "You stay right here. If the phone rings, you answer it."

The local taxi driver was now addressing a small group of men on the green bench outside the newspaper store. "That's right, the G-men are here. It's something about spies. I bet they're out in Sconset. They've got a whole nest of them out there."

"Good place for them," said one man. "They probably been signalling them Nazi submarines offshore..."

"But the war's over!" said another.

"Don't make no difference. They're still enemy aliens to me, and I don't trust them damn foreigners anyway..."

In a few minutes, Chief Mooney returned to the police station with a young patrolman in tow. He introduced the FBI man to Wendell Howes, one of the youngest officers on the force, whom the Chief relied upon to handle heavy cases. The agent repeated the story about the escaped prisoner.

"Sure I know him," said Howes. "I was painting a house in Sconset one day and he borrowed a ladder from me. He said he was a Swiss or something; anyway, he had a foreign accent. He's been living at the old Wander Inn on Sankaty Road, painting and doing odd jobs, all over Sconset. Hell, he can't be a spy, he's a regular feller."

"He's really not a spy," said the agent. "But he is one of 43 escaped prisoners of war, still at large in this country. We have to round them up. I guess they want to stay here forever."

"Wendell, you mean you knew this guy all this time?" asked the Chief.

"I even know his girl friend," said Howes. "Her name is Hamilton and she brought him down here last winter as her handyman. He's been around Nantucket since last February."

FBI Agent Homer Wilbur and Patrolman Howes then took the Nantucket police cruiser out to Sconset where they quickly found their man, still working at the house on Sankaty Road. Upon being questioned, he gave the name of Robert LaForge, and said he was of Swiss-French extraction, a native of Alsace, but he had no papers to prove it. After a few minutes, he broke down and admitted he was the long-lost Fred Kammerdiner, and told them the whole story.

He was 29 years old, having been a sergeant in the German Army when he was captured at Messina during the German retreat from Sicily. After being transported to Fort Devens prisoner of war camp in Massachusetts, he was interned with thousands of other prisoners. While at the camp, he became friendly with Anna Hamilton, who was a civilian truck driver at the time, and she eventually helped him escape in a laundry truck. Early in 1945, they met in New York, and she felt sorry for him, so she purchased a cottage in Sconset and moved there with him in February of 1945. While in Sconset, he worked on her house and did odd jobs for the neighbors in the village. In the meantime, the war ended, but he remained.

Fred Kammerdiner, now a prisoner of the FBI, made one final statement before leaving the Island. "Yes, I knew the war was over, and it was time to give up, but I loved Sconset and hated to leave this place."

He had made a few friends among the neighbors in Sconset, and a small group gathered near the post office as the word of his arrest swept through the village. As the last survivor of Hitler's army was being driven out of Sconset toward town and the long ride home, one of the men was heard to comment:

"Well, I guess the FBI got their man, all right. Too bad it had to be good old Fred. He wasn't bothering anybody."

After the soldier was returned to Fort Devens, he was eventually sent back to his native Austria, and never returned to the Island. The final chapter in the story unfolded in a Boston courtroom. The FBI also arrested Anna Hamilton, age 40, and charged her with aiding the enemy in wartime and harboring an escaped prisoner of war. Heartbroken and penniless, she was confined in East Cambridge jail for lack of bail money. She stated that she had paid $1,000 for the cottage in Sconset--one of the last of the wartime bargain sales--but it was now burdened by a $1,500 mortgage.

She was finally brought in to Federal Court in Boston, where she presented a pitiful sight, weeping as she told her story to the judge. She said she had met Fred Kammerdiner in Fort Devens, where they exchanged notes and he professed his love for her, vowing to return to her after the war. She helped him out because she felt sorry for him. The U.S. Attorney demanded a prison sentence for her, claiming her action would provoke an "open season" on such crimes. However, the judge found there was no evidence of disloyalty on her part, and no collaboration with any enemy government, and declined the government recommendation. Then the brilliant and worldly-wise

Judge Charles E. Wyzanski released her on probation, with the comment:

"There is a big difference between treason and passion!"

> "When erring virtue asks excuse,
> 'Tis free good nature grants it,
> And that which else would be abuse
> Is winked by laws of Sconset."

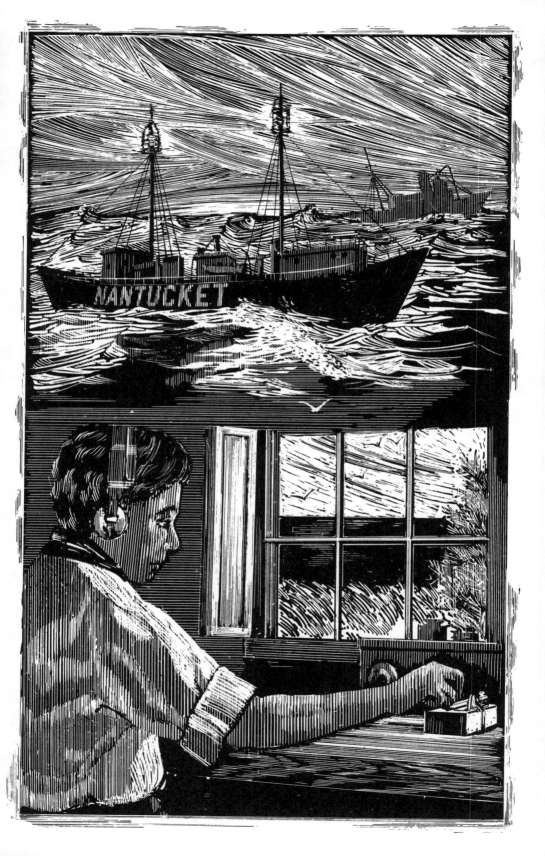

CHAPTER THIRTEEN

THE RESCUE OF RCA

Modern radio and television trace their beginnings to the Italian genius, Guglielmo Marconi, the Wizard of Wireless, who won the Nobel Prize in 1909 for his invention of the wireless telegraph. Born in humble circumstances in Bologna, Italy, in 1874, Marconi gained fame for his scientific skill and made a fortune from his business ability. Upon his death in 1937, he was honored by two minutes of radio silence around the world. In the present day, the value of his inventions to navigation and communication in the modern world is taken for granted, but when his first wireless instruments were put into operation, they were works of wonder. As Marconi extended his energies and inventions from the hilltops of Italy to the continent of Europe, the world watched in amazement. Then he spanned the English Channel with his marvelous messages. Finally, he brought his wireless system to America.

In 1901, the first wireless station in America was established in the village of Siasconset on Nantucket Island for the purpose of transmitting and receiving messages from steamships on the Atlantic Ocean. The project was originally financed by the *New York Herald* for the purpose of announcing early ship arrivals to New York City a day earlier than was previously possible. The *Herald* was proud of its connection with the Nantucket station and lavishly advertised its latest accomplishment in the field of high-speed journalism. The advantage of Nantucket was its geographical location from which a low-powered station could maintain direct communication with Nantucket Lightship, then the first lightship sighted by vessels sailing from Europe to New York. The wireless station at Nantucket was connected by a loop from the underwater telegraph cable which ran to Martha's Vineyard and thence to Woods Hole on the mainland.

This combination provided the first 24-hour communication ever established between ships at sea and the mainland of the United States.

In the same year, Marconi began construction of his famous wireless station, which was delayed by storm damage and construction difficulties, at South Wellfleet on Cape Cod. From this station a message was sent on January 18, 1903, sending greeting from President Theodore Roosevelt to His Majesty Edward VII of England, a distance of 3000 miles, the first message ever sent across the Atlantic. This was followed by a message of thanks and greeting from the King to the President. The news of these first transatlantic communications was quickly sped to a thrilled international audience.

The small station at Nantucket now assumed greater importance and the town came to appreciate the wonderful work being done on the eastern end of the island. At the Nantucket station, Marconi relied upon his personally-selected engineers and technicians to organize and operate the station, and there is no record of his personal presence on Nantucket. He did manage to visit the Cape Cod station, but was dismayed at the rural life of the Outer Cape to such an extent that he ordered his favorite food and wine sent him by train from New York. It is not likely he would have found the cuisine of Siasconset any more appealing.

The Marconi Wireless Company took over the station at Siasconset in 1904 from the *New York Herald* and used it exclusively for ship-to-shore communications. The original station was destroyed by fire caused by its electrical equipment on November 15, 1907, and the company sought a new location. The company then purchased a small house which still stands alongside the highway at the entrance to Siasconset. On the slight hill known as Bunker Hill where the Milestone Road becomes Main Street of the village, the company established its station and continued in business from 1907 through the World War I until 1922. This cottage became a source of great interest as a tall antenna pole was erected in the back yard and the hum of heavy electrical equipment drummed through the quiet evenings in Sconset.

In the early days of the Sconset wireless, traffic was confined to messages from ships at sea and transmissions between other Marconi stations on the mainland. Soon it was utilized to transmit private messages to Nantucket and occasional new bulletins of great importance. The daily newspapers from the mainland usually reached Sconset two days late, a situation which the summer visitors found intolerable. During the summer season, special arrangements were made to send daily bulletins of the score of the New York Giants baseball games to the many members of the Lambs' Club who summered in Sconset during their vacations from the New York theater. In those days before the advent of Babe Ruth, the Giants were the overwhelming favorite of the New Yorkers, and their fans in Sconset could not be denied their daily results. As reported by Margaret Fawcett Barnes, the news of the Giants' score was received each afternoon with great anticipation, as a messenger rushed from the Marconi Station to the Ocean View Hotel on the south bank of Sconset, where the actors responded to each victory with another round of rejoicing, and solemnly announced each defeat by lowering the flag which towered over Sconset to half-staff, while the faithful fans drowned their sorrows.

The early telegraph system was transmitted entirely by Morse code, and required the services of relays of trained wireless operators, skilled in the code, working day and night listening on the earphones and tapping out their signals to the ships at sea. These men occupied the most remote outpost in the early United States radio empire. They became the first pioneers in the field of wireless telegraphy and many of them continued their careers in the modern world of radio and television.

The first dramatic use of the Sconset wireless station took place on the early morning of January 23, 1909, while the waters around Nantucket were blanketed in a thick fog. Near the Nantucket Lightship, the White Star liner *Republic*, carrying 540 passengers bound from New York to Europe, was suddenly struck by the Italian liner *Florida*, which was bringing 880 immigrants from Italy to New York. Within minutes, the wireless operator on the *Republic* flashed out the international distress signal "C Q D" in Morse code. The signal was heard immediately at the Sconset station on Nantucket, where Station Manager A.H. Ginman casually acknowledged the emergency with the following:

"All right, old man, Where are you?"

The Nantucket station then turned up its full power and began sending the rescue message out to all stations and ships within a radius of 150 miles. As the calls from the *Republic* became weaker, the men in the Nantucket station were cheered to hear a response from the steamship *Baltic*, in the vicinity of the collision and headed for the rescue. At this time, both the *Republic* and the *Florida*, which had backed off after the collision, were shrouded in such thick fog they could not even see each other. The *Republic* was settling fast with no help in sight.

With the entire eastern seaboard wireless system listening to the dramatic scene, the *Baltic* closed on the sinking ship and arrived in the early evening of January 23, guided entirely by position reports from the Nantucket station. In a remarkable rescue operation on the open ocean, the *Baltic* managed to take on board a total of 1650 people, passengers and crew from both the *Republic* and the *Florida*, transferred by open boats across the swell of winter sea, without the loss of a single life. The *Baltic* then sailed on her way to New York with her tremendous burden of humanity.

This was the first rescue at sea by means of wireless. Without the connection between the *Republic* and the Sconset wireless station, a disaster of titanic proportions might have resulted. All the news the world received came from the little wooden building in Sconset and the cable which connected it to the mainland of the United States. Marconi's wireless had proven its value in both international communication and maritime life saving.

Many of the wireless operators at the Sconset station were bored and lonely with their remote location and lack of social life, but some fit into the community and found friends in the village. Some of these men came back in later years to meet with old friends and others found companions and even romance during their tour of duty in Sconset. One of these was Harry Holden, who fell in love and married Maria Folger, the cashier at the local Sconset market, where the men went for their daily provisions. Holden was to become the man in charge of the Marconi Station before he retired and settled down in Sconset with his bride.

For the young radio operators at the Sconset station, most of their days were dull and routine, as they spent long hours on the round-the-clock shifts, copying and acknowledging messages from the many ships at sea. One of these young men was a teenage lad named David Sarnoff, who had immigrated from Russia and studied wireless telegraphy. After being trained by the Marconi Company, he was expecting to see more of his new country than the loneliest outpost on the Atlantic Coast. He was soon to achieve his first taste of fame when he played a dramatic part in the most famous marine disaster of all time.

While in Nantucket, David Sarnoff developed his skills to the point where he was promoted to the New York station of the Marconi Company. On the night of April 15, 1912, when the *Titanic* struck an iceberg on the approaches to North America, the Cape Cod Marconi station had finished its scheduled agenda and gone off the air. When the *Titanic* sent out its startling SOS message for assistance, it was first heard by Sarnoff at the station in New York. The entire Atlantic community was immediately alerted to the disaster, and through the miracle of wireless, 712 passengers were saved by the steamer *Carpathia*. The story was on the front pages of the New York newspapers the next morning, and the name of David Sarnoff came to world attention for the first time.

In his early years at the Sconset station, young Sarnoff was a working lad with little time or money for recreation. On his afternoons off duty, he spent his time on the beach and enjoyed the swimming of Sconset. One summer afternoon during the summer of 1910, Sarnoff decided to take a lone swim from the beach, unaware that a summer storm had left a surging surf and dangerous undertow. There were few people on the beach and no other swimmers in the area when he entered the water. Under these circumstances, Sarnoff soon found himself in trouble, caught in the dangerous undertow and dragged out beyond the breakers.

Fortunately, walking along the beach that afternoon were two young women who had experience with the conditions at Sconset. Louise Campbell and Ruth Updegraff were both summer residents of Sconset and popular members of the summer colony which frequented the beach and played tennis at the Sconset Casino. Their social position in the summer community was far removed from that of the young immigrant lad, whom they had never seen before this day. Once they saw the young man being carried out to sea, they were quick to respond. Both dove into the surf and managed to reach him as he was about to go down for the third time. They succeeded in dragging him back to the beach where he collapsed and lay still.

When David Sarnoff was landed on the beach at Sconset, he was waterlogged and unconscious. This was an era before public lifeguards and emergency facilities, but the Nantucketers who quickly gathered on the beach seemed to know instinctively what to do with a drowning victim. Some men arrived to help out, and they immediately turned Sarnoff upside down over a barrel, wrapped him in blankets and stimulated him with several shots of local whiskey. This was considered a miraculous event, since Nantucket was supposed to be legally "dry" at that time. The victim responded to the emergency treatment and was soon able to return to his lonely post at the wireless station.

When his older and more sophisticated colleagues at the wireless station heard about Sarnoff's close call, they gathered to remind him of an ancient obligation. He was told that any boy saved from drowning by a single girl had the obligation and responsibility of proposing marriage to her, upon the principle that he owed the rest of his life to this girl. The innocent immigrant lad was anxious to conform to the customs of his new country and took their advice seriously. He donned his first pair of white flannel trousers, slicked down his hair, and took the long hike up the road to Sankaty Bluff.

At the home of Ruth Updegraff, a servant announced that a strange young man was at the front door, asking to see her. Ruth had him admitted to the house, whereupon he gravely shook hands with her and proceeded to propose matrimony. She was shocked by the suggestion, but took the entire occasion with a casual manner, as she politely thanked him for the compliment and sent him back to his telegraph station.

As Sarnoff later wrote: "It is one thing for a girl to take risks in saving a man's life, but it is another thing to take risks in sharing that life afterward. The first takes courage and the second takes wisdom."

A half century passed before the participants in the rescue at

Sconset had an opportunity to relive that incident at Sconset Beach during the summer of 1910. As Chairman of the Board of Radio Corporation of America, David Sarnoff vividly recalled every part of the adventure. When asked what went through the mind of a drowning man as he was going down for the third time, he remembered the rule of the Marconi Company that allowed not more than ten words in a telegram, with an extra charge for every word over ten. Therefore, he remembered, his mind was occupied with composing a telegram to his mother, telling her that he had drowned, in ten words or less.

After Sarnoff finished his tour of duty at Nantucket, he returned to New York, where his career continued upward until he became the Chairman of RCA. Acknowledged as a pioneer in radio and one of the founders of modern television, he never forgot his early connection with Nantucket, and he returned for many years to become a popular figure of the summer colony and a familiar sight on the green benches of Main Street in Nantucket. His brilliant career won him international fame and his contributions to the great communications industry were celebrated throughout the world. He was a worthy successor to the tradition of his mentor Marconi in the age of wireless, which led to modern radio and television. David Sarnoff, who pioneered the development of lifesaving radio which saved so many lives at sea, always remembered the day when he was himself saved by the fortunate help of two girls of summer and a few friends who happened to be on the beach at Sconset so many years ago.

CHAPTER FOURTEEN

GRAVEYARD
OF THE ATLANTIC

Thirty miles at sea, the Island of Nantucket has always occupied a perilous position in the Atlantic Ocean, off the southeastern extremity of New England. Located at the crossroads of the sea lanes from America to Europe, it early became an important landmark in the world of international shipping. Before the construction of the Cape Cod Canal in 1915, all coastal shipping had to pass within sight of Nantucket, and the long reach of Nantucket Sound was a constant panorama of merchant ships under sail and steam. Circling the shores of the Island, dangerous shifting shoals often seemed to reach out and snare the unfortunate vessels which strayed too close to land. Above the sea and the shoals, there always loomed the constant threat of New England weather, with its sudden storms and treacherous coastal fogs which threatened unwary mariners at all times of year.

The waters off Nantucket have witnessed many shipwrecks in the past. They have also seen two spectacular modern disasters in more recent years, reminding the world that neither powerful ships nor electronic navigation is a guarantee of safety at sea. In 1956, the great Italian liner, *Andrea Doria*, one of the most modern of transatlantic liners, went to the bottom of Nantucket Shoals after a collision with the Swedish liner *Stockholm* in dense fog. The early arrival of rescue craft resulted in the saving of many lives, and some of the injured were flown to Nantucket for treatment. Twenty years later, in 1976, and within thirty miles of Nantucket, the huge oil tanker, *Argo Merchant*, ran aground on the shoals during a winter storm, causing an ecological alarm which aroused the Atlantic Coast. Although no lives were lost, the sinking tanker released millions of gallons of crude oil which threatened to engulf the beaches of Nantucket and the coast of New England, to destroy thousands of coastal waterfowl, and to endanger the rich fishing grounds on the Grand Banks. Only the powerful tides, which created the problem, produced its timely solution by pulling the pollution out to sink in the open sea.

Many marine disasters have become part of Nantucket history and legend. The tales of tragedy related here include two vastly different vessels and two incredible catastrophes which happened within sight of Nantucket Island, and one great modern disaster, separated by more than a century, but linked by the principle that disaster awaits the unwary at sea.

The JOSEPH STARBUCK - 1842

Every visitor to Nantucket is familiar with the spectacular architecture of the Island, the stately homes of the whaling masters and merchants who reigned over the great years of maritime glory on the Island. Non of the homes rank higher in public admiration than the famous Three Bricks. The three identical brick mansions were built on upper Main Street in 1838 by the island's leading shipowner, Joseph Starbuck. Built by the patriarch to house his descendents, the three homes were built alike so his boys would not quibble, and were destined for his three sons, George, William, and Matthew Starbuck.

Following the completion of the Three Bricks, Joseph Starbuck set himself to the task of building another whaleship, the greatest of his illustrious career. Most of the Starbuck ships had been built in Old Rochester, along the shores of Buzzard's Bay, where many of New England's finest vessels had been built since the earliest days. That area, now known as Wareham, Marion, Mattapoisett, and Rochester, had the men and material to build the best for the sailing fleets. From 1811 to 1838, the Rochester yards created eight large and eminently successful whaling ships for the Starbuck family. One of the Rochester-built ships, *Young Hero*, built in 1837 at a cost of $13,000, returned from her first voyage, and netted $39,294 to Joseph Starbuck. From such enterprise, fortunes were made.

Now the Starbucks turned themselves toward a proud and adventurous goal, building a great whaleship right in Nantucket, within sight of their homes and their neighbors. Elisha Smith and his shipyard had been in business on the inside of Brant Point for several years. The yard was used mainly for repairing the local fleet, although Smith had built three whalers since 1832. To build a great whaleship for the Starbucks would be a proud accomplishment for the local shipyard, creating a whaler before the eyes of the critical Nantucket public. For Joseph Starbuck and his three sons, it would become a monument to the founding father. The enthusiasm of the age caught the patriarch in his 64th year, and he became determined to see it through. Furthermore, he decided, he would show the world how fast a whaleship could be built.

The new ship was to be called the *Joseph Starbuck*, and she was commenced May 1, 1838, and launched in October, 1838. That was a phenomenal bit of shipbuilding in five months, with all the major components imported from the mainland. Yet, it was accomplished, at a cost of $15,612. The great ship set sail for her first voyage to the Pacific in November, 1838, and returned in April, 1842, with 3321 barrels of sperm oil, valued at $63,838.

After six months at Nantucket, the *Joseph Starbuck* was ready for her second voyage. This was to be a three-year cruise to the Pacific which held the promise of being even more successful than the first voyage. Nantucket whaling was at its peak in 1842, and the Starbuck ship, built by Nantucketers, manned by Nantucketers, and owned by the greatest of the Island merchants, represented the proudest pinnacle of the glory days. The captain of the ship was not only a veteran whaling master but also a one-sixteenth owner of the vessel. Joseph Starbuck owned the other fifteen-sixteenths of the ship. The scheduled sailing date was November 27, 1842, which fell on a Sunday, a day marine superstition deemed unlucky.

The departure was to be a special event for the Starbuck ship, because she was scheduled for a few days' visit to Edgartown on Martha's Vineyard to take on stores before heading for the high seas. Thus, the ship arranged to carry a party of guests, six women and several prominent men from Nantucket, who were invited to come along for the three-hour sail to Edgartown, where they would spend a few days before returning to Nantucket on the packet boat. Altogether, it was quite a gala occasion as the *Joseph Starbuck* left Nantucket that Sunday morning at 7:15, under tow of the Steamer *Telegraph*, heading around Brant Point for the short cruise with a favorable wind.

The pilot of the ship, John H. Pease, was the first man to notice a problem as the two vessels approached Tuckernuck Shoal. About 10:30 in the morning, the wind swung to the west and increased in velocity. The *Starbuck* was sailing without ballast, prior to taking on stores, and was therefore riding high on the windy seas. After crossing the Nantucket Bar at the harbor entrance, she began to fill the casks in her lower hold with salt water for ballast. As the westerly wind increased, the small *Telegraph* proved unable to make any headway, and the paddle-wheel steamer let go the tow line. Just west of the Tuckernuck Lightship on the shoals, the *Starbuck* let go her bow anchor to hold her position until the wind abated. When this was not enough, the ship dropped her second anchor about noon, and payed out more cable to ride out the blow.

As the wind increased to gale force from the northwest, the captain sought to lighten the top-heavy ship by bringing down the topmasts and yards, but the ship was caught in the teeth of the sudden storm. About 3:30 in the afternoon, the starboard anchor cable parted at the windlass, and the ship was now in serious trouble. In the gathering darkness of the late November day, she was dragging her remaining anchor while being driven eastward across Nantucket Sound for several hours. The force of the gale drove the great ship from Tuckernuck Shoals toward the Chord of the Bay between Great Point and Nantucket Harbor, with only one anchor to keep her from being driven ashore. After standing up to the strain for several hours, that last anchor cable let go about 10 PM, and the ship was headed for Nantucket Bar, the dangerous sandbar which stretched along the northern shore of Nantucket Island and practically blocked the entrance to the harbor. The captain had hopes of bringing the ship over the bar and back into Nantucket port. However, the damage was too great and the ship too far gone to control, and for a while, she was in serious danger of being blown out to sea around Great Point. Captain Veeder now took his most desperate measures, ordering the mizzenmast chopped away to lighten the ship and setting the foresail on the foremast to make the ship run before the wind and prevent her from rolling over. By midnight, the wind was churning the sea to mountainous heights. Driven by gale force winds, the ship was violently driven up on the eastern end of Nantucket bar, about four miles from Nantucket Harbor. With a violent shudder, the *Joseph Starbuck* struck the sands of the shoal and rolled over on her beam ends, while shattering waves threw huge seas over her masthead.

A day of celebration had turned into a night of terror for the 35 men and women aboard the *Joseph Starbuck*, most of whom thought they would never see another day. Yet, the ship held together on the shoal until morning, when it was sighted by the watchman in the South Tower. By good fortune, the steamer *Massachusetts* was at the wharf and she soon mustered a crew of volunteers to attempt the rescue. The *Massachusetts* was a new vessel, built in 1842, and much more powerful than the *Telegraph*. This was her first appearance in a salvage role, and she performed to perfection. She arrived at the scene of the wreck about 9 in the morning, to find the survivors clinging to the rigging as the waves crashed over the decks of the ship on the shoal. By tremendous effort, the steamer churned in close enough to make fast to the lee side of the *Starbuck*. Then, a single whaleboat was launched and rowed across by the volunteer crew. That whaleboat made five trips to the wreck, returning each time with seven persons. When the rescue was complete, the steamer *Massachusetts* steamed back into harbor with all 35 survivors of the

Joseph Starbuck, leaving behind the last remains of Nantucket's proudest whaleship.

Although no lives were lost, the wreck of the great ship within sight of Nantucket Harbor was a cause of much comment and speculation. Leaving port on a Sunday was considered a bad omen by many mariners; carrying women on a pleasure cruise was bound to be cause for suspicion. An unhealthy optimism lay behind the decision to sail into the uncertain November seas without any ballast, for the ship had proven too light to ride out the storm. Captains ashore would always outnumber and outguess the captain at sea. But for many in Nantucket, there was no mystery to the loss of the *Joseph Starbuck*: it was just the pride of the Starbucks, wrecked on Nantucket Bar.

The CONSTANCE - 1949

The last days of summer in 1949 produced a marine tragedy in Nantucket waters which remains a vivid memory to many Islanders who remember the fate of the *Constance*. Although the *Constance* was a cabin cruiser headed home to Falmouth after a short pleasure cruise, she met a tragic fate in the same waters which had claimed the proud whaleship *Joseph Starbuck* 107 years earlier. This time, while the loss of the vessel was unfortunate, the loss of life was appalling.

The winds of September can be unpredictable on Nantucket and the history of the island is replete with tales of summer storms of mid-September as the "line gales" which produced violent wind and rain, usually downing the power lines and causing great damage. The most famous hurricane of New England history struck on September 21, 1938, in an age before modern weather warnings, and caused havoc in New England. Later hurricanes gained fame and publicity and glamorous names as modern systems tracked them up the coast. The Nantucketers always viewed the days of September with caution.

The *Constance* left Falmouth on September 9 on a one-day excursion cruise to Nantucket, with a party of eleven passengers. They were the Reverend Hubert Allenby of Falmouth, his wife, his children, their friends and guests, all the young people being college students and graduates in their teens and twenties. The skipper of the *Constance* was Russell Palmer, 23, of Falmouth. The vessel was a 38-foot twin engine cabin cruiser, built in 1934 at a cost of $14,000 and was a veteran of many years in Nantucket waters. She had recently been overhauled and was considered quite seaworthy. After arriving about 11 AM, the party went for picnic lunch at Surfside, followed by a swim at the beach. Everything went well except for some rain squalls which passed over the island during the afternoon.

About 4:15 in the afternoon, the *Constance* filled her gas tanks at the Island Service Company on Old South Wharf and departed, clearing the Coast Guard Station at Brant Point at 4:20, heading for Falmouth. The rains had stopped and the winds were moderate as she headed toward Tuckernuck Shoal. No storm warnings were flying at Brant Point, but heavy gray cumulus clouds hovered on the western horizon.

When she was fifty minutes from Nantucket, the vessel encountered high winds and a sudden thunderstorm. The winds came on from the northwest, battering the boat with head-on breakers as she approached the choppy shoals north of Tuckernuck Island. Suddenly, a huge wave crashed over the bow and swamped the port engine. Unable to restart the engine, the skipper dropped anchor in fifty feet of water, on the easterly edge of Tuckernuck Shoal.

The deadly combination of time, distance and weather all came down on the *Constance*. As night fell over Nantucket Sound, the wind blew strongly from the northwest bringing heavy rain showers. The tide was running to the east and the wooden hull of the *Constance* started to buckle and break up in the high seas. First the forward cockpit flooded. Next, the passengers were forced on deck with the prospect of leaving the sinking ship in the darkness. Skipper Palmer gave each passenger a life jacket and lashed them together with mooring line to form a circle in the water. He tried to keep them tied to the wreck of the ship, but the line parted and in the attempt to join it again, he became separated from the circle of survivors.

The passengers remaining within the circle were out of the sea lane between Nantucket and the mainland, but within sight of help.

They saw the lights of the evening steamship pass them by, too far away to hear their cries. They could see the light towers of the microwave station on the north shore of Nantucket. There were no rescue boats in sight and nothing to save them from the cold waters and pounding waves which gradually took their toll on the survivors.

Only one man on shore knew the *Constance* was in trouble. Carl Palmer, of Falmouth, owner of the vessel and father of Russell Palmer, was anxious as night fell with no word from the missing cruiser. He set out in his own boat to look for her, but heavy seas forced him to Martha's Vineyard, where he telephoned the Woods Hole Coast Guard Station. Woods Hole sent out an 83-foot cutter to search the waters, and notified Brant Point Station that the *Constance* was missing. Another alert was sent to the Search and Rescue Unit in Salem, but they did nothing until dawn. The cutter completed its search and returned to port. The Nantucket station sent a search along the north shore and found nothing, returning to the station. The night of September 9 ended in gloom and nothingness.

The morning of September 10 dawned as a bright sun shone over a clear, windy morning with high seas running through Nantucket Sound. Carl Palmer was up early, calling his friend Marvin Odum at the Falmouth Airport to fly him over the sound. He flew several times over the area but could not spot any survivors in the breaking whitecaps. He radioed for help to the Civil Aeronautical Administration communications center at Nantucket Memorial Airport, where its chief, Lester Bachman, quickly took charge of communications between planes and land stations. Odum then landed at Nantucket, where he met with Allen Holdgate, a veteran Nantucket pilot, who ran a combination office and lunch counter at Nantucket Flying Service. This was the first news Nantucket had received of the impending disaster since the call from Woods Hole to Brant Point the previous evening.

Meanwhile, a solitary figure was staggering across the beach on Nantucket's north shore, near a summer home at Dionis. About 8:30 in the morning, after a night drifting in his life jacket, Russell Palmer waded through the shallow waters and collapsed on the beach. Summer beachgoers paid him no attention; he was so weak some thought he was just sleeping off an evening party on the beach. Finally, he was noticed and taken to the Fitch home overlooking the beach, where he began to tell his story. About 9 o'clock, a call was made to the Brant Point Coast Guard Station. They said they would send a man out to investigate.

While the Coast Guard was questioning Russell Palmer, Allen Holdgate was taking off from the airport with a small crew which was destined to be the first to sight the survivors. Holdgate patrolled the area from Great Point to Eel Point, until his volunteer spotter, George Lusk, sighted the first survivors in the waters north of Dionis Beach, a couple of miles off shore. Holdgate radioed the location to the CAA, then began circling the scene to alert the rescue boats which he assumed were on their way to pick up the survivors.

The news of the disaster was slowly circulating in Nantucket. On the Island Service Wharf, a Coast Guard jeep stopped at the gas station, and asked where they could get a boat, because "there are some people out there in trouble."

"Can you imagine that," asked the attendant, "the Coast Guard asking a filling station man where they could get a boat?"

State Trooper Edgar Lindstrom heard about the situation at 10:21, when he received a radio message from the State Police Oak Bluffs Barracks, at Martha's Vineyard. He hurried to the Brant Point Station, where he met the veteran local mariner, George "Bunt" Mackey, an expert skipper who owned a boat powered with twin Chrysler engines, capable of 29 knots, who was offering to help out the Coast Guard. They took aboard the experienced boatman, Joe King, and set off toward the scene of the disaster.

"Bunt" Mackey was to make the bitterest comment about the entire procedure, when he later said, "If the Coast Guard had alerted the boatmen on the waterfront, we would have been out there at the crack of dawn and saved most of those people."

It was over one hour after Russell Palmer came ashore when word of the events reached the Nantucket Police Department. Chief Lawrence F. Mooney, smoking his pipe on a bench outside the station, was informed of the news by a tip from a newspaperman. He immediately sent Patrolman Wendell H. Howes to the Brant Point Station, where he found a crew of sailors getting ready to ride to Dionis, which they thought was on the south shore of the Island. Howes quickly straightened them out and led them to Dionis. "I was amazed," said Howes, "to learn they didn't know where Dionis was!"

The Coast Guard arrived on the beach at Dionis in time to start collecting debris from the *Constance* as it began floating ashore. There were no survivors in sight.

The Coast Guard also dispatched the amphibious duck from Brant Point for Tuckernuck and Muskeget. It was stopped at Madaket, by a telephone call from the station to "Madaket Millie" Jewett, who operated a small general store and informal Coast Guard station of her own at the western end of the island. She relayed the order that the two men were to take the 26-foot motor surfboat moored in Hither Creek and search the waters north of Nantucket for people in the water.

When Allen Holdgate first spotted the survivors off Dionis Beach at 10:20 in the morning, they were about two miles from the shore. The Coast Guard cutter was patrolling six miles out in Nantucket Sound. The local picket boat, radio-equipped and well-qualified for rescue work, had been dispatched eastward toward Great Point. The amphibious duck had driven to Madaket, completely by-passing the rescue scene at Dionis, and never took part in the operation. The 26-foot motor whaleboat was now getting underway from Madaket, manned by two men with no radio.

At the airport, Lester Bachman of the CAA called the state and local police and notified the hospital of the disaster, the first official news being sent out at 10:30 AM, two hours after Russell Palmer had landed at Dionis Beach. Bachman then learned that Air-Sea Rescue had not been contacted, and immediately radioed the Naval Air Station at Quonset Point to send two helicopters and pulmotor respiratory equipment.

The scene shifted to the windy beach and bluff at Dionis, where scores of people had gathered after 11 o'clock to witness the rescue. While Allen Holdgate circled overhead to mark the survivors, the

Coast Guard 26-foot motor surfboat approached the area. The men in the boat, one forward and one aft, were having trouble handling the boat and finding the survivors in the choppy seas. They could see four people lashed together in the water, one of them frantically waving for help. One of the men gasped, "Take her first!" motioning to the girl slumped beside him. With great difficulty, the sailors managed to haul the girl from the water into the heaving boat. Then they used both their efforts to drag the man into the boat. While they were doing this, the sailors had to leave the helm to grasp the survivors. The surfboat, with its engine idling, came down on the windward side into the circle of the remaining survivors. One of the lines connecting the survivors fouled the propeller, and the final act of the tragedy was played out. The slowly turning shaft pulled two survivors, a man and a woman, down into the churning sea where they disappeared.

The surfboat returned to the beach with one survivor, H. Alfred Allenby, Jr., age 23, the only survivor of his entire family. As young Allenby was met on the beach by Officer Howes, he stopped to look at the girl's body being lifted from the boat. It was his fiancee, the girl he was to marry within the week.

"That's Emily," he said. "We were together all night. I can breathe all right. They're all out there. Go and get them."

When Allen Holdgate first spotted the survivors, he saw four people, alive and waving for help, with one other lying weakly in the water. He could note the slow progress of the motor surfboat, as its two crewman struggled to attempt the rescue, and he urgently called for more help. "Get more help out here!" he shouted into the radio. "These people are alive but they're getting weak. They need help."

Help was forthcoming, but time and distance steadily took their toll, adding to the tragedy. The only boat on the rescue scene, the motor surfboat, was disabled on the beach at Dionis. The Coast Guard picket boat, after a fruitless chase across Nantucket Sound, returned to Nantucket Harbor for further orders. Although this vessel was radio-equipped, the radio was found to be out of order. Thus the Brant Point station commander had to run down to the rocks at the harbor entrance to shout orders to return to Dionis. The Coast Guard duck, considered unwieldy in this situation, had returned to town. Meanwhile, the help requested by Lester Bachman from his CAA tower was immediately forthcoming. The Naval Air Station at Quonset Point launched two helicopters and they were underway at 10:58, arriving in thirty minutes. The Navy also sent a plane with ten pulmotors, doctors and hospital corpsmen, who arrived at noon.

By this time, there was nothing more to be done but recover bodies. George Mackey and the Whistler came in with four bodies, one more was found close to the beach, and the Coast Guard Cutter came in with the final three. By 12:30 Chief Mooney advised the CAA that the search could be called off as all persons were accounted for; two survivors, nine dead.

Nantucket had known many maritime disasters and loss of life at sea was not a new experience to the Island, but this sinking of the *Constance* was a very personal tragedy which had great impact on the town. The loss of so many lives so close to rescue seemed incredible. The criticism levelled at the Coast Guard was particularly serious. The island had a long and cordial relationship with the service and several Nantucketers had served in the local Coast Guard stations, but it seemed the establishment had failed badly in its search and rescue efforts on this occasion.

The Coast Guard immediately convened a Board of Inquiry headed by Rear Admiral Edward H. Smith, Commandant of the Eastern Area, which heard witnesses for several days and issued a formal report in February of 1950. The Board reported in detail on the events surrounding the search and rescue efforts, which lead up to "a tragic and heart-rendering scene, culminating in an unsuccessful attempt to save life, when rescue was literally within grasp." It made many recommendations for improving the personnel, training and equipment of the various stations, and it handed down seven charges of negligence and inefficiency against officers and enlisted men for their failures during the emergency. Most of the charges concerned the slow and inefficient search efforts mounted after learning of the disappearance of the *Constance* under dangerous circumstances. Boatswain James F. Beaumont, Officer in Charge of the Brant Point Station, was cited for negligence for failure to make prompt search for the vessel. Boatswain's Mate First Class Harold J. Thurston, a Nantucket man in charge of the motor surfboat, and his crew, were cited for failure to wear life jackets under hazardous conditions, but praised for performing their duties under extremely adverse conditions of wind and seas, resulting in the rescue of the one passenger saved.

The Board report concerned itself only with the performance of service personnel. It did mention, "In the present case there are such questions as the seaworthiness of the craft itself, and the seamanship and navigation of the operator, none of which come within the scope of the present Board." Its summary gave the opinion: "It is also rather ironical,...that if all the inefficiency and negligence on the part of this one and that one, in the Coast Guard, in the *Constance* case, be totalled, it is not sufficient to have altered materially the course of the tragedy or the loss of life that occured."

There was plenty of blame to be shared for the tragedy, but the Board also gave credit by issuing letters of thanks to the following Nantucketers who assisted the Coast Guard in the search and rescue: Miss Mildred Jewett, Captain George H. Mackey, Pilot Allen Holdgate, Chief Lawrence F. Mooney, State Trooper Edgar T. Lindstrom, and CAA Chief Lester W. Bachman.

The sad tale of the sinking of the *Constance* was the greatest small boat disaster in the history of Nantucket. From this tragedy, the Island emerged into the reality of modern maritime life. The need to be prepared for the emergencies brought on by increasing numbers of pleasure boats and private planes, was recognized. Allen Holdgate helped form a local search and rescue unit of 25 civilian pilots. Based in part upon the recommendations of the Board of Inquiry, the Coast Guard developed into a vastly improved service, with better training, equipment and communications. Safety and communications were gradually improved for all small boats, and coordinated efforts became established between all concerned organizations. Whether by fate or foresight, the disaster of the *Constance* has not been repeated, but the Island will never forget its tragic lesson.

The ANDREA DORIA - 1956

When the great Italian luxury liner *Andrea Doria* sank off Nantucket in the summer of 1956 after a collision with the Swedish liner *Stockholm*, Nantucket Island became the center of world attention and international news stories. This time, the rescue of the survivors was carried out with great speed and efficiency, taking maximum advantage of modern equipment and coordinated efforts on land and sea. As a result, over 1600 people were safely rescued in the biggest rescue effort since the sinking of the *Titanic* in 1912.

On the evening of July 25, 1956, the *Andrea Doria* was steaming past Nantucket Lightship, headed due west for the port of New York with 1706 persons, including passengers and crew, returning from Europe. She was the pride of the Italian fleet, built in 1953, at 29,100 tons, and was one of the largest and fastest ships in the world. She was also considered the most luxurious and beautiful ship afloat.

At the same time, the Swedish liner, *Stockholm*, a smaller passenger liner carrying 534 passengers, was headed due east from New York to Copenhagen. She was a veteran of the north Atlantic waters, built in 1948 at 12,165 gross tons, and featured an extra heavy bow which was designed to follow ice breakers in Scandinavian waters.

Both ships were operating at full speed despite the heavy ocean fog in the area of Nantucket Lightship, relying upon their radar and lookouts to avoid close contact with other vessels. Despite the fact they were on a collision course, neither took timely action to escape the inevitable, and the two ships collided about 11 p.m., when the sharp bow of the *Stockholm* smashed into the starboard side of the *Andrea Doria*. The Italian liner immediately listed to starboard and soon appeared to be beyond hope of salvage.

The captain of the *Andrea Doria* immediately flashed the SOS message, giving his position and calling "Need Immediate Assistance."

This message was received by the U.S. Coast Guard radio stations in Chatham, Massachusetts, Mackay, New Jersey, and East Moriches, Long Island. The Long Island station relayed to New York at 11:25 P.M.:

> "*Andrea Doria* and *Stockholm* collided 11:22 local
> time, Lat. 40-30 N, Long. 69-53 W."

This message set the U.S. Coast Guard Sea and Air Rescue Coordination Center into action. From Sandy Hook, the 180' Cutter *Tamaroa*, ready for immediate action, got underway in three minutes. From Cape Cod, the cutters *Yakutat* and *Cambell* headed for the area. The Coast Guard ships, *Hornbeam* from Woods Hole and *Legare* from New Bedford soon were underway. The Cutter *Evergreen* steamed out of Boston and arrived at the scene by 8:06 AM

This massive response was a reaction to the identity of the ship involved. Since, the *Andrea Doria* carried over 1700 persons, it was apparent that many rescue ships would be needed to save the survivors. Although the captain of the *Andrea Doria* never sent word that his ship was actually sinking, only that he needed assistance, the additional help was valuable for another reason. As the *Doria* was listing to starboard over 22 degrees, it became impossible to launch her port life boats, and thus the stricken ship had only half the boats needed to off-load her passengers.

Navy and Coast Guard air rescue units were also alerted, together with the Otis Air Force base on Cape Cod, but they could not get airborne until morning and then coastal morning fog delayed their arrival at the scene.

The site of the collision was about 45 miles south of Nantucket, and the Island became the nearest landing field for aircraft rescue operations. At dawn, planes and helicopters began to arrive at Nantucket Memorial Airport, carrying rescue equipment, medical supplies and medical personnel. Equally prompt were the newsmen, who flew in by chartered planes and helicopters from Boston and New York. The first one arrived at 4 AM, followed by 50 or 60 others from reporters to cameramen. Their Nantucket byline was sent to all corners of the world, and was especially awaited in Genoa and Stockholm, the home ports of the two ships.

The first ship to answer the SOS during the night was the U.S. Navy transport *William H. Thomas*, which was 19 miles away from the collision, steaming home with returning troops from Europe. The cargo ship, *Cape Ann*, returning from Europe, responded to the SOS, and radioed that she would be there in thirty minutes, with two lifeboats. The *Doria* flashed back the message: "Danger Immediate. Need Boats to Evacuate 1000 Passengers and 500 Crew. We Need Boats."

The huge French ocean line, *Ile de France*, 44,500 tons, was 44 miles away when she heard the SOS at 11:30 PM. Carrying 940 passengers and a crew of 826, she was on the way to France, keeping to a tight schedule as is necessary for so important and expensive a vessel. Because of her distance from the collision, she was under no strict legal obligation to make the rescue, but in view of the need for lifeboats, she responded to the call of the mariner in distress. She swung in a complete circle and headed for the *Andrea Doria*, churning through the fog at 22 knots.

In the early morning darkness, with the arrival of the rescue vessels, responding to the SOS, and the Coast Guard cutters, the boats began plying from the starboard side of the *Andrea Doria* to their various rescuers. The *Stockholm*, with her bow sheared off but still seaworthy, took on 234 crewmen and 311 passengers from the *Doria*. The Coast Guard cutters took on some, until the *Ile de France* arrived on the scene. With the appearance of the huge French liner, the passengers in the lifeboats had a choice of rescuers, and 753 of them reached the *Ile de France* and safety during the night.

One sad tale involved a little Italian girl, four-year old Norma DiSandro, who was travelling from Italy with her parents. As the lifeboats were being loaded alongside the *Andrea Doria*, her father dropped her from the deck into a lifeboat, where she fell head-first and received a fractured skull. She was taken to the *Stockholm* for later helicopter rescue. Flown to Nantucket, she was photographed coming off the helicopter on a stretcher, a photo which identified the tragedy in human terms. She was, later, flown to Brighton Marine Hospital in Boston, where she died a few days later.

There were 43 people killed on the *Andrea Doria*, most of whom had been in the area of the collision, whose bodies went down with the ship. The injured were taken to the *Stockholm* in the first boats, from which they were air-lifted for medical attention. The helicopters, delayed by fog, stopped at Nantucket for doctors, and proceeded to the scene by 7:30 AM. They came from Salem Coast Guard Station and Otis Air Force Base. Over the *Stockholm*, they lowered stretchers to take on the injured, using a technique developed during the Korean War. From there, they flew into Nantucket.

On Nantucket, the injured were given emergency treatment at Nantucket Cottage Hospital, where dozens of doctors and nurses had volunteered for emergency duty. Many of the injured were seamen from the *Stockholm*, suffering from fractures and shock. All the injured were eventually transferred to Boston for further treatment.

The first pilots to arrive over the *Andrea Doria* shortly after she was abandoned at 5:30 AM, found a startling scene of beauty amid tragedy. As the sun rose on a sparkling blue sea, the graceful Italian liner "never looked more beautiful." Her gleaming white lines, bright sun decks, triple swimming pools and glistening brasswork looked like new. Only the dangling life lines and the sickening 45 degree list to starboard showed her impending doom. As the great ship keeled slowly to starboard and her bow went down, one photographer earned the Pulitzer Prize for taking the last dramatic photos of the sinking ship. She went under at 10:09 AM.

The loss of the ship was a true maritime tragedy, but the rescue of 1,662 persons from the *Andrea Doria* was  the most successful rescue operation in maritime history. The *Ile de France* and *Stockholm* returned to New York with most of the survivors, the Coast Guard bringing in the remainder. So prompt and effective was the response of the seaborne rescue units, that the scene off Nantucket Lightship began to look like a maritime convention of ships. There were so many Coast Guard cutters that the command ship was forced to radio: "Plenty of ships--no further assistance needed." The prompt response of the Coast Guard on land and sea had prevented a disaster of titanic proportions.

Thus ends the latest and greatest of the maritime tragedies off the shores of Nantucket, an incident in which the Island played a small part in the endless story of men, ships and the sea.

CHAPTER FIFTEEN

THE MOST
BAFFLING MYSTERY

Nantucket's greatest modern mystery began on a cold winter weekend in January 1980, while the Island was enduring a stretch of dull wintry days with ice in the harbor and a sharp wind cutting across the land. One afternoon, a well-dressed woman with striking red hair swept into the A&P Supermarket on Harbor Square and began a dynamic shopping excursion which began to attract attention. Hurrying through the aisles of the store, she gathered in a huge quantity of food, loading several shopping carts. Her purchases included three roasts of beef, a dozen steaks and twelve toothbrushes. By the time she reached the checkout counter, several people had taken notice, and some gasped when the cashier loudly announced: "Six hundred and fifty dollars!"

The red-haired woman smiled as she wrote out a Nantucket check for the exact amount. Then she called to a waiting taxi driver to pick up the goods and meet her at the nearby liquor store. The cashier commented on the size of her order and asked the woman about her plans for her stay in Nantucket.

"I'm having a party," she announced in a loud voice. "A great party, for lots of people. I will need three houses for all my friends and the people coming for the press conference. You will hear about it when they announce my discovery. This is going to be my prize party—maybe a *Nobel* prize party!"

The cashier stood in silence as the woman gathered her things and rushed out of the store. Slowly shaking her head, she looked down at the check and read its large, bold signature: Margaret Kilcoyne, M.D.

Dr. Margaret Kilcoyne was a remarkable person in many respects. She was born in Worcester, Massachusetts, and was trained as a registered nurse before making the decision to become a doctor. She put herself through college and medical school, and decided to forego the usual medical practice in favor of rigorous medical research. By the age of 50, she had achieved success in her career when she became a member of the research staff at the prestigious Columbia Presbyterian Medical Center in New York City. There she was highly regarded in the competitive field of advanced research, where she was performing pioneering work in the study of adolescent hypertension.

Doctor Kilcoyne never married and enjoyed the independent life of a successful professional person. She was witty and colorful, fond of music and tennis, and enthusiastic in her pursuit of a healthy lifestyle. She purchased property in Nantucket in 1970, and had a comfortable two-bedroom home constructed at Tom Nevers, a new development about six miles from the center of town, on a hillside overlooking the south shore of the Island. She had the house fully winterized so it could be used at all times of the year, and it was tastefully furnished. While in Nantucket she occasionally worked on her research, but spent most of her time relaxing, working about the house, and entertaining her friends. She loved her home and planned to retire to Nantucket when she completed her professional career.

On the bitter-cold morning of January 26, 1980, a telephone rang at the office of the Nantucket Police Department. The caller identified himself as Leo Kilcoyne, and said his sister, Margaret Kilcoyne, was missing from her home. He gave the address on Flintlock Road in the Tom Nevers district. The police responded as Patrolman Randolph Norris drove out to the house, thus beginning a series of events which soon spread the story of Doctor Kilcoyne far beyond the shores of the Island.

Captain George Rezendes, a veteran of 22 years on the local department, was in charge of the investigation. After a quick check of the area near the Kilcoyne house showed no signs of the missing woman, he interviewed Leo Kilcoyne about his sister. At 53, Leo was an executive with IBM Corporation in Canada, who had flown to Nantucket the previous day. He was plainly disturbed about his sister's fate, and told the police she was in a state of agitation and spiritual confusion which indicated to him that she was on the verge of suicide. Margaret had invited him to Nantucket for the weekend and he had responded because he was concerned about her condition.

When the initial search indicated that there had been no forced entry of the house, the police quickly ordered a watch for the missing person at the local airport and steamship wharf. These terminals were watched for several days without result. It was reported that no person resembling Doctor Kilcoyne had taken the boat that morning, and the presence of ice in the harbor precluded the possibility of departure by private boat. No aircraft had landed or taken off from the airport during the night, nor did any private aircraft leave Nantucket the following day. There was the possibility that an unscheduled airplane could have landed elsewhere on the island, without using the airport, or taken off after dark when the control tower was closed. Some rumors to this effect were circulated, but the possibilities were discarded as most unlikely.

Satisfied that all means of departure were covered, Captain Rezendes ordered a full search of the area around the Kilcoyne house which was conducted on Saturday and Sunday in very cold weather. Using the services of auxiliary police, firemen and volunteers, most on foot and some in four-wheel-drive vehicles, the force swept through the Tom Nevers area for two days, while volunteer pilots flew over the countryside. This area of Nantucket was sparsely settled, with few houses occupied in winter. Most of the land was covered by dense underbrush of scrub oaks and wild bushes, six to ten feet high. It was difficult terrain, hard to traverse for anyone but an experienced rabbit hunter. The frozen ground did not reveal any sign of tracks. At the base of a low ridge in front of the Kilcoyne house, the land leveled off into a large swamp and freshwater pond known as Tom Nevers Pond, which was surrounded by small creeks and marsh grass. The waters of the pond were searched and dragged through holes in the ice with no results. At the end of the long weekend, Leo Kilcoyne, with resignation on his face, told the police he was convinced his sister had taken her own life by walking into the ocean. Captain Rezendes agreed with him and concluded he was dealing with "a case of a water suicide."

On Saturday afternoon, the newly appointed Chief of Police, Paul

Hunter, arrived on the Island to take up his duties. He immediately found himself in the middle of a strange missing-person case which looked to him like more than a suicide. He ordered Captain Rezendes to continue in charge of the investigation while he began to explore other angles of the case.

Chief Hunter focused upon two unusual articles of evidence that were found in the study of Margaret Kilcoyne's home and seemed to have been left there as tantalizing clues to her disappearance. On her desk, the police noticed a portable tape recorder and two tapes, which Leo turned over to them for examination. When played over in the Chief's office, these tapes proved to be lengthy recordings of Margaret's voice on a one-sided telephone call. Leo said they were Margaret's recordings of her end of a long conversation with him, which took place a few days before she left for Nantucket. On the tapes, Margaret's voice talked about the pressures and conflicts in her work, her thoughts about Leo and his family, and the spiritual crisis she was experiencing. In her distinctive and colorful language, Margaret described her excitement about her prospects and plans for the future. Leo believed this conversation showed such anxiety and confusion that he came to Nantucket hoping to talk Margaret into taking a vacation and seeking some help for her mental state. However, he never had the opportunity to discuss this proposal before her disappearance.

The Kilcoyne tapes added another element of mystery to the missing person and started speculation on the reasons for her disappearance. This was increased when the Chief released the contents of the tapes to the press. Overnight, the writers began to comment on the many forces working upon the missing doctor and the pressures of her highly competitive professional life, dramatizing the intensity of her spiritual crisis. One professional investigator listened to the tapes and described them as "a verbal suicide note." Chief Hunter thought he found ominous undertones which increased his suspicions.

One week after the first search, four young people were walking a dog through Tom Nevers Swamp when they made a startling discovery. Stacked neatly in a pile on the marsh grass were a pair of leather sandals, a passport, a Nantucket Savings bankbook, and a wallet containing a $100 bill. All these items belonged to Margaret Kilcoyne, and had been with her before her disappearance. Nearby was a crumpled brown blouse, bearing the label "The Birds," later identified as hers. Although the items were found about a mile from her house they were located in a spot away from the direction of the ocean. Furthermore, this area had been thoroughly searched on foot the previous weekend. If Margaret had placed the items there, she had taken a roundabout route to the ocean; if she had not done this, someone else had. Now the case began to take on more sinister overtones.

The first snow of the year fell on Nantucket February 7, making further ground search useless. Chief Hunter decided to widen the search to find out more about Doctor Kilcoyne, convinced that there was some missing element in her disappearance. On February 8, Captain Rezendes and Town Prosecutor Robert F. Mooney flew to New York City to continue the investigation.* They flew into La Guardia Airport, where they were startled to find several reporters waiting for them, demanding interviews. They learned that *The New York Times* had picked up the story that morning and given it full coverage, dwelling upon the influential connections of the New York medical establishment with the Cape Cod-Nantucket vacation community. One radio reporter insisted upon an interview in a phone booth and a live broadcast from atop a bridge. When Rezendes and Mooney arrived at the New York police precinct, they found the police station surrounded by more press and television cameras. The Nantucketers could not believe the amount of publicity that the case had generated.

Accompanied by New York detectives, they proceeded to the Columbia Presbyterian Medical Center, where they interviewed her research associates. Each doctor described Margaret Kilcoyne as hard-working, sincere, and dedicated to her work. She had been conducting very important work in the field of adolescent hypertension, and was preparing a scholarly paper for presentation at the Symposium of Hypertension Research in New Orleans in May. She had mentioned the possibility of a Nobel Prize for her work but had not mentioned any plans for a party in Nantucket. Some associates described her

---

* The author was a legal advisor to the police department and had been attorney for Doctor Kilcoyne when she bought her property.

as overexcited, but since she habitually used colorful and hyperbolic manners of speech, that was accepted. Although everyone agreed she was overworked and in need of a rest, no member of the staff thought her to be in any danger. The hospital Chief of Staff later expressed his regret that the many doctors on the Columbia Presbyterian staff had not diagnosed a potential problem in one of their colleagues.

From the hospital, the investigators went to the Kilcoyne apartment at 330 East 33rd Street. There they had arranged to meet Leo Kilcoyne and his wife, who had flown from Canada to make arrangements to clear Margaret's personal belongings from the apartment. They found the Kilcoynes cooperative but very upset at the swarm of reporters and television cameramen in the lobby of the apartment house. The apartment was a one-bedroom suite, somewhat cluttered in the manner typical of a busy professional person. In the bedroom closet, Captain Rezendes found other blouses bearing "The Birds" label. There was nothing unusual nor any indication of any unusual event or sudden change of plans. As they returned to Nantucket, Rezendes was convinced that Doctor Kilcoyne was a suicide; Mooney was not certain and remained hopeful she might be found.

The New York investigation indicated that Doctor Kilcoyne was a very private person, one who lived alone and had no close friends, male or female. Her sole confidant was her brother, Leo, whom she normally kept informed of her plans. She frequently attended opera and concerts alone. Due to the nature of her work, she often worked nights and weekends, which caused some conflict with her laboratory technicians, but she had never disappeared without giving notice of her destination because she detested publicity and would never wish to become a public spectacle.

Just before leaving for Nantucket, Doctor Kilcoyne met with Doctor Rosamund Kane, a professional acquaintance and fellow staff member, and discussed her plans for the future. She asked Doctor Kane to write her a prescription for ampicillin, which she was taking for a minor skin infection on a ten-day routine. Doctor Kane also mentioned her plans to bring Doctor Kilcoyne a tire for her Volvo upon her return, since they drove similar cars. Kane described Kilcoyne as being in excellent spirits, eager to continue with her work, and definitely not suicidal. Although they were both Roman Catholics, Margaret made no mention of religion or spiritual experiences to her. Doctor Kane described her as a very private person, with a clever mind and ingenious personality. She jokingly remarked, "If Margaret Kilcoyne wanted to leave that island, she would have known how to hire a submarine!"

After returning to Nantucket, Captain Rezendes received an unusual telephone call from a young woman in Stamford, Connecticut, who said she had met Doctor Kilcoyne and had a story to tell the police. On February 11, Rezendes and Mooney flew to Connecticut, to interview the woman and hear the story of Doctor Kilcoyne's journey from New York to Nantucket.

On January 23, Doctor Kilcoyne left New York in her green Volvo for her weekend in Nantucket. Early that evening, she stopped outside the Avon Products plant in Stamford and spoke to a young woman, Andrea Principe, who was just leaving work. The doctor said she was tired and nervous and could drive no farther. She asked for directions to the nearest motel, so Andrea led her to the nearby Marriott Hotel in Stamford. Doctor Kilcoyne was so grateful for Andrea's help that she invited her to stay for dinner as her guest. While they enjoyed dinner, Doctor Kilcoyne talked continuously in a steady and excited stream about her work and her plans for the future. She spoke about her research and said she had made a major discovery in hypertension which would soon be reported in the *New York Times*. She talked about the politics at the hospital and her troubles with her lab technicians, asking Andrea if she would be interested in working for her in the laboratory. The doctor also showed an interest in the waitress, Susan Prince, and told her to call the hospital if she were interested in a job in February. She wrote the waitress' name and address on a slip of paper, and told both women she would be back at work in two or three weeks, when they should call her.

Doctor Kilcoyne told Andrea she had three homes: one in New York, one in Nantucket and one in the Boston area. She said she had three cars, one in each place. She also said she had been working hard and was going to Nantucket to unwind, saying she must let her brother know, as "he is the only one who is smarter then I am and he knows what I am doing all the time." Her entire conversation was one of enthusiasm and plans for the future, which Andrea described as "a happy high."

During the course of the dinner, the doctor announced it was an occasion to celebrate, so she ordered an expensive bottle of Chateau LaFite-Rothschild. She drank very little of it, and told the waitress she could have the remainder of the bottle, but to save her the label. When the long dinner was finished, they found that there were no rooms available at the Marriott, so Andrea invited the doctor to spend the night at her apartment. She had never done this before, but felt a genuine sympathy for the doctor and admiration for her as a person. At the apartment, Doctor Kilcoyne asked if she could put a vial of peptide in the refrigerator, saying she was carrying it with her to continue her research. She did so, and then tied a red scarf on the refrigerator door to remind herself. The two women talked until 1:30 A.M., when Andrea retired to her bedroom and Doctor Kilcoyne slept on the couch in the living room.

Andrea arose at about 6:00 A.M. to find that the doctor had departed and taken the peptide with her. A half-hour later, the doctor called to say she had only slept two hours and was now on the highway. She thanked Andrea for her help and promised to call when she returned to New York. Later that day, she left her Volvo in the Hyannis Airport parking lot, purchased a round-trip ticket with an open return, and took the Gull Airlines flight to Nantucket.

After visiting her home in Nantucket, Margaret Kilcoyne went into town and began the most unusual shopping spree in recent history. At the A&P market, she purchased large quantities of food and meat, to a total of $650. She loudly announced to the cashier that she was making preparations for a large party and press conference to announce her medical discovery. She said she was planning to rent and provision three houses for the crowd that would gather near her home, and all her purchases were in multiples of three: steaks, roasts, towels, and a dozen toothbrushes. She then went to the liquor store and ordered $250 worth of liquor—three bottles of everything per house.

The recurrence of the threes in the Kilcoyne case is curious. Doctor Kilcoyne told Andrea Principe about three houses and three cars; she talked of renting three houses in Nantucket and bought all her supplies in threes. Her New York apartment was located at 330 East 33rd Street.

While on Nantucket, Margaret Kilcoyne spent most of her time with a few friends. On January 24, her neighbor, Donald Smith, a Nantucket teacher, saw the light in her home and dropped in to say hello. While they had a drink together, the doctor talked animatedly about her research work and told him she was receiving spiritual messages from Heaven. He reached the conclusion that she was on the verge of a nervous breakdown, but was reassured to know her brother was coming to stay with her on Nantucket.

She also visited with Richard and Grace Coffin, Nantucket realtors who had known her since she purchased her property. During the visit, she talked constantly about her medical work and the forthcoming visit of her brother, exhibiting very energetic behavior, but making no mention of any party or press conference.

On Friday, January 25, the Coffins drove Margaret to the Nantucket Airport to meet Leo Kilcoyne when he arrived in the late afternoon. The four then returned to her house in Tom Nevers for drinks and dinner. It proved to be an unusual evening, with the conversation dominated by Margaret, talking incessantly about her research work and the crisis she was going through. She was drinking her usual Scotch highballs, but none of the guests thought she had too much to drink. After the evening of constant conversation, Margaret announced that she was tired and went to her room at about 10:30 P.M., reminding Leo to awaken her early next morning. They both planned to attend the 7:00 A.M. Mass at St. Mary's Church. The Coffins left shortly thereafter. Leo retired to the guest bedroom, which was separated from Margaret's room by a bathroom and a short corridor.

The weather outside the house was very cold, with a north wind blowing about 40 miles per hour. There was no snow on the frozen ground, but the bitter wind resulted in a chill factor close to zero. The darkness was total.

At about 6:30 the next morning, Leo Kilcoyne awoke to hear the alarm clock running down in his sister's room. When she did not appear, he went to her room and found it empty. The bed had been slept in. The sliding glass door which led to the yard was closed but not locked. Margaret's winter coat, boots, and pocketbook were still in the room. Leo quickly dressed and made a hurried survey around the house. Then he called the police to report his sister missing.

Chief Hunter believed the discovery of Doctor Kilcoyne's belongings, located on the marsh away from the ocean, was very suspicious, and became skeptical of the likelihood that she had taken her own life. He felt they were deliberately deposited to mislead the investigation and cover the possibility of her removal from the island, perhaps to a mental institution.

Captain Rezendes persisted in his belief that Margaret was a suicide. He thought it likely that the belongings on the marsh had simply been overlooked in the area search, and felt the personal items were left as a final statement by Margaret that she would not need money or passport where she was going.

The increasing publicity created some bizarre incidents as the search for Doctor Kilcoyne continued. On February 12, Rezendes and Mooney were again sent to investigate reports that the doctor had been sighted in Quincy, Massachusetts. The day after the doctor had disappeared, a woman answering her description had rented a small apartment in a residential area of Quincy, loaded the apartment with groceries and liquor, and installed herself behind locked doors and drawn shades. In the company of Quincy detectives, the Nantucketers banged on the door of the apartment, only to be told, "Go away and leave me alone!" Dozens of neighbors and several real estate agents positively identified the woman inside from Margaret Kilcoyne's passport photo. They said she came from New York and had been inside the apartment for two weeks, refusing to leave or speak to anyone. When the officers persisted in pounding on her door, she turned on a blast of rock music to drive them away.

While reporters gathered outside the building, expecting the police to kick in the door and drag Margaret Kilcoyne outside, Captain Rezendes asked a real estate agent again about the woman in the apartment. He suddenly remembered that she had a sister living in Quincy, and Doctor Kilcoyne had no sister. That evening the sister was located and shown the picture of Margaret Kilcoyne. "Glory be to God!" she exclaimed. "She's the exact lookalike!" She then explained that her sister was recently widowed and moved to Quincy, where she lived with a drinking problem. Again the investigation had come to a dead end, leaving everyone suspicious of the value of eyewitness identifications.

For several months, the police continued to investigate reports of sightings of Doctor Kilcoyne which proved fruitless. They were also contacted by psychics and mystics, people with dreams and theories which they were anxious to prove about the fate of the missing doctor. One had her leaving with a mysterious lover, another had her joining a convent, and the possibility of her removal to a mental institution, perhaps in Canada, was uppermost in the minds of others. None of these theories had any basis in fact, and as the time went by, the mystery continued.

Amid all the disappointments and dead ends, the search for Margaret Kilcoyne occasionally produced some lighter moments. The original police search of the area did not have the advantage of trained tracking dogs because there were no such police dogs resident on the Island. Later, the frozen snow on the ground hampered any further search. Finally, the melting snows of March gave the opportunity to import tracking animals from the Barnstable County Sheriff's Department on Cape Cod. Two large German shepherds, with their handlers, were flown in for a two-day search. The dogs proved immensely popular with the media, posing for photographs and panting for interviews on the local TV station. Their stay on Nantucket was an expensive vacation, for they lived at the Jared Coffin House and dined on roast beef. One dog cut his foot and had to be fitted with a pair of small sneakers. They swept the underbrush for two days, flushed hundreds of cottontail rabbits, but found no trace of the missing doctor.

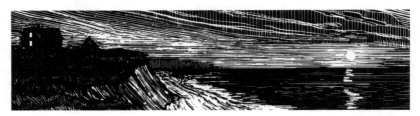

Eight years after his sister disappeared, Leo Kilcoyne petitioned the Nantucket Probate Court for a declaration of the death of Margaret Kilcoyne, a procedure based upon the common-law presumption of death after an unexplained absence of over seven years. The petition was supported by affidavits from friends and relatives who swore she had not been seen nor heard from since that fateful night in 1980.

A hearing was held in Nantucket in July, 1989, at which Leo Kilcoyne testified to the facts of his sister's last day on Nantucket, a day on which she told him she had seen the most beautiful sunrise of her life, and felt that God was calling her to be with Him. He described her emotional state and the reasons for his early conclusion that she had taken her own life in a state of elation. At the conclusion of the uncontested hearing, Judge Eliot K. Cohen ruled that the preponderance of the evidence indicated that Margaret Kilcoyne was deceased, and ordered the court record filed as evidence of her death.

The mysterious disappearance of Margaret Kilcoyne proved to be the latest of Nantucket's strange stories, perplexing in its circumstances and intensified by the glare of modern publicity. As the drama was played out on a remote island in the dead of winter, the case of the missing doctor developed into a major news story and something of a modern mystery. The decree of the Probate Court may have settled the fate of Margaret Kilcoyne for legal purposes, but it did not end the speculation on the island. Rumors, suspicion and speculation will always surround this case, and the mysterious fate of Doctor Kilcoyne will always haunt Nantucket with memories of that cold night and that lonely house on the hillside at Tom Nevers.

Promoting Inquiry in Undergraduate Learning

Frederick Stirton Weaver, *Editor*
Hampshire College

NEW DIRECTIONS FOR TEACHING AND LEARNING
ROBERT E. YOUNG, *Editor-in-Chief*
University of Wisconsin

Number 38, Summer 1989

Paperback sourcebooks in
The Jossey-Bass Higher Education Series

Jossey-Bass Inc., Publishers
San Francisco • London

Frederick Stirton Weaver (ed.).
Promoting Inquiry in Undergraduate Learning.
New Directions for Teaching and Learning, no. 38.
San Francisco: Jossey-Bass, 1989.

New Directions for Teaching and Learning
Robert E. Young, *Editor-in-Chief*

New Directions for Teaching and Learning is published quarterly
by Jossey-Bass Inc., Publishers, 350 Sansome Street, San Francisco,
California, 94104. Second-class postage rates paid at San Francisco,
California, and at additional mailing offices. POSTMASTER: Send
address changes to *New Directions for Teaching and Learning,*
Jossey-Bass Inc., Publishers, 350 Sansome Street, San Francisco,
California 94104.

Editorial correspondence should be sent to the Editor-in-Chief,
Robert E. Young, Dean, University of Wisconsin Center, Fox Valley,
1478 Midway Rd., Menasha, Wisconsin 54952.

Library of Congress Catalog Card Number LC 85-644763

International Standard Serial Number ISSN 0271-0633

International Standard Book Number ISBN 1-55542-879-7

378.17
P965w

Cover art by WILLI BAUM

Manufactured in the United States of America. Printed on acid-free paper.

240320

Ordering Information

The paperback sourcebooks listed below are published quarterly and can be ordered either by subscription or single copy.

Subscriptions cost $52.00 per year for institutions, agencies, and libraries. Individuals can subscribe at the special rate of $39.00 per year *if payment is by personal check.* (Note that the full rate of $52.00 applies if payment is by institutional check, even if the subscription is designated for an individual.) Standing orders are accepted.

Single copies are available at $12.95 when payment accompanies order. (California, New Jersey, New York, and Washington, D.C., residents please include appropriate sales tax.) For billed orders, cost per copy is $12.95 plus postage and handling.

Substantial discounts are offered to organizations and individuals wishing to purchase bulk quantities of Jossey-Bass sourcebooks. Please inquire.

Please note that these prices are for the calendar year 1989 and are subject to change without notice. Also, some titles may be out of print and therefore not available for sale.

To ensure correct and prompt delivery, all orders must give either the *name of an individual* or an *official purchase order number.* Please submit your order as follows:

Subscriptions: specify series and year subscription is to begin.
Single Copies: specify sourcebook code (such as, TL1) and first two words of title.

Mail orders for United States and Possessions, Latin America, Canada, Japan, Australia, and New Zealand to:
   Jossey-Bass Inc., Publishers
   350 Sansome Street
   San Francisco, California 94104

Mail orders for all other parts of the world to:
   Jossey-Bass Limited
   28 Banner Street
   London EC1Y 8QE

New Directions for Teaching and Learning Series
Robert E. Young, *Editor-in-Chief*

Contents

Editor's Notes

The idea of inquiry education is an important component of the national debate about higher education. The idea, however, is an elusive one. The purpose of this sourcebook is to present the notion of inquiry education more clearly and tangibly than general discussions have done.

The reason that these chapters are more specific than usual is that all the contributors have taught for years in Hampshire College's inquiry-based curriculum. Therefore, this volume is first and foremost a book about the practice of inquiry education.

Even so, the first chapter is similar to many writings about inquiry education. It discusses some general theoretical issues in higher education, proposes a set of goals for undergraduate liberal education, and shows how liberal education may be distinct from education in the liberal arts. Nevertheless, the chapter quickly becomes different from much writing in this genre because it immediately proceeds to describe how a working curriculum, which has been operating for almost twenty years, is structured to accomplish these goals.

The following ten chapters describe specific inquiry-oriented courses and teaching strategies. The subject matter of these chapters on teaching ranges from literature to mathematics to biochemistry to cognitive psychology to bibliographical instruction and beyond.

Even though there is one chapter on bibliographical instruction and, generally speaking, three chapters apiece on the humanities, the social sciences, and science and mathematics, this volume is somewhat weighted toward the sciences and the "harder" side of the social sciences. This is not a balanced representation of the pattern of inquiry teaching at Hampshire College, any more than is the relative underrepresentation of women among the authors. One advantage in the subject-matter composition, however, is that it may help to counter the belief that pedagogy in the sciences and in mathematics is governed, within very strict limits, by the internal logic and technical character of these areas of inquiry. The contention that a teacher's pedagogical options in the sciences, in mathematics, and in methodologically allied endeavors are narrowly restricted—in a way that they are not, for instance, in the teaching of history and literature—is a shibboleth that I hope these chapters will help lay to rest.

If lucky, one becomes deeply indebted to many people while putting together a volume of this nature. Because I have indeed been fortunate in this regard, I must acknowledge only the people who have made the most direct and immediate contributions; otherwise, the list would simply be too long. In addition to several of this volume's authors, whose aid

2

went far beyond their individual chapters, I wish to thank Mark Feinstein, Penina Glazer, Michael Gross, Frank Holmquist, Kelley Piccicuto, Nancy Sherman, Adele Simmons, Miriam Slater, Jacqueline Tuthill, Woodward Wickham, and Robert Young for their varied kinds of help. I am also grateful for the financial support that this effort received from the Exxon Education Foundation, the Gwyndaf Jones and Ariel Philips Fund, and the Hewlett-Mellon Presidential Discretionary Fund.

Frederick Stirton Weaver
Editor

Frederick Stirton Weaver, professor of economics and history, served for seven years as dean of the School of Social Science at Hampshire College. He is a cofounder of the college's Third-World Studies Program.

Inquiry education cuts across conventional distinctions between liberal arts and professional programs and is supported by specially designed curricula and pedagogies.

Liberal Education, Inquiry, and Academic Organization

Frederick Stirton Weaver

Between 1984 and 1987, three separate groups of nationally recognized educational leaders issued reports on undergraduate education in the United States. Although the tone of the reports' criticisms varies from mild to scathing, all three recommend significant changes in the prevailing conceptions and practices of undergraduate education. Not only do they invite serious reconsideration of educational goals, they also endorse changes in curricular organization and pedagogy to achieve even more ambitious goals. These reports' influence on the national debate about what is desirable and feasible in reforming undergraduate education makes especially timely an understanding of Hampshire College's inquiry curriculum, which embodies many of the reports' prescriptions. A brief review of some of the reports' principal recommendations will aid that understanding.

The Study Group on the Conditions of Excellence in American Higher Education (1984) strongly recommended that students participate extensively and actively in their own education. Furthermore, the group exhorted faculties to maintain high expectations for students' work and suggested that evaluative devices, such as multiple-choice examinations and grades, be replaced by more informative methods of assessment.

F. S. Weaver (ed.). *Promoting Inquiry in Undergraduate Learning.*
New Directions for Teaching and Learning, no. 38. San Francisco: Jossey-Bass, Summer 1989.

The Project on Redefining the Meaning and Purpose of Baccalaureate Degrees (1985) emphatically condemned two practices: departmental particularism in curricular matters, and the rewarding of faculty more for research than for teaching. On the positive side, this report listed a desirable curriculum of minimum requirements. The authors described this curriculum in terms that explicitly endorsed inquiry education, and the description contains a strong (but undefined) emphasis on the need for coherence.

The report written by Boyer (1987) and sponsored by the Carnegie Foundation for the Advancement of Teaching was the most extensive of the three. At the most general level, the report recommended that the best and most experienced teachers be available to teach first-year students, that teaching be the principal criterion for faculty retention and advancement, and that the newness of a field not be considered a reason to disparage its potential as an excellent vehicle for liberal education. More specifically, the report recommended that the library be integrated into the curriculum through bibliographical instruction, that senior theses and community service be required of undergraduate students, that students' academic progress be measured otherwise than through accretion of course credits, and that students be able to explain their work orally.

Planning for Reform

After nearly fifteen years of discussion and planning, Hampshire College opened in 1970. Two major documents date from this early period. The first (Committee for New College, 1958) was written by faculty members from Amherst College, Mount Holyoke College, Smith College, and the University of Massachusetts at Amherst. These four institutions, together with Hampshire, form a highly successful consortium called Five College, Inc. The second document (Patterson and Longsworth, 1966) was coauthored by Hampshire's founding president and its founding vice-president and second president. A strong thread running through both documents is the idea that undergraduate education should promote students' intellectual independence and initiative to a far greater extent than did current best practice, but the two documents differ in the significance and implications they attach to this idea.

New Means, Not New Ends. Committee for New College (1958) did not consider this aim to be a particularly radical departure from the generally accepted aims of liberal arts education. The committee's plan repeatedly stressed that the new program was "a proposal for changes, not in ends but in means" (p. 5). For instance, the authors recommended against departments based on disciplines, but they did so because they saw departments as sources of an unnecessary proliferation of courses and of an inefficiency that conflicted with the imperative for low-cost operation. Nevertheless, even though there were to be no departments, "the intellectual life of a college must be structured to a large extent by the specialized disciplines" (p. 10).

Although astutely critical of conventional educational processes, this plan was cautious about new directions in the content of undergraduate education. The committee warned, "To call for novel content in a whole curriculum is to invite the superficial and the faddist" (p. 17). The authors were concerned that the recruitment of students and faculty members who were too experimental would result in intellectual slovenliness, over-emphasis on the arts, and the feeling that "the educational community should be set up in opposition to the society as a whole. . . . Such utopian and Bohemian aims are not part of the New College proposal, which . . . is concerned chiefly with modifying the *means* for achieving the generally accepted ends of rigorous liberal education" (pp. 30–31).

Active Inquiry. In vital respects, Patterson and Longsworth (1966) stand in sharp contrast, asserting that the Hampshire College "academic program will be distinctive in its ends as in its means" (p. xii). Drawing heavily on Bell (1966), the authors declare that the organizing principle for Hampshire's academic program will be "conceptual inquiry . . . exercising the intellect to learn, use, test, and revise ideas, concepts, theoretical constructs, propositions, and methodological principles in active inquiry. This process is at the heart of Hampshire's intention and program" (p. xiv). Thus, an orientation toward conceptual inquiry is thought to develop necessary and often neglected analytical skills, so that students can be active and independent learners throughout their lives.

Patterson and Longsworth also criticized the hegemony of graduate departments over undergraduate education, argued that the student must become acquainted with several disciplines in order to gain multiple perspectives on issues, disapproved of organizing faculty members according to discipline-based departments, and advocated that the student's program of study be defined by subject matter rather than by discipline.

Although there are some ambiguities in their arguments, and although some of their specific curricular recommendations (especially for the lower division) were quickly supplanted by faculty and student initiatives, Patterson and Longsworth established Hampshire College's educational principles and, in general terms, outlined an academic organization to effect them. Both accomplishments permanently influenced Hampshire College's development.

Inquiry and Liberal Education

Since 1966, the inquiry approach has received widespread endorsement by educational leaders, but its curricular and pedagogical implications are not widely understood. Aarons (1985), Brann (1979), Dressel and

Marcus (1982), Gamson and Associates (1984), Kavaloski (1979), Lee (1967), McPeck (1981), Mitroff (1982), Weaver (1981), Wegener (1978), and Woditsch, Schlesinger, and Giardina (1987) all advocate inquiry education (whether or not they give it that name), although from very different perspectives. None, however, is particularly clear about the curricular organization appropriate to inquiry education.

Liberal education of the inquiry type stands in contrast, not to professional education, but rather to training (defined as a style of teaching in which the student is to acquire a given set of information and techniques). When training is emphasized, the teacher's function is to transmit a body of information and techniques to students and to judge their abilities to reproduce and apply it by following prescribed procedures. It is easy to recognize courses that have training as their principal objective. Such courses are defined in terms of "covering" a particular subject, and students in them are all expected to come up with the same answers to assigned questions and problems.

According to inquiry principles, the primary difference between training and liberal education is the approach to knowledge. Liberal education at Hampshire means the cultivation of students' capacities for interpretation, discovery, creation, and the critical ability to recognize and understand the significance of competing theories and models. A teacher helps develop students' abilities to use logic, rules of evidence, and sense of context to identify the role of selection, premises, and perspectives in other people's analyses and to construct and defend interpretations of their own. This view of teaching requires students to engage self-consciously and critically in the processes of their own education. It also denies the putatively sharp distinction between "creating knowledge" and "transmitting knowledge." Teaching, therefore, is unambiguously an intellectual enterprise, rather than a packaging and distributing function that transfers knowledge no longer in question.

I do not mean to dismiss the important role of training, which clearly is necessary for liberal education. Each Hampshire student's program of studies, and usually each course, contains both types of learning. In an inquiry curriculum, however, faculty members and students alike recognize that training is a vehicle for establishing a more sophisticated way to address issues that are still open to lively intellectual debate.

Inquiry and Academic Disciplines

It should be clear by now that education in the disciplines of the liberal arts does not necessarily comprise a liberal education. Any subject in the liberal arts, including ancient history and the calculus, can be taught in the form of training, to encourage the same habits of mind as the worst caricature of a professional course. Moreover, the liberal arts hold no monopoly on the subject matter appropriate to liberal education.

For example, business management and elementary education, usually placed outside the liberal arts, are subjects whose complexity requires treatment from a variety of angles and at different levels of abstraction. Both subjects can be taught in ways that promote the development of critical intellect.

It is difficult to achieve the goals of inquiry-based liberal education through curricula organized exclusively along the lines of academic disciplines (or according to any other preset, codified categories of knowledge). Well-developed disciplines supposedly have solved basic conceptual problems. It is all too easy for disciplinary curricula to point students in directions already set by those solutions and to discourage questioning of the intellectual grounds for those directions. Since disciplinary curricula seldom include examination of the implications of disciplinary categories, they often expose students to the results of thinking, rather than involving them as active participants in the processes of that thinking. "Learning a discipline" is not an adequate goal for liberal education.

This criticism of discipline-based curricula is very different from the argument that disciplines are inappropriate to undergraduate study because of their narrowness and high specialization. On the contrary, Hampshire's interdisciplinary approach depends on continually creating new kinds of specialization; there is even concern that study programs defined by interdisciplinary themes and questions are occasionally too specialized.

Disciplinary versus interdisciplinary study is not a major issue at Hampshire. Disciplinary content remains a vitally important feature of the intellectual terrain at Hampshire, but the disciplines are considered tools rather than subjects of study—that is, the disciplines are treated in fundamentally instrumental ways. They are repositories of methods, theories, analytical typologies, and data, to be drawn on pragmatically in illuminating particular problems and questions.

The Organization of an Inquiry Curriculum

The Hampshire College curriculum is structured along two distinct dimensions: course offerings and an examination system, both supported by an intensive faculty-based student advising system. The student's experience is divided into three divisions of work. The purpose of Division I—Hampshire's distribution requirement—is to introduce students to the general nature of intellectual inquiry. Students must formulate substantive questions on a range of specific subjects and then reflect critically on the implications of the analytical frameworks and methods they used in pursuing the questions. Satisfying the Division I distribution requirement entails significant learning in courses and independent projects in all four of our academic units: the School of Communications and Cognitive Science, the School of Humanities and Arts, the School of Natural Science, and the School of Social Science.

Hampshire courses at the 100 level support this conception of the distribution requirement by focusing on narrowly defined subject matter and emphasizing analytical and interpretive issues. Courses numbered in the 200s, designed for students working on their concentrations (structurally equivalent to majors), are more broadly gauged. The 300-level courses are advanced seminars.

Each student, then, working closely with at least two or three faculty members, fashions a Division II concentration and a Division III project (senior thesis or artistic project). A Division II student, with help from faculty members, first defines a substantive area of study and specifies key questions that will serve as general guides throughout the concentration. In the second step, again with the faculty's advice and consent, the student designs a program of study, including courses, field work, internships, and independent study. These preliminary steps are in themselves critically important aspects of teaching and learning at Hampshire.

Upon completing the concentration (for which the plan has probably been revised at least once), the student must be able to describe how a particular pattern of learning experiences contributed to the concentration. Moreover, he or she must also demonstrate the ability to synthesize and critically evaluate the substance of those different learning experiences, through papers and oral presentations not necessarily related to any course. Students' community service projects are evaluated during the Division II phase of their studies, and a multicultural component will probably have been included as an integral part of the concentration.

The nature of the college's inquiry curriculum is clearly illustrated by the way it asks students to construct the multicultural aspect of their work. This requirement is met in terms consistent with each student's concentration. It is not simply an "add on," a base to be touched by completing a course. Instead, as the policy reads, each student is asked to include as an integral part of his or her concentration "an intellectually substantive engagement with the experiences of the peoples of Asia, Africa, and Latin America (including North America's own domestic 'third world')." For example, a film concentration may include an assessment of Western and indigenous influences on African films. A computer science concentration may include research on the effects of computer technology on workplace organization, with particular attention to the implications for minority employment and advancement. A theater concentration may involve helping to produce a set of short Chinese plays. A physics concentration may include critical exploration of the argument that Western science is a culturally specific endeavor that has dubious implications for the peoples of Africa, Asia, and Latin America. The possibilities are endless, interesting, and educationally productive.

The purpose of the multicultural component is not only to learn more about the majority of the world's population—an important goal—

but also to enrich and deepen students' understanding of their specialized studies by looking at those studies from new perspectives. As noted, this is an excellent example of how an inquiry approach to undergraduate education structures a form of breadth requirement so that it becomes more than a matter of coverage.

The final year of a Hampshire student's education is primarily devoted to a Division III thesis or artistic project, which culminates with an oral examination. During the Division III year, students take one or two advanced seminars and either periodically present their specialized works in progress to audiences other than their committees or teach in the course or examination system.

Some Consequences of an Inquiry Curriculum

Because of this curricular organization, students' advanced studies are cumulative. Work submitted to Division II committee faculty members must reflect previous courses and learning experiences, as well as current ones. Unlike course instructors, faculty members on students' examination committees see students and their work over a period of time and are therefore in a position to ask that current work build on past work in a clear and productive way.

These qualities of coherence and cumulative learning stem in good part from the definition of Division I projects, Division II concentrations, and Division III theses thematically, by substantive issues. We strive for an ideal of liberal education, defined in terms of intellectual skills and critical habits of mind, while recognizing that the achievement of this ideal requires every student's program to be substantive and complex.

As a consequence, there is an interesting and somewhat anomalous relationship between process and content at Hampshire. In respect to the goal of liberal education (or intellectual process), content is apparently instrumental, a means for accomplishing the process goal; but this liberal education goal is an institutional goal. The principal commitments of faculty members and students are primarily to the substantive questions themselves. From this second angle, the intellectual process of inquiry-based liberal education looks instrumental: faculty members and students believe that attention to theories and concepts, which instigate questions and frame the responses to them, is the most productive way to engage issues and subject matter that interest them. Thus, content and intellectual process are inextricably intertwined, as they should be, and the belief that one or the other must be primary becomes specious.

Students as Active Learners

All three levels of Hampshire's examination system require substantial initiative from students, especially in proposing the questions to be pursued. In this and other aspects, Hampshire owes a largely unacknowledged debt to the colleges founded or transformed in the 1920s and 1930s along the lines of the Progressive Education Movement.

Hampshire shares with these colleges a student-centered approach intended to stimulate and capitalize on students' interest and motivation. The motivating effect of this student-centeredness is not its only function, however. Students' active involvement is an essential part of learning itself, not just a means of keeping them interested in their studies. Hampshire students' responsibility for defending the significance and coherence of their academic programs at every stage also distinguishes Hampshire sharply from colleges identified with the Progressive Education Movement, as well as from the free-elective system in many leading U.S. colleges and universities at the turn of the twentieth century and today. "Freedom" at Hampshire is an academic requirement that is unusually demanding for undergraduates.

Constructive Evaluation

In the three levels of the divisional examination system, students routinely revise and refine their work in response to the faculty's criticism. The faculty members are committed to this central pedagogical device, but it exacts a high price in terms of faculty workload, including lack of clarity about where the faculty's obligation to students' work ends.

The divisional examination system also allows students' work to be evaluated over time and in detail. The six divisional examination reports—short evaluative essays (four for Division I, one for Division II, and one for Division III)—constitute the student's official transcript, which may also be accompanied by a portfolio of course evaluations, grades for Five College courses, and other evidence of academic achievement. The examination reports also record what the student has learned during the divisional experience, including progress in overcoming particular problems and weaknesses. Hampshire's evaluations thus incorporate assessments of the "value added" dimension of learning advocated by several leading educational researchers (Winter, McClelland, and Stewart, 1981; Astin, 1985). Finally, the Division III thesis or project gives the faculty committee a clear and tangible indication of the student's intellectual and esthetic abilities at the conclusion of his or her studies at Hampshire.

Students (and their parents) occasionally have trouble getting used to this style of work and evaluation, but it is a vital component of the Hampshire system. By regarding students' work as a continuing effort in an area of inquiry, rather than simply as a basis of judging achievement, Hampshire produces a climate for students' intellectual responsibility. Students are encouraged to take risks. Mistakes are seen as instructive, and errors are explicitly acknowledged as an integral part of effective learning. The cost of mistakes is therefore minimized for students.

Courses at Hampshire: Vehicles for Inquiry Education

Much of what is distinctive and significant about a Hampshire education resides in the character of the examination system. Courses are important only as they serve students' educational purposes, expressed through their individually formulated divisional examination endeavors. In this sense, the early aspiration of the college's planners—to dethrone the course—has been realized.

Nevertheless, courses at Hampshire have not been displaced by other formats; they remain a centrally important mode of instruction. Most Division I projects, as well as the vast majority of the academic accomplishments recorded in students' Division II concentration portfolios, have their origins in courses, and even the Division III student, who is deeply involved in a thesis, must take at least one advanced seminar.

Courses have not merely held their own; their importance in the college seems to have increased over the last few years. Faculty members routinely stipulate what a student must achieve in a course in order to receive a course evaluation. If this minimum requirement has not been met, the student's file records that fact.

The extent to which the sentiment of the community has changed in regard to courses is even more graphically illustrated by a second major change. Since the fall of 1985, students have had the option of completing the Division I requirements in one or two schools, by satisfactorily completing two courses in a school (but only courses designed so that students can cogently demonstrate their ability to engage in critical inquiry). This change is clearly built on the first, and its adoption was and continues to be controversial among faculty members and students.

There are at least three interlocking reasons for the survival and even the expansion of the role of courses. First, there is a definite efficiency in exploring interesting ideas or examining an analytical tool with, say, fifteen or twenty students at a time. This efficiency is particularly appealing to faculty members who have substantial examination and advising responsibilities. Second, faculty members have primary responsibility for designing and conducting courses. As a consequence, courses offer dedicated teachers an opportunity for systematically testing their ideas about issues and pedagogy. The attractiveness of teaching is enhanced at Hampshire by the significant latitude that faculty members have in defining the nature and content of their courses and in teaching jointly with colleagues. The third and probably most important reason for the prominence of courses at Hampshire is that they have proved to work extremely well for students. While the examination system itself contributes to the particular spirit of the courses, there is more to it. Courses are collaborative enterprises in a highly individualized academic program, and faculty members and students enjoy and are stimulated and educated by participating with others in grappling with new types of understanding. Mark Hopkins, with the single student at the other end of a log (Rudolph, 1956), represents a limited, even tepid, pedagogy when compared to the excitement of a Hampshire seminar that works for an active and committed group. In good measure, learning is a social enterprise.

While courses are definitely not the only teaching mode in Hampshire's inquiry curriculum, they serve vital educational functions for students and faculty members alike and continue to have a central place in teaching and learning. Even though the highly individualized teaching that occurs on the examination side of the Hampshire curriculum is central to Hampshire's pedagogy and to students' educational experiences, this volume focuses on courses because of their importance to students, their status as a major province of the faculty's intention and skill, and their position as common currency in U.S. college teaching. Thus, courses are the aspect of Hampshire's inquiry experience of most immediate relevance to audiences beyond Hampshire. Even though all courses, by virtue of their format, tend to possess many similarities, this volume's chapters on course teaching vividly illustrate some of the unique qualities of teaching at an institution dedicated to inquiry education.

The Chapters of This Volume

Each of the following ten chapters describes the organization and pedagogy of individual courses. Because of the variety of subjects, questions, and personalities, there is a considerable range of approach and tone. The sequence in which the chapters are presented deliberately contrasts and underscores differences in subject matter, to emphasize their underlying unity. All the chapters demonstrate the authors' common educational convictions about the central importance of inquiry and active learning.

One of this volume's messages, then, is that a plurality of substantive questions, techniques, and styles is consistent with successful inquiry teaching. At the level of specific pedagogy, there are no formulas or party lines. The particular structure of course materials, patterns of assignments, and presentations must reflect the nature of the material, the purpose and level of the course, the background of the students, and the personality and abilities of the teacher.

Several other common themes run through all or most of the chapters. There is the importance of reducing competitiveness among students and facilitating collaborative forms of learning. More general, however, is the theme that active learning requires active teaching. Giving more responsibility to students and involving them more directly in their own education does not reduce the responsibility and involvement of teachers; teaching and learning is not a hydraulic process, in which greater student responsibility means less faculty involvement.

A second aspect of active teaching is that when a teacher does not regard education as primarily transmitting information and techniques, the teacher must have a broader command of the subject, its methodologies, and the surrounding issues. When teachers do not set themselves up as the ultimate sources of correct answers, the resulting flexibility and spontaneity require teachers to respond to unpredictable questions and intellectual challenges.

Moreover, in these chapters, the common theme that good undergraduate inquiry teaching is primarily an intellectual enterprise is apparent in a more fundamental way. Because there are no preset programs of study, few courses are preset. Apart from a handful of basics (for example, Introductory Economics and Organic Chemistry), courses must be defined consciously by the faculty, who do not abdicate these definitions to textbook publishers. The faculty explicitly pose the central questions around which courses are organized and choose appropriate categories of knowledge, levels of generality, interpretive frameworks to give information meaning, and so forth. This intellectual side of curriculum building probably constitutes the most exciting aspect of educational innovation at Hampshire College. Consequently, the institution must encourage and support the faculty members' continuing active involvement with their fields in order to ensure that teachers are able to demonstrate the necessary knowledge, informed imagination, intellectual flexibility, confidence, and enthusiasm for inquiry teaching.

The strongly intellectual function of teachers in an inquiry curriculum also means that there is very little prospect of teachers' being supplanted by electronic teaching devices. (In contrast, teachers who emphasize the acquisition of information and techniques clearly risk becoming prime victims of technological unemployment.) Several of the courses described in these chapters use computers quite extensively, but computers are not surrogate teachers in any of those courses.

Chapter Two, by Ann P. McNeal, argues for the effectiveness of introducing students to science through courses focused on specific topics and organized around professional research articles and laboratory research. This ambitious effort entails special pedagogical efforts and has particular implications for making the study of science accessible to and rewarding for women. This chapter is one of the many expressions of a concerted and successful effort, organized under the rubric "Women and Science," to attract women to the study of science at Hampshire. A major aim of this project has been to identify and avoid pedagogies and attitudes that chronically discourage women from pursuing studies and careers in science.

Chapter Three, by Stanley L. Warner and Myrna M. Breitbart, describes a course that entails role playing by students in a sophisticated computer simulation. The principal purpose of the course is to introduce students to the complex issues surrounding a plant's closing and its moving away from a community where it was the principal employer. The simulation gives students a sense of immediacy about the issues, and it is designed to lead the students to an understanding of and appreciation for alternative theoretical and interpretive frameworks.

Roberto Márquez (Chapter Four) argues that bringing together the social, political, and intellectual dimensions of Hispanic American history is not merely a nice "extra." The failure to systematically link diverse dimensions of life leaves students with a distorted view of the past and an impaired sense of historical motion.

John M. Foster (Chapter Five) emphasizes the importance of the laboratory as a site for teaching, where students produce their own experimental data and learn the principles of scientific research. While this laboratory experience is structured and guided by the teacher, it is crucial that the teacher and the teaching materials avoid inhibiting students' creativity and ability to learn by doing.

Neil A. Stillings (Chapter Six) reflects both on how he has taught inquiry in several different cognitive psychology courses and on the implications of these efforts. It is important to remember that cognitive psychology is one of the constituent elements of a program in cognitive science, which also includes linguistics, philosophy, and computer science. Hampshire's cognitive science program, of which Stillings was one of the principal architects, was the first such undergraduate program in the United States. The promise of this new field for undergraduate inquiry is evident in the chapter.

Ralph Lutts (Chapter Seven) demonstrates how a course can teach both literary analysis and greater personal sensitivity to the environment. Virtually all the chapters evince an awareness of the role of values in education, but this chapter is the only one that treats values education explicitly.

Chapter Eight is by Kenneth R. Hoffman, and it discusses the implications of computers for the design of mathematics courses that serve students in the life sciences and the social sciences. Hoffman argues that the standard calculus sequence is simply no longer adequate (if it ever was), and he describes how the use of computers enables a service course to include a range of mathematical tools especially relevant to the life and social sciences. While the orientation of the course is toward applied mathematics, the power of computers nevertheless makes it easier for students to appreciate the logical properties and beauty of mathematical thought.

In Chapter Nine, David E. Smith describes how literary and anthropological analyses complement each other in teaching students the importance and implications of a point of view in a text.

Chapter Ten concerns an introductory statistics course in the social sciences, a type of course notable throughout academia for its deadly dullness. The chapter argues that by emphasizing descriptive statistics and addressing serious content, this course can become vital and exciting, as befits its importance.

Chapter Eleven, by Helaine Selin, describes the role of the library and the library staff in the teaching mission of Hampshire College. The author argues that bibliographical instruction is especially important for a project-oriented inquiry curriculum, and that its function is more than the teaching of research skills.

These chapters all discuss teaching in specific settings, analyzing the experiences and pedagogies of specific courses (or, in the case of Helaine Selin's chapter, a set of teaching sessions). While they vary significantly in substance, expression, and stance toward the material and express distinct personal styles, they reveal a common idea about what undergraduate education should be.

References

Aarons, A. B. "Critical Thinking and the Baccalaureate Curriculum." *Liberal Education*, 1985, *71* (2), 141–157.

Astin, A. *Achieving Educational Excellence: A Critical Assessment of Priorities and Practices in Higher Education*. San Francisco: Jossey-Bass, 1985.

Bell, D. *The Reforming of General Education*. New York: Columbia University Press, 1966.

Boyer, E. L. *College: The Undergraduate Experience in America*. New York: Harper & Row, 1987.

Brann, E. T. *Paradoxes of Education in a Republic*. Chicago: University of Chicago Press, 1979.

Committee for New College. *New College Plan*. Amherst, Mass.: Committee for New College, 1958.

Dressel, P. L., and Marcus, D. *On Teaching and Learning in College: Reemphasizing the Roles of Learners and the Disciplines in Liberal Education*. San Francisco: Jossey-Bass, 1982.

Gamson, Z., and Associates. *Liberating Education*. San Francisco: Jossey-Bass, 1984.

Kavaloski, V. C. "Interdisciplinary Education and Humanistic Aspiration." In J. J. Kochelmans (ed.), *Interdisciplinarity and Higher Education*. University Park: Pennsylvania State University Press, 1979.

Lee, C.B.T. "Knowledge Structure and Curriculum Development." In C.B.T. Lee (ed.), *Improving College Teaching*. Washington, D.C.: American Council on Education, 1967.

McPeck, J. E. *Critical Thinking and Education*. New York: St. Martin's Press, 1981.

Mitroff, I. I. "Secure Versus Insecure Forms of Knowing in University Settings: Two Archetypes of Inquiry." *Journal of Higher Education*, 1982, *53* (6), 640–655.

Patterson, F., and Longsworth, C. R. *The Making of a College: Plans for a New Departure in Higher Education*. Cambridge, Mass.: MIT Press, 1966.

Project on Redefining the Meaning and Purpose of Baccalaureate Degrees. *Integ-*

rity in the College Curriculum: A Report to the Academic Community. Washington, D.C.: American Association of Colleges, 1985.

Rudolph, F. *Mark Hopkins and the Log: Williams College, 1836–1872.* New Haven: Yale University Press, 1956.

Study Group on the Conditions of Excellence in American Higher Education. *Involvement in Learning: Realizing the Potential of American Higher Education.* Washington, D.C.: National Institute of Education, U.S. Department of Education, 1984.

Weaver, F. S. "Academic Disciplines and Undergraduate Liberal Arts Education." *Liberal Education,* 1981, *67* (2), 151–165.

Wegener, C. *Liberal Education and the Modern University.* Chicago: University of Chicago Press, 1978.

Winter, D. G., McClelland, D. C., and Stewart, A. J. *A New Case for the Liberal Arts: Assessing Institutional Goals and Student Development.* San Francisco: Jossey-Bass, 1981.

Woditsch, G. A., Schlesinger, M. A., and Giardina, R. C. "The Skillful Baccalaureate: Doing What Liberal Education Does Best." *Change,* 1987, *19* (6), 48–57.

Frederick Stirton Weaver, professor of economics and history, served for seven years as dean of the School of Social Science at Hampshire College. He is a cofounder of the Third-World Studies Program.

*Introductory science courses can demonstrate the excitement
and rewards of science by involving students directly in
scientific research, rather than in its watered-down results.*

Real Science in the
Introductory Course

Ann P. McNeal

After students in high school have been drilled by rote in the scientific
method, it is difficult for them to realize that the essence of science really
is a way of inquiry. Teachers, too, often believe that although the frontiers
of science consist of inquiry, the humble student must traverse vast tracts
of fact and technique before getting to the point of inquiry. One consequence of this belief is the presentation of science as a powerful "pill"
that students must swallow dry. Even the discovery method, superior to
standard approaches, asks students to rediscover correct answers by way
of contrived experiments.

There are alternatives. Even at the introductory level in college, it is
possible to teach science as inquiry in a rigorous way that excites students
to ask and answer original questions.

At some colleges, science departments adamantly resist the idea of
introducing students to inquiry before they have a sufficient basis of fact
and technique. Often the argument is in terms of the long list of courses
that undergraduate science majors must complete in order to compete for
places in graduate schools. Science is too often seen as an area in which
it is necessary to have years of background before intelligent inquiry can
be undertaken. I argue that, on the contrary, science is an area in which
it is extraordinarily easy for undergraduates to pose meaningful questions

F. S. Weaver (ed.). *Promoting Inquiry in Undergraduate Learning.*
New Directions for Teaching and Learning, no. 38. San Francisco: Jossey-Bass, Summer 1989.

and to answer them analytically and reflectively. This involves judicious choices of content and pedagogy, and these choices have important implications for making science accessible to students, perhaps for the first time.

While the approaches and aspirations of Hampshire College's science faculty are, in a general way, similar to those of the college's faculty in other areas, science is distinctive because of the inordinate numbers of students who come to college already convinced that science is not for them. Whether this phobia is based on personal experience or on some mystique, this antiscience attitude is widespread and especially serious among women and minority students. For this reason, I will emphasize the significance of our type of science teaching for women—one of the groups of students who historically have had the most difficulty entering scientific professions or even achieving a scientific background adequate for being well informed on scientific issues.

The Content and Pedagogy of Inquiry in Science

The applied sciences offer a number of excellent subjects and questions on which students can do original research on a modest scale with a modest background and yet learn exactly the same principles of inquiry as if they were working in a pioneering basic-science laboratory. For an introductory course, the subject and questions should be narrowly defined; courses that purport to survey a broad area of scientific knowledge too easily present science in a forbidding, misleading, and boring way. Hampshire's introductory science seminars for first-year students enable students to delve into specific and comprehensible areas of scientific research and learn about the nature of the scientific enterprise.

On the pedagogical side, our introductory science seminars emphasize developing students' abilities to read primary research literature and to construct scientifically answerable questions (Goddard and Henifin, 1984). Epstein (1970, 1972) presents a method of teaching students from the primary literature in science and has deeply influenced our thinking about teaching at Hampshire. In our eighteen years of practice, however, the science faculty at Hampshire has modified Epstein's method by requiring students to begin defining and answering their own research questions (rather than simply learning how scientists have inquired), and by including elements of collaborative learning (Trimbur, 1985; Wiener, 1986).

To illustrate and develop these points, I shall describe an introductory science seminar that I have taught for twelve years. The subject matter—the physiology of human movement—is good for such a course, because many students (for instance, dancers and athletes) come to the course with prior interest in it, and because the current research literature is relatively accessible to beginners, in contrast to the literature in such fields as modern physics and molecular biology.

The course meets for two hours, twice a week, throughout the thirteen-week semester. Its principal aims are to get students to learn how to analyze problems (including attention to the pitfalls and assumptions contained in methods that others have used); ask testable questions; distinguish among data, assumptions, and hypotheses; work with colleagues (mostly one another, and sometimes the instructor); and develop the skills of expository writing, data analysis, oral presentation and discussion, and bibliographical search and retrieval.

The first six weeks give students enough background and practice in thinking about the topic to use the electromyograph (EMG) for independent work on projects in small groups over the next four weeks and to present results as papers and talks during the final three weeks. The relative narrowness of the topic (movement physiology, rather than all of human physiology) is a great advantage here, since beginning students can get familiar enough with it in a short time to proceed on their own. Milestones along the way are project proposals (written and rewritten in weeks four to six) and final papers about projects (due a week before the course ends).

In the first six weeks, the general agenda comprises the following:

- Learning to read scientific papers in the field of kinesiology
- Getting some background from lectures, as well as from discussions of the papers
- Becoming familiar with the use of the EMG for measuring muscle activity
- Learning library techniques, such as the use of *Biological Abstracts* to find articles
- Developing ideas into project topics.

Much of the background material comes up as explanations of things students do not understand about the papers, but some outright lectures and readings of secondary sources also fill in the gaps.

Primary Sources. In the second class session, after a brief lecture on the stretch reflex, the students are a bit startled to be handed a research paper on leg muscles in males (Joseph and Nightingale, 1952). It is over their heads, they fear, involving many words and concepts they do not know. The reading of this and subsequent papers is carefully structured so that they can always do the work, so that their questions and confusions are positive contributions to class discussion, and so that they get a chance right away to develop their thinking about the scientific method and their ability to be critical.

The instructions for reading the first paper are: "You will read this paper three times altogether. Read it twice before the next class meeting. The first time is just glancing through, noting headings, whether there are figures, how long it is, when it was published, not trying to get the essence, just looking. The second time through you read it word by word, underlining *every word* you do not understand. It is important that you do this, because we will spend the next class going through all the words and many concepts, defining and explaining. You do not have to understand the paper—we will go through the process of coming to an understanding in class, so just bring all your questions. The third time through, after the next class, you will try for understanding."

In the following class, after students have read the paper, I first ask them to tell me all the words and phrases they did not understand, and I write these on the board. It is important to allow plenty of time and encourage students to bring out all the words they did not understand or only understood somewhat. I express pleasure at getting as long a list as possible at this stage, since the better students can get at identifying their own areas of ignorance, the faster they will be able to learn on their own. When all the words are up on the board, I define and explain them, usually starting with the most straightforward and grouping the words by topic. For example, in the paper on the electromyographic study of leg muscles in males, there is a whole group of technical words concerned with electricity and electromyographs, and so I give a minilecture on the topic that ties together all the unknown words. These explanations take up at least one class period.

After the definitions and explanations have been given, the students are asked to read the paper again (which is a relief to them, since they now can understand a lot more of it) and to come prepared to discuss what was actually being done by the experimenters. I guide the discussion by asking what was done and what the results were. We go through the results section, frequently referring back to the methods section. I lay special emphasis on graphs and tables, since students often shy away from them. Throughout these discussions, my attitude is one of encouraging them—by my sense of ease, my own admissions of ignorance, and positive direct comments—to air their ignorance and their assumptions, as well as their knowledge, and to get help in understanding (from other students, whenever possible). A class of twenty students usually has enough ideas and facts to move forward but needs the chance to pool resources and winnow out good ideas from bad. Every bit of this time-consuming process is worthwhile, since the students are learning to educate themselves and one another.

After we have gone through the definitions and the main body of the paper, it is time to ask what the paper is really about and to ask about the differences between data and hypotheses. One way of provoking and sustaining a discussion that will involve most of the students is to start a list of hypotheses and a list of data and to talk about the connections. Any paper contains many hypotheses and assumptions, as well as a lot of data that are more or less relevant to the hypotheses. Usually the students place many hypotheses in the list of data and then argue them out until the hypotheses wind up correctly placed.

This process is a real eye-opener to the students, since we find a number of hypotheses and assumptions unsupported and usually some loose ends in the data. After these are laid out, I can ask what the major hypothesis of the paper is and discuss it until a clear statement can be written on the blackboard. Then we discuss what other studies might be done, what factors were not adequately controlled, what alternative hypotheses might be supported by the researcher's data, and how the study was biased by its sample, its methods, and so on.

When the next paper is read, the same procedure is followed, but students are asked to look up as many words as possible themselves. Then, after the unknown words are all put up on the board, the students, as well as the teacher, get a chance to do some defining. Here it is important to make sure that the students are really being of use to one another. I watch closely to see whether the students who do not know the word seem to understand the explanation. If not, I tell them to question the student explaining the word, until they can make him or her give a clear definition. This is part of a campaign to get students to talk substantively to one another. As time goes on, I get increasingly directive about stepping out of an argument and saying, "Phil, it seems that your hypothesis contradicts Marie's. Why don't you two explain your positions to everyone?"

The progression in reading papers is toward getting students to do more of the work of gaining understanding, through looking up words and concepts, being able to tackle and work through tables and figures, and having discussions with one another. It is a manageable series of steps that students are asked to do, but at the same time it provokes more anxiety than a carefully graded series of text readings would. They are asked to confront confusion and masses of unknowns, just as in the real world, while being given a system for working problems out (underlining unknown words and bringing questions to class). After watching students cope with this way of learning, and on the basis of what I know of the creative process (Poincaré, 1956; Taylor and Barron, 1975), I think that they gain an invaluable ability to work and keep working when surrounded by things that are unclear.

As I have noted, this method of teaching through reading papers is derived from Epstein (1970, 1972), but it differs in emphasis. Students are aimed toward independence from the teacher; and they know it, because they are going to be doing projects that involve reading papers without the teacher's aid by the end of the course. They are encouraged to talk to one another and not to aim all dialogue at getting answers from the teacher. Finally, the discussions examine the thinking process of science and the gaps as well as the truths arising from the papers. Students are encouraged to see both the limitations and the powers of the techniques that are used.

Why read original scientific papers with beginning students? First, these papers are the sources, and students can research anything once they know how to read such papers. Second, the papers present a concrete experience that is similar to what happens in a laboratory; they reveal the nitty-gritty of science. Third, reading and discussing papers in the way outlined here enables students to understand the hypothetico-deductive method of science better than from reading any number of passages in a text about how science is done. Fourth, such readings are a strong antidote to the "solid facts" view of science that encourages many students to memorize and discourages them from thinking. Finally, such readings seem to motivate students to a remarkable degree: They appreciate that they are reading the real thing, and not just another watered-down version. I use textbooks only with more advanced students, because when beginning students buy textbooks, they tend to believe that they are buying ideas, believing that the textbook has all the answers already.

The Project. During the fourth week, the requirement to propose a project starts students thinking and gives me a fairly accurate idea of where each student is, so that those who need extra attention can get it. Rewriting is a hallmark of the Hampshire system, and project proposals, as well as the students' research papers, are considered to be drafts and are usually rewritten in response to my suggestions and criticisms about content, organization, use of evidence, and writing.

The planning and execution of original projects requires a good deal of attention by the instructor. Since there are real limits to this attention, each teacher must devise feasible mechanisms. For example, I use class times as office hours on alternate days for weeks six through ten. In addition, however, having students spend time in class reporting on their individual or group projects is also surprisingly productive, since students hear from one another about lab and research techniques and watch one another's ideas develop.

The projects must be quite structured, but actual applications or questions to be addressed are extremely open. Students are asked to compare muscle activity in the same muscle on the same subject under two different conditions and to repeat the measurements at least ten times. Thus, they can try to assess abdominal muscle activity during different exercises, muscle activity in different postures or positions, the effects of different loads or carrying techniques, the effects of verbal suggestion, or whatever suits their fancy. Many of the ideas come from the students' own experiences as runners, dancers, or skiers. Because they must present data to the class, they learn to analyze data quantitatively and present them in charts or graphs. The main lesson, however, is usually how difficult it is to control conditions well enough to get consistent results from human subjects.

Besides the EMG, the other major research tool is the library. Our library staff members give expert introductory lectures on the techniques of researching primary and secondary scientific literature. The students receive this instruction early in the semester, and they are immediately given an assignment that will use and reinforce this knowledge. Often I require them to find primary articles and to summarize them orally or in writing. Students must also use the library to put their research in the context of the literature.

Although I give quite direct guidance in many ways, there is little danger of the projects' degenerating into "cookbook" exercises. Designing an experiment and finding specific muscles, machine settings, standardizing procedures, and so forth are all left to the ingenuity of the students, with help from time to time. Best of all, there are no "right answers," because most of these experiments have not been reported in the literature. Students' sense of exploring the unknown, as well as of their peers' scrutiny, proves to be a strong motivator for accuracy and conscientiousness in lab work.

Results

Introducing students to college-level science through active inquiry is both feasible and rewarding, but choosing to teach in this way entails abandoning broad coverage in favor of critical skills. The topic for such a course must be carefully chosen to be accessible and exciting to students, many of whom arrive on campus with strong negative feelings about science. The applied sciences provide good subjects and questions, such as those involving technology, nutrition, and other health-related areas, all of which have direct and obvious connections with students' lives.

As I have already mentioned, the choice of content is extremely important, but pedagogy is at least equally so. Hampshire science teachers have found several elements of teaching style to be especially important in drawing women students into active participation in science courses and frequently into science concentrations. One of these elements is the encouragement of active questioning in a manner that validates students' willingness and eagerness to push ideas or reexamine things that may have slipped by too quickly. For this element, the establishment of a noncompetitive environment is crucial. Teachers can contribute to such a setting by fostering cooperation among students as part of the course, by encouraging students to build on one another's ideas, by respecting students' ideas, and by presenting themselves as people who are eager to learn but who value their own knowledge (Woodhull [McNeal], Lowry, and Henifin, 1985). This pedagogical style, although it also makes science accessible and attractive to women when it is practiced by men, is clearly enhanced at Hampshire, where 40 percent of the science faculty members are women.

24

The major point is more general: This approach to science education empowers all students, for they create their own teaching devices. They make up projects that (with guidance) teach them how to run controlled experiments, they do statistical analyses, and they package, present, and defend scientific ideas. Since these ideas are their own, there is no question that they are perceived as tangible, relevant, and worth pursuing.

Teaching in this way also motivates the faculty. Students who are taking responsibility for original projects show a startling amount of seriousness and dedication, in contrast to their often negligent attitudes upon entering a course. Moreover, beginners, who have not yet been indoctrinated into the limitations of the various disciplines, are very creative in their project ideas. Hence, a beginning course becomes a source of stimulation rather than repetition to the teacher.

The nature of education, as opposed to training, is that it gives the skills for lifelong learning. The ability to keep learning and judging science is particularly crucial in modern society and will outlast particular facts.

References

Epstein, H. T. *A Strategy for Education*. New York: Oxford University Press, 1970.

Epstein, H. T. "An Experiment in Education." *Nature*, 1972, *235*, 203-205.

Goddard, N., and Henifin, M. S. "A Feminist Approach to the Biology of Women." *Women's Studies Quarterly*, 1984, *12* (4), 11-18.

Joseph, J., and Nightingale, A. "Electromyography of Muscles of Posture: Leg Muscles in Males." *Journal of Physiology*, 1952, *117*, 484.

Poincaré, H. "Mathematical Creation." In J. R. Newman (ed.), *The World of Mathematics*. New York: Simon & Schuster, 1956.

Taylor, C. W., and Barron, F. (eds.). *Scientific Creativity: Its Recognition and Development*. New York: Krieger, 1975.

Trimbur, J. "Collaborative Learning and Teaching Writing." In B. W. McClelland and T. R. Donovan (eds.), *Perspectives on Research and Scholarship in Composition*. New York: Modern Language Association, 1985.

Wiener, H. S. "Collaborative Learning in the Classroom." *College English*, 1986, *48*, 52-61.

Woodhull [McNeal], A., Lowry, N., and Henifin, M. "Teaching for Change: Feminism and the Sciences." *Journal of Thought*, 1985, *20* (3), 162-173.

Ann P. McNeal, professor of physiology, earned her B.A. at Swarthmore College and her Ph.D at the University of Washington. She has taught at Hampshire College since 1972, where she has been active in the Women in Science and Feminist Studies programs. Her research interests are on the biomechanics of standing and on muscular activity during different tasks, but she is also interested in health issues in the Third World, especially Africa, where she taught for two years.

Well-designed computer simulations allow students to work within the variety of options, conflicts, and uncertainties that characterize complex situations.

Plant Closings and Capital Flight: A Computer-Assisted Simulation

Stanley L. Warner, Myrna M. Breitbart

The increasing mobility of capital, both nationally and internationally, has intensified the process by which some communities and regions are dismantled while others are reconstructed. A contemporary national debate has become framed in the language of deindustrialization, the Rust Belt versus the Sun Belt, the Japanese challenge, and the international competitiveness of U.S. industry. In 1988, a plant-closing notification law reflected congressional compromises and the threat of a presidential veto. How does one assess the social costs that arise when corporate capital withdraws from one territory and relocates in another, and what possibilities for community and regional intervention are both realistic and justified?

These questions led the present authors—one an economist, the other a social geographer—to design a teaching framework that would simulate

The authors are grateful for the support of this project by a grant from the Annenberg Foundation and by the loan of equipment from IBM. We also thank Richard Muller, George Moryades, and Tom Hull for their contributions to designing and improving the computer software.

F. S. Weaver (ed.). *Promoting Inquiry in Undergraduate Learning.*
New Directions for Teaching and Learning, no. 38. San Francisco: Jossey-Bass, Summer 1989.

the decision-making environment in which various constituencies in a medium-sized U.S. city would respond to the closing and relocation of a major corporate plant. We decided on a simulation approach for three reasons. First, we wanted to emphasize critical inquiry in an issue not defined by prior "right" answers. Second, we sought a framework that would combine both quantitative and qualitative patterns of thinking. Third, we were in search of a format that would require students to engage one another in a context that offered a high level of real-world immediacy. The project as a whole was constructed as a role simulation. Within that framework, we use a computer component that seeks to model the ways in which computers are typically used as an aid to analysis.

As in most other upper-division Hampshire College courses, there are no content-specific prerequisites rather, we expect students to have developed the skills of reading and thinking critically, of using the library, and of coherently presenting their work orally and in writing. Students typically are in the middle or later stages of their individually designed concentrations. Approximately half our class time is spent on developing the technical and theoretical background necessary for this subject, and we draw on such areas as the economics of the firm, location theory, urban and regional sociology, labor and women's studies, political geography, and so forth. The other half is devoted to the simulation process, to students' presentations, and to discussions of conflicting positions, as set out in the current literature.

No established text provides a reading "backbone." We use three or four specialized paperbacks and provide (at cost) a four-hundred-page package of simulation materials and current articles. In the latest versions, we have made more explicit the treatment of gender-based issues and the analysis of the First World/Third World dimensions of capital mobility.

We spend the first few class sessions discussing some of the readings. The first assignment is to write a research report on a local corporation. Students do this assignment in teams. We have recently used General Motors in Framingham and General Electric in Pittsfield, both in Massachusetts and both within a few miles of Hampshire. Students use library sources and visit these two firms, interviewing key personnel, to acquire the information required by our structured questions. These questions (in addition to the standard ones on profitability and so on), emphasize relationships between the local plant and the parent corporation and between the local plant and the community. While students must work cooperatively with their research teams, they submit individual essays. This preliminary exercise gives students experience in researching a corporation, as well as a concrete sense of the issues evoked by the simulation.

The Simulation

As the first step, we assign each student a role: plant manager, union president, personnel director, city planner, real-estate developer, or one of ten other roles. (Roles may be combined or multiply assigned, to accommodate class size.) Students are provided with personal biographies outlining education, life experience, and work history and are given detailed packages of information describing the standard metropolitan area of "Culpepper" and its largest employer, "Plastico." The simulation proceeds through three stages: predicting corporate closure, assessing the community impact of job loss, and designing alternative responses to capital flight. At the conclusion of each stage, students present oral and written reports. We have developed computer programs for the first two projects, and we are working on the third.

Several considerations guided our design of the computer software, as follows:

1. The programs should be able to run on a desktop personal computer comparable to what a city planner or a plant manager might use. (At the moment, we are stretching the limits of 192K memory on an IBM XT.)

2. The programs should assume little or no computer experience on the part of the user. Our intent is to demystify what computers are and what they can do. (This has meant building in a silent background of "dummy-proofing" that blocks certain keystrokes, provides escape routes, and offers onscreen assistance, if needed.)

3. There should be no predetermined "right" answers or conclusions. Persons using the program must experience it as a framework for organizing information and developing answers that still require independent interpretation and analysis.

These are not easy objectives to achieve simultaneously. Desktop limitations on memory are partially alleviated by the partitioning of exercises onto separate floppy disks. The larger problem—joining the "no computer background" assumption with an open-ended problem-solving capability—is full of thorns and compromises. Our approach was to begin with a narrow range of options and then increase the degree of user choice and initiative.

Project I: Predicting Corporate Closure. Students are asked to evaluate the financial condition of the hypothetical firm, Plastico, and determine the likelihood of a plant shutdown. The first few screens of the program set the context, introduce the problem, and offer a menu of options for proceeding. The corporate balance sheet, income statement, and capital investment record may be examined, with the standby aid of a directory of financial definitions, if one is needed. Plastico shows low reported profits but a high depreciation contribution to cash flow, which indicates the possibility of a "cash cow" strategy of deliberate underinvestment by a parent corporation, to maximize the short-term transfer of funds.

Under one option in the program, it is possible to introduce changes in revenues or costs and explore the impact on profitability. Another subroutine, based on the research of Edward Altman (for instance, Altman and McGough, 1974), asks students to provide income and balance-sheet ratios, which are then used to calculate a weighted score that predicts the possibility of a shutdown. Users may type in their conclusions and print all parts of the data, including their own modifications. This first exercise introduces the framework of nested menus, the notion of interaction with the computer, and the expectation of a personal analysis. While the content requires reasonably sophisticated input and judgment, the computer format tries to anticipate and block the most common errors. A student typically requires thirty minutes to one hour to complete work at the computer.

Project II: Assessing the Community Impact of Job Loss. The second project expands both the analytical task and the range of independent computer interaction. This program presents a data base for Culpepper that covers (1) employment in fifty-three industries and sectors, (2) occupational distribution, (3) age and income distribution, and (4) education level, with all four categories subdivided by race and sex. The program begins with the following text:

> Welcome back to the community of Culpepper. Recent events now suggest the metropolitan area's largest employer, Plastico, will shut down. Your task is to assess the economic and social impact. That assessment includes not only the direct loss of jobs at Plastico but also a variety of "rippling" effects throughout the larger community. These effects are social as well as economic and include a consideration of such factors as job and income loss, physical and mental health, erosion of the local tax base, and changes in the composition of jobs available. The program provides you with a data base for the community of Culpepper and challenges you to discover what patterns of significance can be extracted.

Different conceptual approaches to estimating the economic and social impact of a plant closing have already been presented in class meetings and readings at this point. Working on the computer, students can manipulate the data base by invoking one of several computational options in order to apply established theoretical models or pursue independent approaches of their own. For example, the percent distribution of employment by industry for Culpepper can be computed and compared with the U.S. distribution, to produce a vector of "location quotients" that indicates the extent to which particular sectors are export-oriented (that is, produce more than is required to meet local demand). Those figures in turn can be used to calculate a local "multiplier," based on the ratio of export to nonexport employment, that then provides an estimate of the additional jobs that would be lost if an export firm such as Plastico were to close.

To take another example, information on Plastico workers according to sex, race, and age can be compared with Culpepper data, to consider the degree to which the loss of jobs by women, minorities, or older workers would create special problems, both in job replacement and in the quality of jobs available. The intent is to provide a more thorough understanding of the range of social impacts triggered by a plant closing, as well as to encourage students to use this information selectively in developing reports consistent with the roles they occupy.

Project III: Designing Alternative Responses to Capital Flight. The last project is even more open-ended. Plastico will in fact close, and the immediate loss of 1,200 jobs will create the possibility of an extended and deep-rooted community crisis. Students are asked to make class presentations that combine the social impact analysis of Project II with their reading of the literature on what other communities and regions have attempted. Moreover, each student must do this in a context that reflects his or her role as a member of management, labor, or the local community. Sometimes sympathy for the plight of dislocated workers leads to an early and easy proposal, which contradicts the reality of most experience. We then remind students of their role constraints (for example, by using a memorandum to plant managers or a letter to the regional and city planners that says they are overreaching the discretionary options of their positions).

Results

The traditional theoretical literature for understanding the relationship between capital flight and the reconstruction of communities and regions is under serious challenge. The "Other Resources" section listed at the end of the chapter offers a guideline to the major contributors of that theoretical debate. The newer literature rejects the "natural endowment" tradition, in which the uneven spatial distributions of minerals, water, or climate becomes commingled with such variables as cheap labor or a stable political environment, to explain growth or its absence. It also questions the "stages of development" theories built around the notion of one-way progress, from underdevelopment to economic maturity. Instead, the more recent work emphasizes the extent to which the social conditions necessary for the profitable use of capital are shaped and reshaped both by past patterns of deployment and by new organizational options for disassembling production across space.

How does this debate at the theoretical level influence the design of a simulation? We reached an early decision that students should confront the full range of theoretical disagreement and yet be faced with reaching resolution by constructing independent responses to concrete situations. The computer-aided part of the simulation should reinforce this emphasis on exploration, discovery, and choice.

We reviewed a number of interactive computer programs for teaching, ranging across such subjects as economics, biology, chemistry, and paramedical training. Some were far more imaginative than others in their latitude for personal input, diagnosis, and participation, but virtually all shared the feature of guiding users to correct responses and returning people to earlier subroutines to learn from their mistakes. In our simulation, participants who move through the stages of predicting a plant shutdown, assessing community impact, and proposing responses encounter not answers but a widening set of analytical possibilities and an overload of empirical information.

The use of computers in this simulation also differs in a more formal sense. This project does not offer computer modeling of the movements of capital across space, in chessboard fashion—a problem to be solved, for example, through game theory or linear programming techniques. Rather, it offers modeling of the normal use of computers in a simulated environment. That distinction at least partly alters the mindset of simulation participants. The computer is not a surrogate teacher; it is a device for assisting problem solving. Among other things, it can be commanded to display, manipulate, and print information on command.

How does the experience of students match these expectations? First, students are not sure whether the open-ended nature of their work on the computer means that all responses are equally acceptable. That uncertainty is dispelled when they begin reading the varied theoretical literature and presenting and critiquing their own findings. They discover (as we do) wide-ranging differences in originality, depth, and organization. (Some ask for their projects back, in order to improve them.)

Second, as the simulation proceeds, students often experience internal conflict as they try to reconcile their role positions (as members of management, labor, local government, or the community) with the moral sense of a just outcome and the analytical sense of a logical outcome. We try to use this frustration, as well as its related ambiguity, to develop a different level of understanding about the way information often is selectively organized and defended.

Finally, the willing suspension of disbelief—necessary both for good theater and for a simulation—is never quite achieved. We send students to the computer (as managers, planners, and so forth) to use it as a problem-solving tool, but they know that we wrote the script, choreographed the data, and, in some cases, loaded the deck. The knowledge that this is, after all, a simulation is often displaced by fascination with the possibilities and by the desire to anticipate and counter positions taken by these on the other side of the debate.

The course, which we call "Capital Versus Community," has been offered four times in the past five years. It continues to evolve as we learn from past experience, expand the simulation options, and change the mix of readings to reflect new published research. Each cohort of participants brings a different group chemistry and engages the simulation in ways that surprise us. Our students sometimes think they are learning too much about the specific subject of plant closings, but we hope they are acquiring the habits of mind that foster good social inquiry.

Other Resources

Altman, E., and McGough, T. "Evaluation of a Company as a Going Concern." *Journal of Accountancy*, Dec. 1974, pp. 50–57.

Bluestone, B., and Harrison, B. *The Deindustrialization of America*. New York: Basic Books, 1982.

Gordon, D., Edwards, R., and Reich, M. *Segmented Work, Divided Workers: The Historical Transformation of Labor in the United States*. New York: Cambridge University Press, 1982.

Lynd, S. *The Fight Against Shutdowns: Youngstown's Steel Mill Closings*. San Pedro, Calif.: Singlejack Books, 1982.

McKenzie, R. (ed.). *Plant Closings: Public or Private Choices?* Washington, D.C.: Cato Institute, 1982.

Massey, D. *Spatial Divisions of Labor: Social Structures and the Geography of Production*. New York: Methuen, 1984.

Noble, D. *Forces of Production: A Social History of Industrial Automation*. New York: Oxford University Press, 1984.

Price, K. (ed.). *Regional Conflict and National Policy*. Washington, D.C.: Resources for the Future, 1982.

Raines, J., Berson, L., and Gracie, D. (eds.). *Community and Capital in Conflict: Plant Closings and Job Loss*. Philadelphia: Temple University Press, 1982.

Sawers, L., and Tabb, W. (eds.). *Sunbelt/Snowbelt: Urban Development and Regional Restructuring*. New York: Oxford University Press, 1982.

Scott, A., and Storper, M. (eds.). *Production, Work, Territory: The Geographical Anatomy of Industrial Capitalism*. Boston: Allen and Unwin, 1986.

Shaiken, H. *Work Transformed: Automation and Labor in the Computer Age*. Lexington, Mass.: Lexington Books, 1986.

Staudohar, P., and Brown, H. (eds.). *Deindustrialization and Plant Closure*. Lexington, Mass.: Lexington Books, 1986.

Stern, R., Wood, K. H., and Hammer, T. *Employee Ownership in Plant Shutdowns*. Kalamazoo, Mich.: W. E. Upjohn Institute for Employment Research, 1979.

Stanley L. Warner, associate professor of economics, did his undergraduate studies at Albion College and earned his Ph.D. at Harvard University. Before joining the Hampshire College faculty in 1973, he taught at the University of California, Santa Cruz, and at Bucknell University. His teaching and research interests include industrial organization and U.S. economic history.

Myrna M. Breitbart, associate professor of geography and urban studies, focuses her teaching and research on examining the ways in which built and social environments reflect and reinforce class, gender, and race relations. She received her B.A. from Clark University, her M.A. from Rutgers University, and her Ph.D. from Clark University. She has taught at Hampshire College since 1977.

*History courses that do not emphasize the dynamic
relationships between ideas and social structure risk teaching
and learning that severely underestimate and distort the
dynamics of historical change.*

A Dialectical Approach to Spanish American History

Roberto Márquez

Hobsbawm (1973, p. 245) has observed, "It is not the fact of thinking independently, or otherwise, which gives intellectuals certain political characteristics, but a particular social situation in which they think." This is the statement of a truth whose implications pose no small problem for those of us interested in developing courses that, lacking neither specific focus nor general efficacy, are themselves expressions of the continuous tension between cultural and social history. A course called "The Social and Intellectual History of Spanish America" represents at least one attempt to come to terms with the challenge implicit in Hobsbawm's succinct observation.

An economist colleague and I designed this course as the basic course for second- and third-year Hampshire College students beginning concentrated work in some aspect of Latin American studies. It does, however, attract students from unrelated fields and from the other four colleges of the Five Colleges Consortium. Far from discouraging this cross-fertilization of disciplines and schools, we believe it to be an important ingredient in the chemistry of the course: As the class gains momentum and as discussion becomes more focused and more generalized, it tends to lend a certain dramatic emphasis to some of the fundamental questions of methodology and context that are central to

F. S. Weaver (ed.). *Promoting Inquiry in Undergraduate Learning.*
New Directions for Teaching and Learning, no. 38. San Francisco: Jossey-Bass, Summer 1989.

the course. That we ourselves come from distinct disciplines—literature and economics—tends further to objectify and dramatize these broader issues and, not incidentally, to provide a learning experience for us as instructors.

Guiding Principles

In designing and teaching the course, our guiding principles are several and interrelated, reflecting aims both modest and ambitious but, on the whole, fairly concrete. On the simplest level, our intentions are entirely within the bounds of the conventional and the more traditional in Latin American studies: to familiarize our students with the progression, key junctures, and general drift of forces and events that are the political and economic history of Spanish America. We also aim, by placing them in this larger context, to present simultaneously the salient facts of Spanish America's intellectual and cultural history. This aim obviously involves a purely informational function, which in a more conventional course or setting can be fulfilled by individual subject courses or by variously tracked departmental requirements.

Our premises, however, involve considerably more than that. It has been our experience that, despite their inextricable relationship and natural complementarity, cultural history, the history of ideas, and history as more conventionally defined continue to be treated in isolation from one another, as if each subject somehow constituted a separate and independent reality.

It might be argued that this separate treatment is merely an efficiency device, nothing more than a part of the division of labor common to colleges and departments of every description. Nevertheless, this procedure, instead of providing students with any genuine sense of history, tends to deemphasize the real complexity—the dialectical nature and mutual interdependence—of the several phenomena in question. More often than not, it fails to meet more than the barest demands for analytical rigor and perspective. On the whole, it encourages compartmentalized thinking, which lacks range and depth and gives students a misleading sense of security with respect to a problematic and shifting body of material. Whereas the more conventional course may succeed in transmitting information, it rarely appears to provide any sense of where the part can be said to relate to the more complex and dynamic whole. Insofar as one is dealing with a pedagogical device, the means have become the end, hardening, if only implicitly, into a very particular philosophy of history whose idealist premises disguise a generally conservative bias.

Equally to the point, this usually unarticulated mode of approaching history in general, and Spanish American history in particular, lacks consistency and rigor and cannot, therefore, instill either quality in students. It is a fundamentally uncritical historical posture. By reintroducing the dimension of historical and thematic simultaneity, we hope to give our students a keener sense of the wholistic sweep of what, as a class, we are analyzing.

Fundamentals

The crux of our course is a concern with providing a context and an opportunity for sensitizing students and engaging them in the conceptual, theoretical, and methodological problems of historical thinking as it applies to Spanish America, especially the dialectical relationship between social and intellectual history. Rather than give students specific answers, our goal is to expose them to different types of answers and approaches, encouraging them to consider the contextual and theoretical premises that serve as a backdrop. The idea is to awaken students' awareness of a theory in practice and, by so doing, to make them equally sensitive to the practice of theory—questions of objectivity and subjectivity in historical analysis.

Since choice (explicit or implicit) is compellingly unavoidable, we seek to encourage the conscious articulation of considered choice. Throughout the course, we are continually concerned with exploring the broader implications of various theoretical positions, and we are careful to avoid mechanistic formulations of any persuasion. To the degree that we touch on these, we impinge on the philosophy of history, but concretely, through the analysis of philosophies of history in their specific and developing context in Spanish America.

Course Structure

Hampshire's semesters are thirteen or fourteen weeks long. We divide our class time as follows: one week for a general introduction, four weeks for an overview of Spanish American history through the early twentieth century, three weeks for a closer look at Argentina, two weeks for Peruvian history, one week for Cuban history, and two weeks for discussion of students' presentations.

In the first week—relying principally on Carr (1967), Williams (1973), Morse (1964), and Fischer (1970)—we present general questions about the relationships among culture, politics, and the economy. We try to define as carefully as possible the issues of historical interpretation and analysis involved in these abstract categories, indicating the very different conceptions of social change that emerge from alternative models and the political or policy implications of their use. An important aspect of this effort involves the critique of idealist and "hero" theories and of axiomatic applications of historical materialism.

In the next four weeks, we try to make these issues more concrete by relating them to Spanish American history. Our major emphases are the material goals of the Spanish monarchy in the New World and the cultural forms of its expression; the role and importance of the confrontations among the Spaniards, the indigenous peoples, and black slaves; the interaction of economic and social forces, European affairs, and political thought in the wars of independence; the impact of foreign trade and investment from the late nineteenth century and its relationship to such phenomena as positivism, naturalism, and realism in literature; and the rise of populist movements, with industrial and urban growth, and their relationship to modernism, *indigenismo,* and other nationalist literary trends in the twentieth century. Readings include selections from Parry (1973), Morner (1967), Zea (1963), Weaver (1980), and Hobsbawm (1962), as well as works by such historical figures as Hernán Cortés (1485–1547), Simón Bolívar (1783–1830), José Joaquín de Olmedo (1780–1847), and others.

In the national case studies of the next six weeks, we move to another level of historical specificity. Against a narrative background of Argentinean social and economic history (Scobie, 1971), the students read such authors as Sarmiento (1961), Martínez Estrada (1971), Corradi (1974), and Romero (1963). Insofar as he manages to crystallize a generational attitude of importance to the whole of Spanish America, we include a discussion of Rodó's *Ariel* (1988) in this section. With a similar background of narrative reading in Peruvian history, which includes Piel's (1970) fine essay, students become acquainted with the work of Prada (Meade, 1953) and Mariátegui (1971). In addition, students read and critically evaluate Dobyns and Doughty (1976) and Klaren (1973).

The Cuban section is the most compressed and abbreviated, because there are already several courses on Cuba available on campus and in the other four colleges of the consortium. During this week, apart from reading some descriptive history, students attempt to engage the thought of José Martí and Fidel Castro in their respective historical moments. We give particular attention to the ways in which the work of Martí can be said to anticipate and embody the intellectual and political development of Fidel Castro and of the revolution he represents.

At the end of the fifth week, we ask for a short paper on some historiographical issue in Spanish American history, a paper drawing only on the course readings and lectures and demonstrating serious reflection on a significant issue of the historical process. This paper may or may not be a preliminary version of the student's longer research paper, due at the end of the week that follows the end of the term.

Results

While the course's basic intentions and structure have remained intact, we have made substantial changes in the readings and presenta-

response to students' suggestions. We have come to appreciate how difficult the conceptual material is for students, many of whom have never
recognized the existence of the issues that we consider so important. This
heightened awareness has led us, in preparing our lectures, to take greater
care in developing the background and comparing alternative historiographical approaches. We also offer more precise examples to illustrate
different positions. We have reworked the syllabus each time we have
offered the course, and we have added an extensive bibliography of suggested readings, becoming more confident that the assignments will mesh
better with our lectures.

Our initial choice of Argentina, Peru, and Cuba as case studies has
worked very well. The significant differences among these societies, despite the common Hispanic component of their histories, effectively illustrate the importance of the general questions we discuss in the first two
sections of the course and demonstrate the sterility of simple, axiomatic
answers. The use of this broad range of examples has its pedagogical
dangers, however: As we painfully realized in our first attempt, it can
lead to considerable confusion and induce an unproductive relativism.
Since we began taking greater care in relating the general to the particular, however, the variety contained in the case studies has appeared to
accomplish its intended purpose.

Despite our initial problems with the course, and despite some rough
spots that still remain, this course has become extraordinarily successful.
Enrollment from all five colleges has grown each year, even though there
are no course requirements at Hampshire, and even though a large number of more conventional alternatives are available in the other four colleges. Moreover, the quality of students' oral and written work for the
class has risen dramatically. The questions raised during class are better
informed and more interesting, and students' written work is considerably
more sophisticated, both in conception and in execution.

One of the most heartening aspects of students' projects over this
period has been the marked decline in papers narrowly defined as being
"on" literature, economics, politics, or any single discipline. Our students
appear to be more comfortable with and capable of effectively pulling
together different dimensions of social life to make coherent arguments
about one dimension. Another encouraging indication of our success
with this course is its increasing influence on the ideas and methods that
appear in students' subsequent work, such as senior theses.

Our own growth as instructors is also evident. Our professional preparation and research emphasize different aspects of a single human reality,
and our own aspirations to enrich our specialized professional work and
broaden its context have been neither incidental nor ancillary to the
design and purpose of the course. We have managed to teach each other
a great deal about our respective fields and, through continuing dialogue,

to transform our interaction into an instrument both pedagogically effective and personally rewarding.

References

Carr, E. H. *What Is History?* New York: Random House, 1967.

Corradi, J. "Argentina." In R. H. Chilcote and J. C. Edelstein (eds.), *Latin America: The Struggle with Dependency and Beyond.* Cambridge, Mass.: Schenkman, 1974.

Dobyns, H. E., and Doughty, P. L. *Peru: A Cultural History.* New York: Oxford University Press, 1976.

Fischer, D. F. *Historians' Fallacies.* New York: Harper & Row, 1970.

Hobsbawm, E. J. *The Age of Revolution, 1789-1848.* New York: New American Library, 1962.

Hobsbawm, E. J. *Revolutionaries: Contemporary Essays.* New York: New American Library, 1973.

Klaren, P. *Modernization, Dislocation, and Aprismo.* Austin: University of Texas Press, 1973.

Mariátegui, J. C. *Seven Interpretive Essays on Peruvian Reality.* Austin: University of Texas Press, 1971.

Martínez Estrada, E. *X-Ray of the Pampa.* Austin: University of Texas Press, 1971.

Meade, R. G. "Manuel González Prada: Peruvian Judge of Spain." *PLMA,* 1953, *68,* 696-715.

Morner, M. *Race Mixture in the History of Latin America.* Boston: Little, Brown, 1967.

Morse, R. M. "The Heritage of Latin America." In L. Hartz (ed.), *The Founding of New Societies: Studies in the History of the United States, Latin America, South Africa, Canada, and Australia.* San Diego, Calif.: Harcourt Brace Jovanovich, 1964.

Parry, J. H. *The Spanish Seaborne Empire.* Baltimore: Penguin Books, 1973.

Piel, J. "The Place of the Peasantry in the National Life of Peru in the Nineteenth Century." *Past and Present,* 1970, *46,* 108-133.

Rodó, J. E. *Ariel.* Austin: University of Texas Press, 1988.

Romero, J. L. *A History of Argentine Political Thought.* Stanford, Calif.: Stanford University Press, 1963.

Sarmiento, D. F. *Life in the Argentine Republic in the Days of the Tyrants, or Civilization and Barbarism.* New York: Collier Books, 1961.

Scobie, J. R. *Argentina: A City and a Nation.* (2nd ed.) New York: Oxford University Press, 1971.

Weaver, F. S. *Class, State, and Industrial Structure: The Historical Process of South American Industrial Growth.* Westport, Conn.: Greenwood Press, 1980.

Williams, R. "Base and Superstructure in Marxist Cultural Theory." *New Left Review,* 1973, *82,* 3-16.

Zea, L. *The Latin American Mind.* Norman: University of Oklahoma Press, 1963.

Roberto Márquez received his B.A. from Brandeis University and his Ph.D. from Harvard University. He taught at Hampshire College from 1970 to 1986 and is now the Clarence J. Robinson, Professor of Hispanic American and Caribbean Culture at George Mason University.

Intensive and open-ended laboratory experience is the only way in which a crucial type of learning for science students can take place.

Teaching Experimental Science: Enzymes and the Laboratory

John M. Foster

If a student intends to do creative and original work in experimental science, he or she must develop, through experimental methods, problem-solving skills based on a thorough understanding of underlying principles and of how those principles operate to yield reliable data that can be interpreted in useful ways.

In the experimental sciences, these skills clearly should be developed through direct experience with laboratory or field investigation. Good laboratory or field research demands rigorous quantitative thinking, careful planning, meticulous attention to detail, and long hours. These analytical and quantitative skills, and an awareness of the time and effort that research requires, are probably of much greater long-term benefit to an undergraduate than is acquiring a prescribed body of concepts and information. Students with good potential can learn specific subject matter and concepts largely on their own. What undergraduate science students need most is to spend more time in the field or the laboratory, learning the quantitative and reasoning skills that can best be taught there, and less time in the classroom listening to lectures.

Unfortunately, the approach most often used in undergraduate labo-

F. S. Weaver (ed.). *Promoting Inquiry in Undergraduate Learning.*
New Directions for Teaching and Learning, no. 38. San Francisco: Jossey-Bass, Summer 1989.

ratory courses is the prefabricated laboratory experiment. In such experiments, the student strives to obtain some correct answer, predetermined by the instructor. Instructions for these exercises are usually elaborate and detailed, to make sure that the student does everything properly. Some published laboratory manuals go so far as to include preprinted data sheets, with most of the calculations already done; the student has merely to fill in the blanks and do the arithmetic. It is clear that under such conditions students can quite readily carry out an exercise and even get good data without really understanding what they are doing.

For Hampshire College to develop a truly inquiry-based curriculum in experimental science, we needed to create the opportunities for advanced undergraduates to have extensive laboratory or field experience and for experiences that would go well beyond the mere replication of prepackaged laboratory exercises. For these reasons, I set out several years ago to develop a course in general biochemistry, to be taught almost entirely in the laboratory. Students who had chosen concentrations in biological science would be exposed directly to arduous and heavily quantitative laboratory work and would learn much of the biochemistry through direct observation.

"Enzymes"

I chose enzymes as a focus for the course, because I believed that enzymes would be intrinsically interesting to the students and because many quantitative biochemical techniques can be used to study enzymes. I can show students how living material, which is familiar to all of them, can be examined in specific quantitative and theoretical ways. I tell the students explicitly that they can expect work that is time-consuming, difficult to understand, and demanding of considerable technical skill. I also tell them that they will learn what it is like to do quantitative experimental work in biochemistry and that they will learn a lot of basic biochemistry in the process.

The response to the course, which I have now taught a number of times in various forms, has been gratifying. The students have gladly accepted the challenge and have worked extremely hard. The subject of enzymes has proved particularly well suited to my basic objectives, but there are clearly other topics in quantitative science that could serve as well.

The semester is divided into two half-semester minicourses. The first, "Enzymes as Catalysts," is a carefully structured sequence of laboratory exercises that builds, step by step, the theoretical basis, laboratory techniques, and quantitative skills necessary to undertake the second minicourse. The second, "Enzymes as Proteins," gives each student group the opportunity to purify an enzyme from a suitable biological source. This arrangement gives a sharp focus to each half of the semester but also gives each half a different perspective.

"Enzymes as Catalysts." The first part of the course is a set of prescribed exercises, but their purpose and organization are different from those of traditional prefabricated experiments. First, I say explicitly that they are exercises, not experiments, and that their purpose is to teach many commonly used techniques in biochemistry, along with the quantitative problem solving that accompanies the use of these techniques. The exercises are also intended to illustrate specific biochemical concepts, but these concepts emerge only when good data have been obtained and properly interpreted. Second, I give students minimal instructions, so that they are left to plan most of the work themselves. They must modify procedures in response to changing conditions, deal with dilution problems, choose appropriate sample sizes, and cope with myriad other technical problems in biochemical laboratory analysis. There is indeed a right answer to each exercise—namely, reliable data obtained by methods whose principles are understood.

Two examples will illustrate how such exercises are implemented in the course. The first concerns an assay for salivary amylase. Because it is the first exercise in the course, the student is given a fairly detailed protocol for the quantitative starch-iodine reaction, which is the basis of the assay, but is given no information on how much to dilute the enzyme or on how many samples to take and how frequently. The student must therefore do a trial run first, figure out from the preliminary data how rapidly the reaction runs, and then use those data to plan a proper sampling schedule. He or she must decide how to modify the procedure to obtain more accurate results near the end of the reaction, when there is very little starch left.

The second example concerns the instructions for an alcohol dehydrogenase assay, as follows:

> The reaction is followed spectrophotometrically by measuring the increase in absorbance at 340 nm (due to the formation of NADH) in a reaction mixture containing 100 mM pyrophosphate buffer (pH 8.5), 100 mM ethanol, 0.5 mM NAD+ and approximately 0.05 units of enzyme in a final volume of 3.0 ml.

The student, whose initial reaction is that these are not instructions at all, soon discovers that they are precise and complete directions. To implement them, however, means learning to work in appropriate units, deal with the calculations necessary to make up a specified reaction mixture from small volumes of concentrated reagents, understand what is meant by a unit of enzyme activity, and perceive how all this relates to absorbance changes registered on a spectrophotometer. Such seemingly mundane material is basic to effective laboratory work in biochemistry, but students are not likely to learn it well unless they are required to get their work done.

To reinforce the requirement for getting work done properly, I ask students to develop basic concepts from their own data, as much as possible. For that reason, they are discouraged from doing outside reading during the first two to three weeks of the semester. Instead, they are urged to spend time in the laboratory, developing their skills and making sure that they have usable data. They become thoroughly familiar with such data and can use them more effectively to develop theoretical ideas.

How this works out in practice is illustrated by my approach to enzyme kinetics. Most textbook treatments of the subject tend to be almost entirely theoretical, and some of the assumptions that are made in deriving the Michaelis-Menten equation (widely used by biochemists as a way of describing the properties of an enzyme) are not readily apparent to students who are new to the subject. I begin with students' own data, asking them to propose simple models to account for their results and then to write equations for these models. On its own, every class has been able to come up with the notion of saturation of an enzyme and of some type of an intermediate complex being formed during an enzyme-catalyzed reaction. The students have little difficulty writing down the simple mechanisms for reactions and can, with some help, write equations for the mechanisms. A computer is then used to gauge how these equations behave if a reasonable set of numerical values, derived from students' own data, is assigned to the variables and rate constants. The computer solution shows that a so-called steady state exists throughout much of the course of an enzyme reaction. This is a prior assumption in most textbooks; here, it develops as a condition predicted by a model based on the students' own data. Introducing the idea of a steady state into the equations the students have developed simplifies the Michaelis-Menten equation.

Next comes an exercise that builds on these basic ideas with a different enzyme, which yields data that do not fit the students' simple models. By having to deal with additional complications, students quickly realize that the usual textbook treatment of the topic represents only the simplest case, but they also perceive that the same basic approach can be used to develop a new mathematical model, which takes the added complexities into account.

The last exercise in "Enzymes as Catalysts" introduces two new enzyme assays, one of which yields data that must be handled quite differently from the assays the students have encountered up to this point. It also has a complex protocol, requiring integration of data from several different experimental procedures. The work is split up among the different student groups, which are required to coordinate their work and pool their data. It emphasizes the need for careful notes and accurate book-keeping. There is a strong temptation here to give students many instructions, to ensure that the exercise will be complete, but I have found it better to offer gentle reminders here and there and leave the rest up to the students, even if that means they have to repeat some of the work because someone forgets to write something down.

By the time "Enzymes as Catalysts" is over, the students have acquired the bulk of the basic conceptual and laboratory skills they will need to do an enzyme purification. About two weeks before the second minicourse begins, the students are given an opportunity to reorganize their laboratory groups, and each group is asked to choose which enzyme it wishes to purify. Copies of several different purification procedures are made available. They are drawn from published laboratory manuals and from the research literature. The groups are free to choose any of these or, if they are more adventurous, to find their own procedures in the literature. In the latter case, I review the procedures for feasibility, special equipment needs, or the use of especially toxic or expensive materials. The choice of enzyme also gives the students an opportunity to pursue their own projects and interests. Such projects often overlap with other courses that students are taking, such as organic chemistry or microbiology.

"Enzymes as Proteins." In contrast to the first minicourse, which is carefully structured, "Enzymes as Proteins" is not. Whatever structure exists is imposed on each laboratory group by the explicit instructions of its purification procedure. Each group is expected to plan and carry out its enzyme purification on its own, calling on the instructor for consultation and help in setting up new equipment and techniques. Because there may be as many as half a dozen different purifications going on simultaneously, there is the potential for chaos. Because the students have already spent several weeks working with a minimum of instruction, however, this potential has never become a reality.

The students' major preoccupation during the second minicourse is with the details of their laboratory work, but their intellectual focus is on enzymes as proteins. Each group is required to report periodically to the class on the progress of its purification, explaining what techniques have been used, what results have been obtained, and what specific properties of protein molecules are being used in each step of the procedure. These reports become the basis of more extended discussions about related experimental methods and about proteins in general. As in the first minicourse, the practical experience that students gain in the laboratory serves as an excellent framework on which to build concepts of the chemical and physical properties of proteins. The application of these principles to the specific problem of isolating an enzyme, by means of techniques with which the students are becoming familiar, gives a substance to ideas that otherwise might seem abstract.

Readings and Problems

After the first two or three weeks, readings are assigned periodically and discussed in detail during a weekly ninety-minute seminar. Once students have learned enough about enzymes to understand technical terminology, papers are assigned. These are applications of enzymological principles to interesting biological problems. No single textbook is used in the course, although a collection of texts on biochemistry, cell physiology, and enzymology is placed on reserve in the library. The students are free to use these for basic information, but most of the conceptual framework of biochemistry is developed around the laboratory work. Standard reference manuals and handbooks are also available in the laboratory. Many questions arise as students cope with each new experimental problem, and these questions present perfect opportunities for the instructor to discuss biochemical principles in a very tangible context.

While students get continual practice in quantitative problem solving and the effective use of units while working in the laboratory, they also have regularly assigned problems for additional practice, which introduce new material. Whenever possible, problems are constructed so that they cannot be solved through the routine application of formulas, and an attempt is made to select problems that lead to interesting, informative, and unexpected results.

Results

The course I have outlined is clearly very demanding and time-consuming for the students and the instructor alike, yet the willingness of the students to work extremely hard, to tolerate frustration, and to repeat unsuccessful experiments, without being asked, attests to the success of this approach. The choice of enzymes as the principal topic of this introduction to biochemistry may have been fortunate, because of the variety of interesting and dynamic phenomena that are encountered. Nevertheless, it seems possible to choose any topic that provides a sharp intellectual focus and a clear set of experimental objectives. The choice depends on the interests and expertise of the instructor and on the relationship of the course to the rest of the curriculum.

Some practical considerations should be kept in mind in implementing a course of this type. First, because it takes time for students to learn how to plan and carry out their work without detailed instructions, it would probably be difficult to implement such a course within the constraints of the traditional laboratory period. At Hampshire College, the laboratory is always open, and students are expected to put in a good deal of work on their own time.

Second, the students have to be prepared for the experience to make good use of it. At Hampshire, students are not allowed to take the course without having passed an examination (or offered equivalent documentation), which shows that they have learned to use the library effectively, have had some exposure to the scientific research literature, and have demonstrated some capacity to work independently. I have found these capacities to be more important prerequisites than whether a student has taken some prescribed body of courses.

Finally, this approach places unusual demands on the instructor. To be effective, he or she must know the subject matter thoroughly and be prepared to lead extemporaneous discussions, without the benefit of prepared notes. Moreover, there will inevitably be technical problems, methods that must be adapted to local conditions, instruments that cease to function, faulty reagents, equipment that must be improvised from materials at hand, and so on. In dealing with such problems, the instructor necessarily becomes a role model of the laboratory scientist at work. Students have clearly said that they find watching the teacher cope with these problems as instructive as any other aspect of the course. Significant and continuing research experience is clearly a great asset to anyone teaching a course of this type.

Supervising five or six groups of students, each of which is trying to learn how to think systematically and creatively about an increasingly complex body of material, is a demanding experience. Nevertheless, the enthusiasm of the students, and the sense that the course has had a substantial impact on their learning, provide rewards that more than justify the effort.

John M. Foster, professor of biology, received his B.A. from Swarthmore and his Ph.D. from Harvard. He taught at the Boston University School of Medicine and was director of the Science Curriculum Improvement Program for the National Science Foundation before joining the Hampshire College faculty in 1969. He is particularly interested in biochemical control mechanisms and in the development of biochemical approaches to environmental biology.

The tension between explanations that stress biological determinants and those that look more to social and cultural causes is especially acute and interesting in cognitive psychology, and it can be used very effectively in courses with a strong experimental orientation.

Inquiry and Cognitive Psychology

Neil A. Stillings

I came to Hampshire College because I wanted to teach inquiry. I arrived with the naive notions that everyone has a strong natural inclination to inquiry and that teaching is largely a matter of not repressing that inclination. Since then, I have had to face some difficult truths. Students recognize that inquiry is hard work and that it is not conspicuously encouraged or rewarded in the world at large. Moreover, it seems that there is a general inclination to relax and curl up with one's received beliefs. It has turned out to be quite a challenge to create situations in which students will ignore the world's reward system and abandon some of their inner comforts for a taste of inquiry.

The Experience of Inquiry

My efforts to teach inquiry are founded on a view of what it is and on an instinct that it should be taught by example and learned from experience. I think of inquiry as a tension among three modes of imagination: imagining that the world is a certain way; imagining that the world is not that way at all; and imagining ways of getting the world to cough up information that will push one's thinking in new directions. These modes can be labeled *creation, self-criticism,* and *observation.* I try

F. S. Weaver (ed.). *Promoting Inquiry in Undergraduate Learning.*
New Directions for Teaching and Learning, no. 38. San Francisco: Jossey-Bass, Summer 1989.

to teach inquiry directly, showing students how the three modes of imagination can be combined in their projects.

Some students need to be encouraged and shown how to construct theories, because they operate exclusively in a critical mode or because they are too discouraged about the potential of their initial research efforts. Other students need to be shown how their prior commitments have shut off their self-critical faculties and led them to construct logically or empirically weak arguments. Still other students need to be initiated into the joys of tricking the world into revealing what one thought could only be speculated about. The occasions when such discussions have moved students have been among the most rewarding in my teaching career.

It has become clear to me that teaching the skills of inquiry by example and suggestion works (when it does work) not so much because the student incrementally acquires the skills with repeated practice but because one or two experiences with inquiry can trigger the beginning of an enduring taste for further experience. It is fun to have insights, to see data that no one else has ever seen, and to sense what it would be like to work as a professional. Of course, sometimes the insights do not come, the data are all garbage, and the student senses what it would be like to be a failure. For some students, it can be maddening that the first steps have to be so small, that the goal has to be so modest, and that the combination of constraint and independence has to be so judicious. Inquiry is in the realm of art and craft, rather than of formula or of "hanging out."

Learning to inquire requires more than overcoming a state of simple inertia. Most people do not want to inquire. They tend to cling tenaciously to their beliefs about the world, whereas inquiry demands a certain relaxation of one's beliefs. Criticism of one's own ideas involves the admission of possible error and the entertainment of ideas that may be threatening. Creatively developing one's ideas and subjecting them to empirical tests involves facing the unknown and indulging in seemingly unnecessary or insincere intellectual play. Inquiry demands a commitment to its own values, which inevitably come into conflict with one's other values. To become an inquiring thinker, some of the drive to maintain one's preexisting beliefs must be brought into the service of inquiry. This motivational transformation seems to be set in motion by initial experiences with inquiry. One's first attempts at creation, self-criticism, and empirical inquiry begin to rearrange one's motivational structure, transforming a simple capacity for belief into a capacity for inquiry that tends to be self-sustaining. The teacher's most important task is moving students to take their first inquiring steps, convincing them that their heartfelt prior commitments need to be at odds with the search for truth.

Promoting Inquiry Through Courses

I have tried to develop courses that, because of their subject matter and structure, can dramatize and create an environment for the emergence of inquiry. One of these courses, "Human Intelligence," had uneven success. The main idea of the course was to use the study of intelligence and ability testing—counterposing meritocratic social theory with opposing theory and data from work by Bowles and Gintis, Jencks, and others—to motivate the study of cognitive psychology, a radically different approach to human intellectual capacities. The uneven results were in part due to my trying to fit too much into the term. Another part of the problem was that the subject matter strongly aroused students' anxieties about their own abilities and life chances, and this particular anxiety seems very difficult to redirect.

A course titled "The Conscious and Unconscious Mind in Psychology" was also designed to dramatize inquiry, and it has been more successful. It begins with the reading of an extraordinary example of psychological inquiry, Freud's *Introductory Lectures* and *New Introductory Lectures*. The lectures not only systematically develop Freud's theories, which are largely anathema to contemporary students, but also pulsate with his remarkable imaginative, critical, and observational facility, as well as with his infuriating blind spots, culturally determined prejudices, and high-handedness. As students argue against (and occasionally for) his hypotheses, and as they are pushed to respond to the sweep and detail of his argument, to pinpoint his failings, and to clarify their own responses, they can begin to sense the excitement of inquiry within themselves, as well as the need to struggle against their own blind spots and prejudices. The contemporary material that follows these readings takes on quite a bit of life for many of the students.

Although students have said nice things about the course in evaluation questionnaires, the best measure of its success is the high quality of the students' writing. In a series of five take-home essay assignments, they turn out forty to fifty pages of critical argument on the interplay of theory and evidence in psychology. It is still something of a mystery to me why this course works for more students than "Human Intelligence" does. One hypothesis is that contemporary students' immediate sexual anxieties are considerably less than their status anxieties, making it easier for them to take on Freud than the IQ test.

An Example of Psychological Inquiry

One of the reasons I was first attracted to psychology, and a reason why I think it is a good subject for the liberal arts, is its methodological pluralism. Psychology, in its dedication to maintaining an independent discipline to study the individual's mental life and behavior, is poised between biology and the social sciences, necessarily informed by both but resisting reduction to either. Psychology is one arena where the many methods of the biological and social sciences knock against one another with enough force to command the student's attention.

It is difficult to illustrate this rather sweeping claim in a brief essay, but I would like to offer an example from my intermediate course, "Cognitive Psychology." One of the topics treated in the course is human memory. Memory performance can be broadly defined as the retrieval of information related to a current situation. In everyday life, memory performance is the outcome of a complex interaction among biological, psychological, and cultural factors. It is impossible to understand a person's memory performance without attending to this web of influences.

A simple example is short-term retention of information that one has just absorbed. A standard measure of short-term retention is the digit-span task, in which the subject is read a series of digits at a rate of about one per second and then asked to repeat them. Digit-span performance varies from person to person, develops with age, and tends to peak at around seven to ten digits. Suppose that we are confronted with the fact that Chinese children have consistently longer digit spans than American children do. Does this fact reflect superior short-term memory physiology, greater experience with numbers, some specific memory skill that Chinese children have mastered, or something else? Stigler, Lee, and Stevenson (1986) were able to show that the difference is almost completely accounted for by a physiologically rooted connection between short-term retention and auditory duration: Chinese digit names are pronounced more quickly, and therefore a greater number of digit names can be pronounced in a fixed time period. When the auditory time span was controlled, short-term retention in the two groups was equal. This is a simple but profound example of a case where a great deal of speculation and controversy about cross-ethnic and cross-cultural variation was cut short by the application of a theory and by findings that originated in seemingly dry laboratory studies of memory.

This does not mean that there is no room for cultural and educational influences on short-term memory performance. The potentially enormous scope of such influences is perhaps best illustrated by another laboratory study (Chase and Ericsson, 1981). Chase and Ericsson paid a single undergraduate volunteer to come to their laboratory and practice the digit-span task in one-hour sessions several days a week for over two years. With about 250 hours of practice, the subject increased his average digit span from seven to eighty. If one looked at his performance alone, it appeared that the subject had increased his short-term memory span just as he had built up his endurance and leg muscles in training for another of his activities, long-distance running. By interviewing the subject and putting him through further controlled tests, however, Chase and Ericsson were able to show that his improvement was entirely due to his invention of a scheme for interpreting the sequences of digits as times in foot races and organizing the times into a set of hierarchical groups. He encoded sequences of digits, such as "9 4 6 2," into running times, such as "a two-mile time of 9:46.2," and he inserted each time into a slot in a well-established grouping structure, such as "the first time in the second group of three times." His mnemonic technique exploited a known phenomenon: that short-term memory performance is affected by a person's ability to relate incoming information to well-established knowledge. This study is a dramatic illustration that much of the cognitive variation we see among individuals and cultures is the result of the emergence of culturally transmittable cognitive skills from a universal, complex, and adaptive biological base.

The example illustrates the way in which my course in cognitive psychology is an exercise in multiple levels of analysis. When we confront the cognitive capacities of the individual, we simultaneously confront a biological structure, a personal history of experience, and a cultural setting that has shaped that experience. Our understanding of the individual's performance is a joint product of our understanding of the constraints and potentials of biology, of the way a given culture has exploited biological possibilities, and of the individual's more or less industrious and creative transformation of the biological and cultural materials he or she has been granted.

My general point is that rigorous focus on the meaningful mental activity and behavior of the individual is precisely what produces creative tension among levels of analysis in psychology, as well as among research strategies that emphasize factors of biology, culture, or personal history. In psychology, the reductive tendencies of any one approach are always subject to criticism from other perspectives. One consequence is that the study of psychology is an excellent way of approaching certain questions that are at the center of liberal education, classically conceived: What is an individual? What is the human potential?

Inquiry in Cognitive Psychology

In one sense, cognitive psychology is the study of the structures and processes underlying human thought, memory, attention, language, perception, and learning. The necessity of multiple levels of analysis stressed in the previous section suggests another profound perspective, however. To study cognition, we must establish a conceptual framework that links mind and body. Cognitive psychology is not only the study of cognitive capacities; it is also the empirical study of the mind-body problem. At the heart of the discipline is the question of how meaning can emerge from mere matter. At a young age, I became convinced that the key to meaning was form and the rule-governed transformation of form. The first examples that impressed me were the grammatical structure of sentences, the formal structure of logically sound arguments, the harmonic structures underlying jazz improvisation, and the compositional structures of abstract paintings. A corollary mystery that emerged from these early examples was the remarkable diversity and beauty that could be built on seemingly simple principles. While in high school, I was impressed first by Euclidean geometry and then by Bertrand Russell's claim that all of mathematics and perhaps even all of thought and meaning could be built up from a handful of simple logical principles. I was enthralled and mystified by the creative powers of rigorously classical, almost minimalist, jazz artists, such as Louis Armstrong and Lester Young. I could see that what they were doing was based on simple principles, but they never failed to surprise me. My interest in psychology developed out of this fascination with the patterns that underlie the meaning and diversity of our thought and behavior.

The view that cognitive psychology is about relationships among matter, form, and meaning is quite abstract. It is parallel to abstract statements that can be made about the underlying questions of other disciplines (What is the nature of matter and energy? What is the nature of life?). In spite of their abstractness, such views have a fundamental power to excite intellectual curiosity. In a sense, modern biology begins with the rejection of vitalism and is sustained by fascination with how life can be founded on inert matter. Analogously, modern psychology begins precisely with the rejection of dualistic accounts of the relation between body and spirit and is sustained by the drive to reconcile them scientifically. Freud, Piaget, the Gestalt psychologists, and the more theoretically minded behaviorists were all driven by this issue. Contemporary cognitive psychology continues the tradition, armed with a less reductionist approach and with vastly improved methods.

The course in cognitive psychology and a topic like human memory invoke fundamental questions about the biological and social, about mind and matter, to link the levels of analysis and to motivate the laboratory research that must be done to sort out competing theories. For each topic in the course, I give a speculative introduction to the ways in which a physical system can accomplish particular symbolic functions. I then tie the various strands and levels of empirical research to the core questions about symbolic representation and process.

To return to the example of memory and the memory performance of Chinese and American children on mathematical tasks, it has also been noted that Chinese children are able to hold mental arithmetic problems in mind by imagining the problems being done on an abacus. A correct analysis of this skill depends in part on questions about whether the imagination involved is a specifically visual system. The analysis thus depends on deep theoretical and empirical questions concerning what it means for a cognitive process to be visual and how we go about showing that a process is visual.

Similarly, analyzing the spectacular digit-span skill of the student runner depends on moving behind surface memory performance to a theory of underlying transient and permanent memory processes and their interrelations. Many other kinds of data then come into play. For example, the notion of a distinctive physiological process at the interface between transient mental activation and long-term memory is supported by research with neurological patients who retain the ability to learn sensorimotor skills (such as swinging a golf club) and much of their normal intelligence, but who lose the ability to retain new autobiographical and factual knowledge. These patients have a massive anterograde amnesia for all that has happened in their lives since they sustained their brain damage. Their condition not only supports one class of theories about long-term memory, but the cessation of their self-development also confirms connections between memory and personality that were explored earlier in this century by Freud and Proust.

Empirical Research

I have already suggested that observation is a distinct mode of imagination. Psychology provides an excellent opportunity for teaching the observational aspects of inquiry because there are no strong technical barriers to undergraduates' empirical research. Many studies at the center of the field can be done either with no equipment or in a small laboratory equipped with moderately priced equipment. The techniques consist largely of the principles of experimental design and statistics, which undergraduates can begin to master fairly easily.

I have tried to do everything I can to encourage students at all levels to do their own empirical studies, especially experiments. Hampshire's Division I project requirement and undergraduate thesis requirement lend themselves to this emphasis. In addition, every student in my intermediate course on research methods is required to do an original experiment for the term project. The course also systematically covers professional standards of design, execution, analysis, and writing.

Training in and experience with the experimental method can be extremely valuable for thinking about any domain. The importance of empirical observation and the logic of inference seem to emerge with unique clarity in experimental research. By learning the practical steps required to arrive at an explanation through the systematic manipulation of variables, randomization, careful sampling, and the inclusion of control conditions, one can learn how to think about more complex situations, where experiments are not possible. By experiencing once or twice the pleasant and unpleasant surprises that experimental data can hold for one's hypotheses, one learns that one should always look and work on new ways of looking. The accompanying logic of statistical inference holds additional general lessons, such as about the importance of sample size and measures of variability.

My belief in the potential importance of this kind of training has been reinforced by a rapidly accumulating body of research on everyday human inference and the development of what Piaget called formal operations. Although the reasoning capacities that evolution has provided us seem good enough to get us around most of the time, these capacities are severely limited when they are evaluated with respect to reasonable criteria of rationality. People have a strong tendency to ignore sample size, variability, base rates, sampling distortions, and so on. They have a tendency to fail to reason from the contrapositive in inductive situations. They tend to interpret correlation as evidence for causation. This list could be extended.

These shortcomings of the intuitive scientist can be at least partially overcome through explicit training in the experimental method and in statistics. (One of the sobering findings of the research is that even professional statisticians and scientists tend to make the same errors, if they are not extremely careful to avoid them.) I now begin my course on research methods with material on the shortcomings of the intuitive scientist, rather than with the simplistic normative material from the traditional philosophy of science that appears in textbooks. Illustration of the strengths and pitfalls of informal inference provides better motivation for students to learn about experimental research and statistics.

Teaching inquiry is the hardest challenge a teacher faces. I do not really know how often I have succeeded. There seems to be no formula for success, and failure with at least some students is always possible. Trying to teach inquiry has helped me keep my own inquiring spirit alive, which in turn helps me to recognize nascent intellectual curiosity and excitement in my students.

References

Chase, W. G., and Ericsson, K. A. "Skilled Memory." In J. R. Anderson (ed.), *Cognitive Skills and Their Acquisition.* Hillsdale, N.J.: Lawrence Erlbaum Associates, 1981.

Stigler, J. W., Lee, S., and Stevenson, H. W. "Digit Memory in Chinese and English: Evidence for a Temporally Limited Store." *Cognition,* 1986, *23,* 1-20.

Neil A. Stillings, professor of psychology, has taught at Hampshire College since 1971. He did his undergraduate work at Amherst College and received his Ph.D. from Stanford University. His main interests are visual perception and cognition, the psychology of language, and the foundations of cognitive science.

Early twentieth-century literature on natural history raises issues of the proper relationship between people and nature in ways that are especially useful for encouraging students to think seriously about current environmental debates and their own beliefs about nature.

Views of Nature:
The Environment,
Values, and Literature

Ralph Lutts

Nature is such a complex idea and phenomenon that it can be defined, approached, and experienced in many ways. Different views of nature represent different facets of our experience and understanding of our environment. Everyone concerned about environmental issues needs to be able to identify and understand the different conceptions and values that underlie different stances toward nature. The absence of such understanding is a fundamental source of disagreement about environmental issues.

A principal goal of my course, "Views of Nature," is to alert students to the existence and significance of this sort of analysis. The course, which I taught at Hampshire College for a number of years, examines the character and history of literary natural history and surveys many of its significant American authors and works, emphasizing the twentieth century. By reflecting on the views of nature represented in the writings of such literary naturalists as John Muir, Henry Beston, Aldo Leopold, Loren Eiseley, and Annie Dillard, students come to grips with questions of values.

In doing so, they confront their own biases and presuppositions that shape and sometimes distort their perceptions and decisions; that is, students examine their own psychological and cultural agendas and over-

F. S. Weaver (ed.). *Promoting Inquiry in Undergraduate Learning.*
New Directions for Teaching and Learning, no. 38. San Francisco: Jossey-Bass, Summer 1989.

come, rather than succumb to, a narrow view of the world and what it can become. This process is necessary to achieve the open-mindedness needed for understanding and evaluating views that are different from their own and avoiding simplistic dichotomies. The study of nature literature is a useful exercise because students usually respect all the authors' views of nature, despite their great diversity. The course promotes students' reflection through readings, class discussions, writing assignments, and values-clarification exercises.

The literature that we read in the course also constitutes a fascinating chapter in American cultural history. Although I use them for broader purposes, these writings give students insight into environmental history and promote informed appreciation for the complexity of environmental issues. Many current environmental concerns, and even the terms in which they are debated, were also current early in the century—a surprise for many young environmentalists, who often lack historical perspective.

Working with nature literature has another benefit as well. The task of the literary naturalist is to report his or her experience of nature to the reader. The report must be grounded in careful and accurate observations of nature. This alone, however, is not sufficient; the author must also be faithful to the experience of nature. What is reported is nature as it has touched the heart and mind of the writer. It is not simply an objective report; it is also the expression of a creative interplay between author and environment. The literary naturalist is one of the few people professionally required to combine the perceptions of both scientist and poet, and study of nature writing is a study of this interplay. A student who steps out of the woods, sits down, and writes a piece of literary natural history is engaging in this interplay in an educationally profound manner, for he or she is beginning to integrate thoughts, feelings, and actions. This is a step toward reuniting the rational, emotional, and physical aspects of our being, among which our culture long ago drove a wedge. This reunion is an important and necessary step toward dealing with environmental problems.

Readings

This course requires a good deal of reading. My students read about a book per week, plus selections from a variety of sources. I want them to gain a good grasp of the range of nature literature, its diversity and significant themes, and its important books and authors. The amount of material covered places quite a burden on them, however, and I have found that I must highlight specific parts of each book for them to focus on; otherwise, it is difficult to ensure that they will be properly prepared for each class. It is also helpful to suggest study questions for them to keep in mind as they read. The following books and articles have often been used in the course, although not all have been used each time it was taught. An additional bibliography can be found in Waage (1985), an excellent resource for anyone teaching environmental literature.

We generally begin with Aldo Leopold's *A Sand County Almanac and Sketches Here and There*. I assign only the almanac section. This is an enjoyable and accessible piece, and many of my students are already familiar with it, which makes it easier to begin analyzing the themes and structure of the writing. With this as an example of nature writing, we can begin to ask, "What is a literary naturalist, and what is he or she trying to do?" In preparations for this discussion, I have my students read John Burroughs's introduction to *Wake Robin*, the introduction to *The Best Nature Writing of Joseph Wood Krutch*, and the introduction to John Steinbeck's *The Log from the Sea of Cortez*. I sometimes include the first chapter of Donald Worster's *Nature's Economy: The Roots of Ecology*. I also distribute a collection of definitions of the term *naturalist,* which I have culled from a variety of sources. I underscore the distinctions among a literary naturalist, a research naturalist, and an interpretive naturalist.

Since I want my students to use the literature as a vehicle for reflecting on their own experiences of nature, I employ a number of books that include biographical or autobiographical elements. Paul Brooks's *The House of Life: Rachel Carson at Work* concentrates on Carson as a writer, and a substantial part of the book consists of excerpts from her work. Sally Carrighar's autobiography, *Home to the Wilderness*, follows her life to the writing of *One Day on Beetle Rock*, which we also read. *The Night Country*, by Loren Eiseley, includes a good deal of autobiographical material, as does much of his other writing. Many of the other books that I have used, although not autobiographies, do include the presence of the author, who reports his or her experiences. It is relatively easy to turn the discussion of these books to the students' experiences by asking such questions as "Does this ring true in terms of your experience? Have any of you experienced something like this?"

I have also found it useful to contrast works and authors. John Burroughs and John Muir, for example, were nature writers, contemporaries, and friends, yet they differ considerably in what they write about and in writing style. Muir strides across glaciers and mountaintops, while Burroughs stops at the edge of a country road to contemplate a flower. Edwin Way Teale's collection of Muir's writings, *The Wilderness World of John Muir,* is a good anthology. I have not found a satisfactory collection of Burroughs's writings and have relied on selected essays from various volumes. Henry Beston's *The Outermost House: A Year of Life on the Great Beach of Cape Cod*, provides a good contrast to Leopold's *A Sand County Almanac*. Beston's approach to nature is largely esthetic, while Leopold sees nature ecologically. Another good contrasting set is Annie Dillard's *Pilgrim at Tinker Creek,* Edward Abbey's *Desert Solitaire: A*

Season in the Wilderness, and just about anything by Loren Eiseley (I have generally used either *The Immense Journey* or *The Night Country*). Dillard's breathless natural theology, Abbey's macho and misanthropic ecoanarchism, and Eiseley's immersion in geological time and the plight of consciousness provide a great deal of material for discussion.

Interest in homesteading and back-to-the-land movements provides an opportunity to explore pastoral themes and examine some of the literature of rural life. The material that we have used includes excerpts from Henry Beston's *Northern Farm: A Chronicle of Maine,* Hal Borland's *Countryman: A Summary of Belief,* John Burroughs's *Leaf and Tendril,* and David Grayson's *Adventures in Contentment,* David Shi's *The Simple Life: Plain Living and High Thinking in American Culture* provides a useful perspective on this theme.

We also examine a debate, from the first decade of the twentieth century, over the accuracy of the natural history reported by a number of literary naturalists. William J. Long, who is now forgotten, received the brunt of the criticism, although some was also directed toward Ernest Thompson Seton (*Trail of an Artist Naturalist*) and other authors. John Burroughs and Theodore Roosevelt were the chief architects of the debate, which has come to be known as the "nature fakers" controversy. They accused the nature fakers of fabricating tall tales, represented as absolutely true, to sell their books. Lutts (1981) reviews the debate and identifies the underlying issues.

An examination of this affair provides an excellent opportunity to discuss the literary naturalist's responsibilities, both as an observer of nature and as a creator of literature. The line between who was right and who was wrong was not so clearly defined as Burroughs and Roosevelt thought, and classroom discussion can become quite lively. One of the underlying issues of the debate was just how much we can empathize with animals. Another was the extent to which a literary naturalist can take liberties with facts and observations. There is bound to be disagreement on these issues in any group of students.

The last book that I assign for the course is John Steinbeck's *Cannery Row.* This is not a work of literary natural history, but it incorporates most of the themes that are likely to have been developed in the course. My purposes in assigning this book are to connect the specialized context of the course to the wider body of literature that my students will encounter and to demonstrate that they do not have to limit themselves to works of literary naturalists in order to discover an author's views of nature. Alexander's (1972) critical essay is quite useful in helping students understand what Steinbeck has done.

At some point early in the course, I have the students read a particularly syrupy, sentimental piece of writing. Although it is relevant to the themes of the course, it is just awful. My students generally share my feelings must have some merit if it was assigned. A discussion of this reluctance helps to loosen their tongues and gives them some confidence in their own opinions. (The reading also provides an example to which I can refer when they write equally syrupy and sentimental essays of their own.)

My library reserve list of suggested readings contains scholarly works related to nature writing, attitudes toward nature, and environmental history, including Foerster ([1923] 1958), Hicks (1924), Huth ([1957] 1972), Marx (1964), and Nash (1982). The most comprehensive (although popularized) review of American literary naturalists is Paul Brooks's *Speaking for Nature: How Literary Naturalists from Henry Thoreau to Rachel Carson Have Shaped America.* I also include published journals of authors including Emerson, Thoreau, Muir, and Burroughs.

Expectations and Evaluation

I expect the following work from every student who will receive an evaluation for the course.

Participation. Each student is expected to attend classes regularly, keep up with assignments, and participate in class discussions.

Journal. Each student maintains a personal journal in which he or she reflects on experiences in nature and responds to the readings and class discussions. I encourage students to use the journals in whatever ways will help them reflect on the course and on their related thoughts and experiences. There are two general categories of entry. The first consists of any that are generated on the student's own initiative. The second category consists of entries made at my request. Sometimes, for example, I give students specific study questions to reflect on in their journals, in preparation for a class discussion. The journals, however, are theirs, and students should not feel constraints on what they write. I explain that the journals will be evaluated two or three times during the semester only to determine that a sincere effort is being made and that students will not be evaluated on their writing or spelling or on the details of their entries. I also suggest that students look at some of the published journals on the reserve list.

I also may point out sections of students' journals that provide good material for nature essays or that are examples of particularly good writing. Many of my students, if not most, have difficulty writing polished essays. It is surprising, though, how much good material does appear in their journals.

Biographical Presentations. Students take turns preparing biographical presentations about the authors who are going to be discussed. These are not written assignments, although they do require good outlines. The students act as teaching assistants during discussion of their particular authors; in effect, each student becomes a resident expert on a particlar authors; in effect, each student becomes a resident expert on a particular writer. I try to give each student the assistance necessary to locate useful biographical sources and to prepare an effective presentation. Generally, this takes more time than doing the presentation myself, but it is often of considerable value to the student.

Childhood Memories. Each student writes an essay evoking the memory of a childhood experience of nature. (I will describe this assignment later, when I examine teaching methods and activities.)

Nature Writing. Each student is expected to produce a polished piece of nature writing. The journals can be very useful sources of ideas and material. I ask them to write about personal experiences in nature. This piece is not a science paper, although it must be factually accurate, grounded in experience rather than in imagination. When I receive the papers, I place them in a folder on reserve in the library, and the students read one another's work, which motivates them to make extra efforts and provides an opportunity for them to learn from others and evaluate their own work in relation to the rest of the class. In class discussions of the essays, we attempt to find common themes and relate the students' work to that of the authors whom we have been reading; I do not permit them to pick one another's work apart.

Research Paper. Each student writes a polished research paper on a chosen topic related to nature literature. The biographical presentations and journals may provide ideas and material. Students are asked to speak with me about their ideas before they go too far. Again, the papers are placed on reserve in the library, and the last few classes are devoted to discussing them. In this case, each student prepares a class presentation that summarizes his or her paper. I organize the presentations in a sequence that seems to make sense and promises to keep the discussion going.

Methods and Activities

Most class meetings consist of discussions of the readings. I try not to lecture very much, and when I do, my lectures are relatively short and designed to set the readings in a broader historical or literary context, or to expand on issues raised in discussion. From time to time, I change the pace by employing exercises to help my students explore their own values and by taking them out of the classroom. These exercises are a very important part of the course, because they connect abstract concepts with students' personal values and experiences. I will briefly describe the exercises here; Lutts (1985) provides greater detail.

Ideal Home. In one of the first class meetings, I employ a values-clarification exercise in which my students fantasize about an ideal living situation. The purpose of this exercise is to help them recognize their own landscape and life-style biases. I begin by explaining that I want to ask them some questions about their ideal style of living. First, however, they must all put some thought into just what that ideal might be. I ask them to sit back, relax, and close their eyes. When they are ready, I begin to talk them through a fantasy trip to an ideal home. It is important to explain to them that there are no "correct" images, as long as they are making a sincere effort to participate.

After they have visualized their fantasies, I ask them to describe the fantasies by writing down their answers to a number of questions. This material fuels a discussion of their own values and biases, as revealed by their images of their ideal homes. (The written answers are not handed in but are added to the journals.)

Picture Show. This exercise is a good follow-up to the first one, and sometimes I manage to do both in one class session. I ask my students to search through their collections of snapshots and slides and select five photographs of places that are special to them, places that have happy or pleasant associations (magazine pictures are also acceptable).

The students begin by taking turns showing their photographs to the group and explaining how they were selected. After the presentation, I broaden the discussion by asking questions about the similarities and differences among the pictures, about the numbers of people and buildings in them and their relationships to one another and to the landscape, about and how the pictures are related to their responses to the Ideal Home exercise. It is important to conclude each exercise by explaining that its purpose is to help students become aware of their environmental values and biases.

Childhood Memories. Some of the readings include authors' reminiscences of their childhoods. It has been useful to follow such readings with discussions of students' childhood involvement with nature. Good introductory readings for this discussion include excerpts from Loren Eiseley's *The Night Country,* Pablo Neruda's *Memoirs,* John Muir's *The Story of My Boyhood and Youth,* John Burroughs's *My Boyhood,* Ernest Seton's *Trail of an Artist Naturalist,* and Elizabeth Coatsworth's *Personal Geography: Almost an Autobiography.*

To prepare for class, I ask students to pick a specific time and place in childhood in which they felt very close to nature and to write about those experiences in their journals. I also ask them to prepare large maps, faithful to their subjective childhood experiences, depicting the landscapes of those experiences and including the people, places, landmarks, and routes that were important to them.

Students then take turns displaying their maps and describing their childhood landscapes. Such personal reflection and conversation generally stimulate a great deal of enthusiasm. I take advantage of it by asking each student to write an essay in which he or she evokes in the reader the special qualities of the childhood landscape that make it personally significant. In writing the essay, the student may draw on journal entries, maps, and class discussion. This writing assignment was first given at the request of my students, which indicates the enthusiasm that this exercise can kindle.

Getting Outside. It is useful to get out of the classroom and into the primary source—nature. This provides a welcome break in the course format and grounds the class in the reality underlying all the words. I generally take my students on nature walks around campus. These walks can build on their interest in the literature, particularly if I am able to show them things in nature about which the authors have written. I also have my students do some "Seton watching." This practice, named after Ernest Thompson Seton, has each of them find a private place to sit quietly and watch the natural world around them. It is the passive counterpart of a nature walk; they wait for nature to come to them.

Results

This is a course on natural history, literature, and writing, and each discipline has intrinsic value. Nevertheless, its principal purpose lies beyond any of these three facets. The varied assemblage of books, exercises, writing assignments, and class discussions is held together by continual reference to basic questions. What is the author's special view of nature? What is the view of the individual student? What are the implications of these views? What alternative views are available? The combination of encountering diverse points of view on nature, using these points of view as a basis of individual reflection, engaging others through class discussions, and using both analytical and personal forms of writing has proved effective in encouraging students to take an important step toward more open-minded inquiry into environmental problems and their solutions.

References

Abbey, E. *Desert Solitaire: A Season in the Wilderness.* New York: McGraw-Hill, 1968.

Alexander, S. "*Cannery Row:* Steinbeck's Pastoral Poem." In R. M. Davis (ed.), *Steinbeck: A Collection of Critical Essays.* Englewood Cliffs, N.J.: Prentice-Hall, 1972.

Beston, H. *The Outermost House: A Year of Life on the Great Beach of Cape Cod.* New York: Doubleday, 1928.

Beston, H. *Northern Farm: A Chronicle of Maine.* New York: Ballantine Books, 1972. (Originally published 1948.)

Borland, H. *Countryman: A Summary of Belief.* Philadelphia: Lippincott, 1965.

Brooks, P. *The House of Life: Rachel Carson at Work.* Boston: Houghton Mifflin, 1972.

Brooks, P. *Speaking for Nature: How Literary Naturalists from Henry Thoreau to Rachel Carson Have Shaped America.* Boston: Houghton Mifflin, 1980.

Burroughs, J. *Wake Robin.* Boston: Houghton Mifflin, 1895.

Burroughs, J. *Leaf and Tendril.* Boston: Houghton Mifflin, 1908.

Burroughs, J. *My Boyhood.* New York: Doubleday, 1922.

Carrighar, S. *One Day on Beetle Rock.* New York: Knopf, 1944.

Carrighar, S. *Home to the Wilderness.* Boston: Houghton Mifflin, 1973.

Coatsworth, E. *Personal Geography: Almost an Autobiography.* Brattleboro, Vt.: Stephen Greene Press, 1976.

Dillard, A. *Pilgrim at Tinker Creek.* New York: Harper's Magazine Press, 1974.

Eiseley, L. *The Immense Journey.* New York: Random House, 1957.

Eiseley, L. *The Night Country.* New York: Scribner's, 1971.

Foerster, N. *Nature in American Literature: Studies in the Modern View of Nature.* New York: Russell & Russell, 1958. (Originally published 1923.)

Grayson, D. [R. S. Baker]. *Adventures in Contentment.* New York: Doubleday, 1907.

Hicks, P. M. *The Development of the Natural History Essay in American Literature.* Philadelphia: University of Pennsylvania Press, 1924.

Huth, H. *Nature and the American.* Lincoln: University of Nebraska Press, 1972. (Originally published 1957.)

Krutch, J. W. *The Best Nature Writing of Joseph Wood Krutch.* New York: Pocket Books, 1971.

Leopold, A. *A Sand County Almanac and Sketches Here and There.* New York: Oxford University Press, 1949.

Lutts, R. H. "The Nature Fakers: Conflicting Perspectives of Nature." In R. C. Schultz and J. D. Hughes (eds.), *Ecological Consciousness: Essays from the Earthday X Colloquium.* Washington, D.C.: University Press of America, 1981.

Lutts, R. H. "Views of Nature: An Interplay of Personal Reflection and Literary Natural History." In F. O. Waage (ed.), *Teaching Environmental Literature: Materials, Methods, Resources.* New York: Modern Language Association of America, 1985.

Marx, L. *The Machine in the Garden: Technology and the Pastoral Ideal in America.* New York: Oxford University Press, 1964.

Muir, J. *The Story of My Boyhood and Youth.* Boston: Houghton Mifflin, 1913.

Nash, R. *Wilderness and the American Mind.* (3rd ed.) New Haven, Conn.: Yale University Press, 1982.

Neruda, P. *Memoirs.* New York: Farrar, Straus & Giroux, 1977.

Seton, E. T. *Trail of an Artist Naturalist.* New York: Scribner's, 1940.

Shi, D. E. *The Simple Life: Plain Living and High Thinking in American Culture.* New York: Oxford University Press, 1985.

Steinbeck, J. *Cannery Row.* New York: Bantam Books, 1971.

Steinbeck, J. *The Log from the Sea of Cortez.* New York: Bantam Books, 1971.

Teale, E. W. (ed.). *The Wilderness World of John Muir.* Boston: Houghton Mifflin, 1954.

Waage, F. O. (ed.). *Teaching Environmental Literature: Materials, Methods, Resources.* New York: Modern Language Association of America, 1985.

Worster, D. *Nature's Economy: The Roots of Ecology.* San Francisco: Sierra Club Books, 1977.

Ralph Lutts, adjunct associate professor of environmental studies, has taught at Hampshire College since 1973. He earned his B.A. at Trinity University and his Ph.D. at the University of Massachusetts, Amherst. Since 1980, he has been director of the Massachusetts Audubon Society's Blue Hills Trailside Museum in Milton, Massachusetts, and he is president of the Alliance of Environmental Education.

Students see mathematical tools for the life sciences and social sciences as useful, interesting, and beautiful when they learn to use them in realistic applications and when computers do the calculations.

Calculus and More: Computers, Finite Mathematics, and an Innovative Service Course

Kenneth R. Hoffman

Over the last few years, the mathematics faculty at Hampshire College has revised the service course for life science and social science students, to take better advantage of the computational power available from computers. For math and physical science majors, we teach an intensive calculus course whose content is roughly equivalent to that taught in most other schools. For all other science concentrators and quantitative-minded social scientists (and curious humanists), we have developed a fundamentally new course. It is not calculus or finite math or computer science, but a combination.

Our typical student is a sophomore going on in the biological or health sciences, although a broad range of other disciplinary interests (economics, music, geology, and so on) is also represented. Seldom has more than 15 percent of the class studied calculus in high school. A larger percentage has had some experience with computers; but for more than half the students, this course is the first extensive experience with computers and programming.

F. S. Weaver (ed.). *Promoting Inquiry in Undergraduate Learning.*
New Directions for Teaching and Learning, no. 38. San Francisco: Jossey-Bass, Summer 1989.

New Views of Calculus and Computers

The first step in this process of course revision was to acknowledge that calculus has always been fairly inappropriate for life scientists and social scientists. Like mathematics teachers throughout the nation, we did our best to concoct "relevant" examples, but we and the students knew that the students would never use a large part of what they were expected to learn. We excused ourselves by saying it would not do them any harm and might teach them to think analytically. This excuse is no longer adequate.

Thinking of the computer simply as a way to make existing math courses more relevant and interesting seriously underestimates the fundamental shift in the kinds of mathematics that computers have now made available to practicing scientists. The computer has enabled us, to a considerably greater extent than we could without electronic computational power, to design a course that develops mathematical skills directly relevant to work in the life and social sciences. Through actively involving students in manipulations and simulations, we enhance their appreciation for the logical and esthetic properties of mathematical tools and their capacity for independent work. The first goal is important in all curricula, and the second and third qualities are vitally important for a college with an inquiry curriculum.

New Content for the Calculus Course

What are the most important tools, skills, and conceptual insights that could reasonably be included in a two-semester sequence? In developing our course, we looked at a number of journals and texts in the relevant fields, to see what tools seemed to be used regularly, we talked to our colleagues in these disciplines and, like all teachers everywhere, relied on our own sense of what would be good for the students. This process has yielded the following observations.

Language Versus Tool. The failure of many math teachers at all levels to distinguish clearly between the role of mathematics as an expressive language and its role as a tool underlies much of the confusion that so many students feel. For example, calculus is ubiquitous, cropping up regularly in all sorts of journals and advanced texts. Nevertheless, its primary role is often to be a language for clearly and concisely expressing the processes and relationships in a problem, rather than to be a tool for solving a problem so expressed. It therefore seems absolutely essential that our students be able to read and write calculus in order to understand thoroughly what is being expressed by sentences like

$$dR/dt = 3R + 7$$

and to perform routine elementary transformations on such sentences.

However, the actual problems so expressed are usually either very simple or essentially unsolvable by the standard tools of calculus. There are few instances where, for instance, partial fractions would be helpful. Similar remarks can be made about linear systems as well.

Differential Equations. The single most common use of calculus is for describing dynamic systems through differential equations. Moreover, these are often not just ordinary differential equations; they may be systems of simultaneous (frequently nonlinear) differential equations. Any course that does not give students a solid feel for such systems and ways of thinking about them, qualitatively and numerically, is seriously inadequate. The traditional division of introductory calculus, into differentiation and integration, is not particular helpful for such problems.

Approximation. Mathematics courses are customarily geared toward finding the right answer to a problem, and students develop a perception that mathematics is only useful in situations with a degree of simplicity and clarity of structure that is rarely found in the life sciences and the social sciences. These fields require a clear understanding of concepts like intelligent estimates, confidence intervals, the trade-off between accuracy of approximation and cost (in computing time or data acquisition), discrete approximations to continuous systems and vice versa, and so on.

Handling Data. Every science student needs a solid grounding in the techniques of displaying, manipulating, and analyzing data. Students who do not know what a t-test is, or (not much better) who know what it is but blindly apply it to all data sets, are simply not prepared to become practicing scientists today.

Modeling. The concept of model building is in vogue these days, but many treatments of the role of modeling place excessive emphasis on its quantitative aspects, giving the impression that modeling is useful only in contexts with atypically simple structures and unusually complete quantitative data. We are in danger of being too influenced by our strong historical ties with physics, where the fit between the model and reality is often so close that we identify the two. This is rarely the case in "messier" disciplines; in fact, the construction of models has always been the heart of much natural science and social science. It is important for students to understand the role of models and the modeling process, even in settings where relationships must be guessed at, where parameters are loosely approximated, and where quantitative predictions are impossible. Much more attention needs to be paid to the qualitative features of classes of models—features like the existence of stable points and cycles, robustness, and order-of-magnitude estimates.

Linear Systems. Emphasis on handling data, approximations, and modeling leads to a strong need for facility in working with linear systems and their transformations. Again, a clear distinction can be made between the language and the tool. Students have to be able to think in terms of vectors and matrices, both geometrically and analytically. With the increased study, in many sciences, of multicomponent systems, a Markov process becomes a superb organizational concept. As the problems tackled by scientists become more sophisticated, there will be an increasing need to command the tools of eigenvectors, eigenfunctions, and inverse calculations, and to be comfortable with the concept of transformation.

The Role of Computers. The presence of computers has shifted many of these topics—Markov process, numerical solutions to systems of differential equations, modeling, and so on—from the esoteric fringes of many disciplines to a central place among the tools needed for dealing with basic problems. Most students will be convinced of this centrality, however, only if these topics are presented with "real enough" (usually meaning computationally "messy") examples. Many students, alas, see neither beauty nor relevance in the working out by hand of the steady-state solution of a simple-minded, three-state regular Markov process. Use ten or fifteen states, though, with calculations done by computer, and students see both beauty and power. In fact, in much of applied mathematics, the beauty of the underlying structure is increasingly apparent to the students of today, who are relieved of the drudgery of the tedious calculations that took so much time in the "bad old days." Therefore it is essential to develop these topics, using the computer throughout. It must be emphasized, though, that this does not necessarily mean teaching computer programming. With the increasing availability of suitably powerful languages, software packages, and professional computer-consulting services, it is possible for even the more quantitative scientists to function effectively, without ever having to write programs.

Elegance Versus Brute Force. Many techniques in classical mathematics were developed to simplify the life of the poor devil who had to do the calculations. While these techniques are often very beautiful and clever, they require a lot of time to master. In addition, they often require the breaking down of a topic into lots of special cases, which thereby obscure much of the underlying coherence and unity of the topic. Ordinary differential equations are an excellent example. If we are willing to forgo the elegance of these techniques, however, and substitute massive computing power, we can now introduce naive audiences to topics that heretofore were considered advanced. For instance, if we are interested in the limiting behavior of a Markov process, we can simply take the transition matrix to a large power, or we can model several hundred iterates of the process on the computer. This brute-force approach gives students a deeper and more immediate understanding of the underlying concepts than do classical approaches, in which the subtle chain of reasoning required to understand a computational technique can obscure the basic simplicity of the problem.

Our Course

The course we have developed at Hampshire attempts to incorporate all these points. A rough breakdown of the first semester is as follows:

- Introductory review of algebra, functions, graphing, and curve sketching; elementary approximation techniques (four classes)
- Introduction to computer modeling and simulation, using the language APL (eight classes)
- Introduction to calculus and differential equations, with emphasis on the language of calculus, on graphical and qualitative analyses of dynamic systems, and on numerical methods for estimating solutions (sixteen classes)
- Matrices and arrays, linear algebra, input-output models, and Markov processes (eleven classes).

Although we are beginning substantial revision of the second-semester course, in which about half the students continue, it still resembles a more traditional linear algebra course. Therefore, I will limit my evaluative comments to the first-semester course.

Results

Since we began with a fairly jaundiced view of the traditional calculus sequence's usefulness for our target audience, we view even modest accomplishments as improvements. Our sense is that the course is working quite well. Students typically emerge with a broad perspective on the ways in which mathematics can be used in their disciplines, greatly enhanced confidence in their own ability to comprehend and use the relevant tools, and an ability to use computers to model processes and make estimates. Let me turn to the different components of our course and present the key issues and insights.

The Computer. In this course, the computer is viewed strictly as a glorified calculator, a tool that lets us do lots of powerful mathematics because it does all the tedious calculations. This is not a computer course, and we spend virtually no time discussing structured programs or other aspects of good programming style. Ideally, students do no programming at all but use predeveloped software, for two reasons. First, programming is a major obstacle for many students and prevents a number of otherwise quite capable students from using the mathematical tools effectively. Second, we believe that there will be widely available, sophisticated software packages for most of the specific applications our students are likely to need once they are on their own.

Our goal has been to get the students to feel comfortable going to the computer for computations and calling up stored programs (some written by previous generations of students). We chose the language APL precisely because one can use the computer for weeks, without having to talk about programming: The language has built-in functions to do all the basic operations we need. The student can sum series, approximate integrals by Simpson's rule, invert matrices, throw darts and count how many fall under a given curve, and perform many other operations, all with straightforward one-line APL commands. When we reach points where programs are necessary, such as for finding solutions to differential equations numerically, we give prototype programs (rarely over ten lines long), which the students then adapt to the parameters of the specific problems they are working on.

We had been using a VAX 750, but now we have moved to micros (the sign-on procedure with the VAX, and the layers of interaction and associated layers of error messages, are sufficiently inhibiting, especially in the initial stages, to justify the change). The students finish the course feeling quite comfortable with the computer.

In the sections on computer models and simulations, probably only a third of the students are able, by the end of the semester, to develop their own programs from scratch. The rest of the class can take a model that someone else has written and, by editing the program, use it as a tool to explore the impact of changing the boundary conditions, to see how sensitive the model is to the parameters, and to generate data to get an overview of stability questions and asymptotic behavior. Given the amount of time available for developing modeling techniques, this is probably the best that can reasonably be expected. Simulations and modeling are explored again in the second semester.

Statistics. One of our early decisions was not to include statistical techniques in this course, beyond elementary descriptive statistics. We believe that a solid grounding in statistical analysis is so important for our students that they need to spend a full semester on it in a separate course.

Calculus. There are topics that we do not cover. We do not prove the basic rules for derivatives (although there are exercises designed to lead the students to make intelligent guesses about these rules), nor do we use these rules extensively in exercises. We do not mention the mean value theorem or discuss integration techniques. We do spend a lot of time using calculus to make estimates, with what used to be called the differential and the focal point, although we do go on to discuss Newton's Method and Taylor Series.

The major goal of this part of the course is to make the students comfortable dealing with systems of differential equations. We develop the idea that differential equations are one of the basic ways in which relationships in the real world can be expressed. The trigonometric and exponential functions are extensively developed as being the solutions to common differential equations, and their properties are deduced from these equations. By the end of this section, students should be able to find equilibrium points, sketch local solutions, use the computer to get numerical solutions and their graphs, explore stability questions, and the like. We use a number of examples, largely drawing from population biology (e.g., the logistic curve and Lotka-Volterra predator-prey models) to develop these concepts.

This is undoubtedly the hardest section of the course, but most of the students are able to master its concepts. While they clearly will not attain the level of sophistication that they would have after four semesters of calculus, they will have sufficient insight to deal intelligently with most of the calculus they are likely to encounter in the professional literature in their fields, a claim that could probably not be made for students completing standard first-year calculus sequences. They will also have had substantial experience in applying and experimenting with nontrivial examples.

Matrices and Linear Algebra. Here is an area that has been transformed by the computer from a collection of interesting theoretical insights to a basic set of tools applicable to almost all sciences. The difference is that we can now routinely handle thirty or forty variables, instead of the three or four we were restricted to twenty years ago, when calculations had to be performed by hand. This increase in complexity means that real problems can now be tackled readily.

We introduce matrices both as devices for displaying and storing data and as algebraic objects that can be added, multiplied, raised to powers, and (sometimes) have inverses. We spend half a class period on how one finds the inverse of a matrix, and we give the students some simple exercises in finding inverses, but all the rest of the time we use the computer to find inverses, products, and powers of matrices. We include the solving of systems of simultaneous equations. We discuss incidence matrices for graphs, transition matrices, and interpretations of the powers of such matrices. We look at matrices for the trophic structure of simple ecosystems, Leslie matrices in population dynamics, and matrices approximating heat flow in two-dimensional systems.

There are two major classes of examples on which we spend a fair amount of time: Markov processes and input-output models. The underlying concepts are straightforward, but—because of the overwhelming computations involved—these examples are almost unteachable to general audiences if no computer is on hand. With computers, though, we have found that students have little difficulty grasping the underlying concepts and interpreting the results of the various manipulations. In fact, this part of the course typically turns out to be the one that the students enjoy most.

It is our overall experience that life science and social science students come out of this course with greater appreciation for the strength and relevance (and hence the beauty) of mathematics, and with more confidence in their ability, than we have typically seen in similar students who have finished traditional calculus courses. While we have tended to adopt a somewhat eighteenth-century approach to math, in our disregard for the niceties of logic and rigor, we have found by the end of the course that students have a context and an interest in the subject that enables them to think about it with insight and pleasure. We believe that the sacrifice of some elegance and rigor is more than compensated by the level of engagement and wide-ranging applicability we have achieved.

Kenneth R. Hoffman, professor of mathematics, taught at Talladega College before joining the Hampshire College faculty in 1970. His undergraduate education was at the College of Wooster, and his graduate work was at Harvard University. His principal teaching interests are mathematical modeling (especially in population biology), algebraic number theory, modern algebra, and natural history.

Bringing together the theories and writings of literature and anthropology teaches students the vital importance of points of view in all texts.

Observer and Observed: Collaboration Between Literature and Anthropology

David E. Smith

Over the past six years, I have worked with Professor Barbara Yngvesson, a cultural anthropologist colleague at Hampshire, to teach a course that joins the literatures and analytical approaches of anthropology with certain texts in English, American, and European literature and modern criticism. In particular, we explore questions of mutual concern to cultural anthropologists and literary critics: problems of the relationship of observer to observed, of author to text, and of audience or reader to text; problems arising from the presumed perspective of an ethnographer or narrator; problems connected with the analysis of literary structure, narration, and strategies; and problems having to do with, on the one hand, the nature of anthropological understanding and, on the other, literary analysis and theory. We approach these questions in both fields from the point of view embodied in the analysis of a text: What kind of text is assumed, how is it produced, what were the authorial intentions, and what kind of description or analysis of the text is to be attempted, and to what end?

In the development of the course we now jointly offer, "Observer and Observed in Literature and Anthropology," we focus on how this com-

F. S. Weaver (ed.). *Promoting Inquiry in Undergraduate Learning.*
New Directions for Teaching and Learning, no. 38. San Francisco: Jossey-Bass, Summer 1989.

bined approach enables us to introduce fruitful new ways to present the understanding of texts. For two years, we were fortunate to have documentary filmmaker and critic Anne Fischel join us. With Anne's help and insight, the course's objectives have been expanded to take into consideration the perspectives of documentary film. With critical material from John Grierson, George Simmel, Elizabeth Fernea, John Marshall, and Fischel herself ("Engagement as an Approach to Documentary Filming"), and with films from a wide variety of sources—from Flaherty to recent experiments putting cameras into the hands of Native Americans—we have benefited extensively from Anne's insight, guidance, and collaboration.

We also pose provocative questions to students about their assumptions of what literature and anthropology are. This approach challenges commonly held assumptions about narrative point of view and stimulates useful debate about authenticity in a work. We apply to the reading of ethnographic description categories and techniques commonly reserved for the analysis of literary work (for example, novel, satire, autobiography). Conversely, we frame questions often connected with an anthropological approach to culture in such a way as to enhance the understanding of fiction.

This approach has proved stimulating for students from a range of disciplines, in the humanities as well as the social sciences, and has helped them develop central questions for advanced study. Our initial interest derived from our awareness—practicing, as we do, in a college that strongly encourages interdisciplinary approaches to teaching—of certain practical problems experienced time and again by anthropologists in the field, writers, journalists, and other investigators who face the often bewildering problems of entering a community, being accepted, and then making sense out of the experience while there and after leaving. In particular, we note the problems surrounding subjectivity and objectivity, as well as questions of whose understanding is being imposed on an experience. Another consideration involves the writer's typical struggle with ethical questions that invariably arise. These concern trust, confidentiality, accurate portrayal, and the use of information.

Narrative as the Basis of Inquiry

The perspectives suggested by the technical discussion of narrative point of view offer a good illustration of our approach. Point of view is usually reserved, in "the rhetoric of fiction," for discussions of where narration originates, but we have used it as a framework for ethnography. In reading Colin Turnbull's controversial portrayal of an African tribe in *The Mountain People* or Jean Briggs's description of Eskimos in *Never in Anger* or Janet Siskind's absorbing description of a South American riverine culture in *To Hunt in the Morning*, it becomes essential to know whose perspective dominates the account. To whom have the ethnographers spoken? How do they introduce and portray "themselves"? What questions did they ask? How long, and under what circumstances, did they visit the community? To what extent is their interpretation of actions and events biased because they have imposed the categories, values, and meanings of one culture on another?

Similarly in literature, the identity of the narrator is often problematic, sometimes intentionally and sometimes characteristically so. The involvement (or lack of involvement) of a narrator in the events of a novel obviously affects the reader's assimilation or interpretation of events in the text and has much to do with the reader's relationship to the text as a production. (This is in contrast to assumptions that the text is either unpremeditated or a naive escape into fantasy.) Deliberate manipulation of narrative point of view—which began in English with the fiction of Defoe and Swift, was developed by Hawthorne, Henry James, and Virginia Woolf, and is pursued constantly in modern literature—enhances "reality," provides verisimilitude, or creates character through distortion and plotted deception. The technique has become commonplace.

Focusing Questions from One Discipline to Another

What we find unique about our work is the constant experimenting to apply analytical questions commonly practiced in one discipline to illuminating material in the other. For example, Turnbull's *The Mountain People* is paired with *Gulliver's Travels*. After we demonstrate, through the use of selected contemporary critical essays, how the character of Gulliver, as narrator, is distinct from his creator Swift, we deliberately propose that the narrator of Turnbull's story is also a contrivance of the author. Students are confronted with the possibility of an invented narrator, a contrived persona. We enhance the effect of this technique by presenting other textual material about the Ik tribe that portrays the culture in quite contradictory terms. This material is first presented as having been written by another distinguished cultural anthropologist (not Turnbull). When the students discover that the contrasting description is also actually by Turnbull, they must deal with this new complexity. In conjunction with the reading of *Gulliver's Travels*, whose narrator is a consciously contrived persona, our inquiry leads to insights about the deeper structure of Turnbull's book as "a text." We raise provocative questions about the ultimate intentions of the author, reopen the issue of self and other in an alien culture, and question the validity of the author's authenticity as he ponders certain profound ethical questions, all mediated by the persona of Turnbull the narrator. Our perspective frees us to ask questions about an ethnography in terms different from those conventionally applicable.

In parallel fashion, when we read *Gulliver's Travels* (without delimiting the historical and literary background necessary to an understanding of the work in conventional terms), we examine the effect of Swift's imposition of his era's assumptions—about savages—on the character of the despicable Yahoos, and we contrast literary descriptions of the savages with those in the accounts of seventeenth- and eighteenth-century traveler-anthropologists. This procedure has the advantage of introducing notions of early ethnographic description and questions of cultural racism, a perspective rarely employed in conventional discussions of Swift in literature classes.

The course allows us to examine other kinds of texts, in which there is significant interplay between careful observation of a culture and narrative invention. Examples include many studies that combine ethnographic description (by an anthropologist in the field) with personal reflection.

Our approach introduces some of the insights of modern literary criticism concerning the "construction of autobiography," the invention—even by the autobiographer, as distinct from the novelist—of a character-narrator who is a reliable witness, and the authorial and editorial decisions that go into the ordering of events, chapter construction, things left out, and so on. We contrast these insights, in the texts under consideration, with discussions of the structures of conventional ethnographies. Our choice of a number of texts by women anthropologists introduces another group of assumptions about women's experience in the field: what is more or less accessible in a culture from the perspective of gender, and what are considered important or unimportant questions. Likewise, in fictional narratives written by women, we can ask some of the same questions, for example, regarding the female narrator and portraits of women in Sarah Orne Jewett's *Country of the Pointed Firs*.

Results

Student response to the course has been extremely positive. It is a distinct advantage to be offering the course at Hampshire, where it can attract concentrators in a wide variety of fields, including anthropology, literary studies and criticism, cultural journalism, film criticism, and writing. The interdisciplinary emphasis of the course is matched by our students' diverse experiences and backgrounds. When possible, we invite guest anthropologists, novelists, and filmmakers to lecture. Short papers and exercises are usually geared to the text in question, but students are encouraged to do longer papers or projects tied to their own central interests.

An additional pedagogical advantage is coteaching. The course demands a full collaborative effort, not one in which an anthropologist lectures for part of a semester and a literary historian for another. Hampshire's unique, nondepartmental structure supports our work. Besides carefully orchestrating individual class sessions to fully exploit our dual presence, we sometimes find it tactically advantageous to disagree openly in class, to challenge each other in order to bring out a further nuance or explanation, and to heighten contrasts or blur distinctions between our separate disciplinary training and experience. Coteaching also enhances the overall resources available to students and heightens the satisfaction that each teacher can derive from a full partnership, shared criticism, and mutual support. In a college that requires periodic performance reviews of all teachers at all ranks, it is encouraging to have one's own teaching reviewed by colleagues who have been full partners in an endeavor, not merely one-time outside visitors to a classroom lecture.

Still another advantage of coteaching across interdisciplinary lines is the intellectual stimulation it provides for the participating colleagues. In this and other courses at Hampshire, collaborations have resulted in new partnerships in research and publication, new directions in scholarship, and, in our case, a reassessment of how texts and materials from a traditional canon can be enlivened by new questions, alternative contexts, and innovative approaches to teaching.

"Observer and Observed in Literature and Anthropology" continues to be offered at Hampshire College. The course has an enduring impact on our perspectives as scholars and on our students' work, for it consistently opens new possibilities for the selection and analysis of texts.

References

Briggs, J. *Never in Anger: Portrait of an Eskimo Family*. Cambridge, Mass.: Harvard University Press, 1970.

Jewett, S. O. *The Country of the Pointed Firs and Other Stories*. New York: W. W. Norton, 1982. (Originally published 1896.)

Siskind, J. *To Hunt in the Morning*. New York: Oxford University Press, 1973.

Swift, J. *Gulliver's Travels*. Baltimore, Md.: Penguin Books, 1970. (Originally published 1726.)

Turnbull, C. *The Mountain People*. New York: Simon & Schuster, 1972.

David E. Smith, professor of English and American Studies and dean of the School of Humanities and Arts, did his undergraduate work at Middlebury College and received his Ph.D. from the University of Minnesota. Before coming to Hampshire College in 1970, he was the director of Indiana University's graduate program in American Studies. His writing and teaching interests are primarily in American social and intellectual attitudes toward land and landscape.

Nothing intrinsically condemns introductory statistics courses in the social sciences to be dull.

Introductory Statistics: Questions, Content, and Approach

Frederick Stirton Weaver

The nineteenth-century English "statistics movement," a product of Victorians' concern with social reform and control, was the primary inspiration for systematically collecting and publishing national social statistics (Cullen, 1975). In the intervening 150 years, the propensity to count everything important has flourished. As a consequence, we are now at the point where so much of our understanding of contemporary social existence is constructed and communicated through the use of statistics that quantitative literacy is crucial for effective participation in social and political life. In our culture, the ability to find and interpret quantitative material is a prerequisite for gaining access to important types of social knowledge, for formulating plausible arguments, and for distinguishing between legitimate and illegitimate use of the statistics with which we are deluged in everyday life.

This importance is reflected in the academy, and the ability to deal effectively with quantitative information is necessary for advanced work in most of the social sciences. All too often, however, introductory statistics courses in the social sciences are the stepchildren of curricula, and

F. S. Weaver (ed.). *Promoting Inquiry in Undergraduate Learning.*
New Directions for Teaching and Learning, no. 38. San Francisco: Jossey-Bass, Summer 1989.

teachers as well as students become involved in these courses only with the greatest reluctance.

The central argument of this chapter is that much of the pall that hangs over such courses is due to the effort to move students too quickly into sophisticated levels of quantitative analysis, at the expense of a thorough grounding in the uses of descriptive statistics (tabular and graphic presentations, properties of averages and other summary statistics, and so on). This haste seriously limits pedagogical possibilities and impedes the inquiry potential of introductory statistics courses in the social sciences.

When more time is spent on descriptive statistics, important skills are imparted and the whole enterprise can be defined and implemented around a set of substantive questions capable of drawing students into the study: An introductory statistics course can be a content course, in which important dimensions of social life are studied through quantitative methods. On that method side, the course is where students confront the realization that quantitative data most certainly do not speak for themselves, and that the same body of data can be (and often is) used to support divergent conclusions that are meaningful for social inquiry.

At a more ambitious level, quantitative materials are especially useful for demonstrating, in a tangible and readily comprehensible fashion, the differences among various kinds of knowing, as well as the imperative of clearly distinguishing among different analytical levels of generality. Another aspect is to help students appreciate the extent to which the selection of what is counted, as well as the very categories in which data are collected and presented, necessarily contains premises, limits the types of questions that can be addressed to the data, and influences the range of answers deemed plausible. These goals are clearly integral to the promotion of educational goals related to critical inquiry.

This approach to statistics, which involves the effort to encourage habits of systematic, critical quantitative thinking through focusing on descriptive statistics, opens up pedagogical formats conducive to convincing students that learning requires continuous and active involvement by them, as well as by the teacher. While the "cookbook" statistics course is a familiar and probably not undeserved caricature, there is no more need for the statistics teacher's function to be reduced to the mere pouring of inert knowledge into passive students than there is in any other field.

When an introductory statistics course stresses the interpretive latitude permitted and required by the quantitative evidence germane to a meaningful question, and even when the boundaries of that latitude are continually stressed, it can introduce students both to the means and to the desire for creating their own interpretations of quantitative evidence and intelligently criticizing others' uses of it. This is more likely to be feasible and rewarding when there is a focus on descriptive statistics and substantive questions, more than on sophisticated statistical techniques.

Numbers and Inquiry

An introductory statistics course is a common requirement for under-graduate economics, psychology, and sociology majors. Even when it is not required, it is frequently recommended for these and other majors. Introductory statistics courses, however, as already noted, are too often viewed as necessary nuisances. While the quantitative skills taught in them are valued for advanced work in the disciplines, the benefits of those skills are realized only elsewhere, and the courses are too often taken and taught only under duress.

I have already asserted that a strong emphasis on descriptive statistics is the best way for an introductory course to achieve broader educational aims for students. While this remains my principal point, there are also strong pedagogical reasons for emphasizing descriptive statistics, even for the more limited goals of disciplinary majors. To address both inquiry education and skills acquisition in a suitably concrete manner, I will focus on the teaching of statistics in one social science—economics. I have chosen economics because it is the discipline I know best, and because the tendencies I have observed in the teaching materials for intro-ductory economics statistics are discernible from a survey of forty-three introductory statistics books in the social sciences (but see Huff, 1954, and Zeisel, 1968, lively books on descriptive statistics for general audiences).

In the introductory statistics course for economics majors, the primary goals in the methodological realm should be a solid introduction to handling and reasoning from descriptive statistics (including the signifi-cance of the categories in which data are collected and presented), to the advantages of different ways in which such statistics can be presented for particular purposes, and to the available sources of systematically col-lected and published economic data.

Instead of starting a course with throwing dice and flipping coins, my experience suggests that there is no substitute for devoting the first few weeks to having students experiment with different tabular and graphic arrangements of data, to increase their ability to use tables and graphs effectively and to appreciate problems of construction and inter-pretation. Through this experience, students should become familiar with how the purpose of displaying data governs the selection of empirical information; with the need to use care with units of measure and their time dimensions (for example, stocks versus flows); with the proper use of averages, measures of dispersion, percentages, index numbers, and so on; and, not quite parallel, with a calculator and perhaps a computer terminal.

These exercises need not be as deadening as they sound, and this is where the content of the course is important. For example, a very large portion of the course might be devoted to income distribution. After some preliminary readings that make various arguments about the distribution of earned income, the teacher can make available sets of figures on wages and salaries for a number of years, cross-classified by industrial and occupational groupings and by race, age, gender, region, and so on. Right away, the teacher can demonstrate, in specific and interesting ways, a variety of techniques for displaying data to illuminate various changes over time, while at the same time introducing the classification schemes by which industrial, occupational, and other data are arranged, all in the context of questions that are worth pursuing through numbers.

After students have been initiated in this manner, price indexes can be introduced, to deflate nominal figures, and used to compare averages over time. The choice of which price indexes are appropriate for this purpose necessarily involves a discussion of coverage, the relative weights given to individual prices, basing periods in which comparisons are made, and other construction problems with direct carry-overs to quantity indexes.

For here, it is an easy step to go beyond wage and salary figures by broadening the assigned reading, circulating data on the distribution of income among families and individuals, and constructing a host of statistical indicators on income distribution, including graphic devices (the Lorenz curve is a favorite).

Meaningful Questions

Again, it cannot be overemphasized that these explorations should be guided by provocative, nontrivial questions on which the data can shed some light. Readings and class discussions will generate a number of plausible ideas. By using a simple device like shift-share analysis, students can try to determine how greatly differences in income are affected by different variables.

From this work, several questions arise naturally: In defining family income, why use the category of Personal Income rather than that of Disposable Income? What difference does it make? Why have these aggregates constituted changing proportions of Gross National Product and of National Income over time? Such concepts and the significance of alternatives should be explored.

After the treatment of national income aggregates, it is feasible to explore national income accounts. By this time, students should be able to look at a wide variety of data presentations and be able to discern what they are about. Thus, they will be ready for input-output tables, flow-of-funds accounts, industrial concentration ratios, and leading indicators of economic activity. With some additional discussion of sampling techniques, they should also deal easily with such survey data as unemployment figures. It cannot be overemphasized that throughout the course, these explorations should be guided by provocative, nontrivial questions on which the data can shed light.

The use of meaningful questions not only helps sustain students' interest in the whole endeavor but is also a means by which students themselves can make arguments and interpretations from the data, without getting distracted by technical considerations or mechanical rules. Furthermore, they must get acquainted with several different sources of economic data. Useful references for these purposes include the *Statistical Abstract of the U.S.*, the *Historical Statistics* volumes, the *Economic Report of the President*, the *Survey of Current Business*, the *Federal Reserve Bulletin*, the *Monthly Labor Review*, and perhaps some census data, including industrial censuses and other surveys by the U.S. Department of Commerce. For international and comparative data, the United Nations' *Statistical Yearbook* and *Demographic Yearbook*, the International Monetary Fund's *International Financial Statistics*, and the World Bank's *World Development Report* are widely available and easily used by undergraduates. (For sources of statistics appropriate to introductory courses, see Wasserman and Bernero, 1977, an extensive and easily used index. The U.S. Congressional Information Service publishes two comprehensive annual indexes, *American Statistical Index* and *Statistical Reference Index*. Students will probably need a reference librarian's help in using either of these complex indexes.)

At any one of several points in the course, students can be exposed to the ideas of probable association between variables (through Phillips curves or cross-sectional versus time-series consumption functions), correlation and causation, frequency distributions, and elementary economic modeling and estimation procedures. The major point here is that this should be done only after students have acquired a sound understanding of descriptive statistics that makes these topics less abstract, serves as an excellent background for an advanced course in econometrics and forecasting, and is immediately applicable to such other aspects of college life as writing term papers or reading newspapers.

Results

It is always gratifying to find underlying harmonies of interest, and the qualities that make descriptive statistics useful for furthering inquiry education also contribute to specialized disciplinary study. By treating descriptive statistics in more than a casual and abbreviated manner, teachers provide a vital pedagogical step for students' comprehension of the more sophisticated quantitative methods essential for advanced study in the social sciences. In economics, confidence in handling descriptive statistics is necessary before students can attach meaning to even such elementary calculations as single-equation least squares and correlation coefficients. Without sufficient care in the more pedestrian realm of data organization and presentation, the idea of fitting a line to a series of data points is extremely abstract for many students. In defense, they learn by rote and avoid more active engagement with quantitative work.

An introductory statistics course, organized around a series of substantive questions, should serve as an initiation into the substance of the discipline for those who will continue their study of the discipline. It ought to be where students learn vitally important quantitative measures, empirical magnitudes of social processes, ways to find reliable data on their own, and first-order issues involved in applying theoretical frameworks to data. The focus on descriptive statistics and on content is necessary to create in students the inquiring habits of mind that will help them in advanced study and research.

At least as important as moving ahead in the study of a discipline, however, is that students, as citizens, will continually have to confront quantitative claims by advertisers and the overwhelming volume of economic data so assiduously reported in the mass media. In addition, citizens are frequently required to assess important arguments purportedly based on quantitative data concerning age, race, gender, family structure, marital status, religion, area of residence, migration, health, crime, public-sector activities, educational attainment, intelligence, voting patterns, and so on. In all of this, the capacity to handle, interpret, and find data on the descriptive level will significantly contribute to people's ability to function as informed citizens capable of independent judgments about what is "proved" by statistics. The confidence, responsible skepticism, and critical patterns of thought acquired in an inquiry course are likely to make them willing to do so, and to lead to their active involvement.

References

Cullen, M. J. *The Statistical Movement in Early Victorian Britain: The Foundations of Empirical Social Research.* New York: Barnes and Noble, 1975.

Huff, D. *How to Lie with Statistics.* New York: Norton, 1954.

Wasserman, P., and Bernero, J. (eds.). *Statistics Sources.* (5th ed.) Detroit, Mich.: Gale, 1977.

Zeisel, H. *Say It with Figures.* (5th ed.) New York: Harper & Row, 1968.

Frederick Stirton Weaver, professor of economics and history, taught at the University of California, Santa Cruz, before joining the Hampshire College faculty in 1971. His B.A. is from the University of California, Berkeley, and his Ph.D. from Cornell University. His principal teaching and research fields are the economic history and development of Latin America.

Teaching research skills is a necessary step, but only the first one in a bibliographical instruction program.

Turning Them Loose in the Library

Helaine Selin

> *"Remember first to possess his books: for without them he's but a sot . . ."*
>
> (The Tempest, *Act III, Sc. 2)*

Colleges that aspire to promote the development of students' critical, independent intellects must have library programs that encourage students to pursue active research, which entails going beyond the acquisition of information and bibliographies. Librarians should enhance students' critical understanding of their fields by helping them to see that there are alternative sources of information and interpretation for every issue. The inquiry curriculum places a double responsibility on the librarian, just as it does on any other teacher.

First, the librarian must help establish basic research skills, enabling students to find their way in the pertinent indexes, bibliographies, electronic data bases, and so on. The first step, of course, is to convince students of the need for well-developed bibliographical skills. After several fairly conventional approaches, we began developing a vigorous bibliographical instruction program in the late 1970s, a program that continues to be our principal means for introducing students to library use. Bibliographical instruction is increasingly recognized as a very effective mode of

F. S. Weaver (ed.). *Promoting Inquiry in Undergraduate Learning.*
New Directions for Teaching and Learning, no. 38. San Francisco: Jossey-Bass, Summer 1989.

teaching research skills. Its importance for inquiry education, as well as our distinctive approach to it, warrant devoting the first section of this chapter to describing what we do. The second part deals with another aspect of bibliographical instruction important for an inquiry curriculum, an aspect that is unique to inquiry education and that seldom has been explored in the library and educational literature: the librarian's role in helping students recognize the methodological disputes, diverse interpretations, and conflicting findings that abound in scholarship about all serious intellectual questions. Moreover, students should appreciate the extent to which organization and availability of information influence the direction of their own research. These two dimensions of bibliographical instruction are conceptually distinct, but they are closely related: You must master research skills before you can tackle the second dimension of library teaching.

Teaching Research Skills

Bibliographical instruction is a relatively new approach to teaching research skills. While it may include general information, such as what part of the collection is found where and whom to ask about getting reserve books, its major purpose is to teach research strategies—how to proceed from an idea to a useful bibliography, and how to acquire the needed materials. It is very different from a library tour, a library orientation seminar, and other such devices, which we found inadequate for our students' educational needs.

In this new approach, one of the first changes we made was to reorganize the reference librarians' responsibilities. Each librarian is now responsible for instruction, collection development, and general liaison for one of the college's four schools. Faculty members, too, are directly involved in the selection and evaluation of reference librarians. A key ingredient of success is the establishment of the librarians' academic credibility in the eyes of the faculty.

The faculty also created a freshman seminar (or proseminar) program. Every first-year student enrolls in one of the proseminars, which combine a narrow focus on subject matter (for instance, the biology of young women) with an introduction to the divisional examination system and a strong emphasis on writing and research skills. Now that library sources and research methods are an explicit part of proseminars, we simply call faculty members to schedule sessions. The timing of this change in the curriculum for first-year students was fortunate, but bibliographical instruction would not have survived in the proseminars if the faculty had not found the library's contribution valuable.

For each session with students, our procedure is to draw up a research guide for the individual course, meet with the class, and go over the material in the guide. We do some annotation, so that students can remember which source is which, but most of the description is oral. For each guide, we choose a subject as if we were going to do research and write a paper. (For the course in young women's biology, we might choose a topic like vitamin therapy for premenstrual syndrome.) We then spend an hour describing our choice of subject headings, how to use our computerized catalogue to find books on the subject, and how to choose relevant indexes and find journal articles.

We attribute some of our success to each library presentation's combining three crucially important elements. The first is timing. We want to schedule our sessions after students have settled into an academic routine, but before they have begun any extensive research projects without us. We want to catch them at a time when they can appreciate research tools' value to their pursuit of interesting questions. At this stage, by showing the ease and rewards of finding interesting material on challenging topics, we significantly increase students' motivation and commitment.

This kind of presentation necessitates close contact with the faculty. For best results, the librarian is scheduled and mentioned in the syllabus; faculty members attend sessions; and during the first two or three weeks of the term, faculty members let the librarian know about projects being planned and students' research needs.

A second element is specificity. We try, for example, never to introduce undergraduate students to the variety of resources available in United States labor history; we will, however, go into great detail on the subject of women's work in the late nineteenth century in the United States. Such specificity is encouraged, even required, by the organization of the proseminars, but we are convinced that it is also a pedagogical necessity for bibliographical instruction. It is much easier to observe the process of information retrieval in one specific area and apply it to another than it is to work from lists of general sources whose relevance is questionable and whose scope is confusing.

The third element, relevance, is actually an extension of the first two: For our examples, we choose topics that some of the students already have said are interesting to them. We avoid hypothetical questions. We never ask anyone to find out which European capital begins with the letter O or how many American households use electric garbage disposals. In an upper-division course on environmental science and politics, for example, we might discuss finding sources on environmental effects of incineration. In this way, at least for some students, the guide and presentation are directly matched with research needs. For the others, the focus is so closely related that many of the sources will be the same, and the process of information retrieval is similar.

Beyond Research Skills

The development of research skills through bibliographical instruction is imperative in a curriculum that requires students to be active participants in their own education and to conduct numerous and extensive independent research projects. Librarians at Hampshire College go another step in encouraging critical inquiry by students: We help students understand that researching a complex question will inevitably involve their having to confront a range of interpretations and conflicting findings. This understanding is extremely important, but it is a less tangible goal than the research-skills side of bibliographical instruction, and it does not lend itself so well to how-to-do-it descriptions.

To perform well in this function, the librarian must be aware of the nature of the materials that students are finding and are likely to find. In the social sciences and the humanities, the librarian explicitly identifies the methodological or political points of view represented by various publishers and journals. In the sciences, where there may be less methodological plurality, there is certainly not complete consensus about the proper questions, procedures, and interpretations of research. In searching for bibliographical materials in the sciences, the librarian can make students aware of debates about research findings, debates informed by criticisms of research designs and by diverse interpretations of findings or theories. Hampshire students are expected to think analytically, and they should also think that way about the search for information. Scientific research is not one-dimensional, and its difference from research in the humanities and the social sciences is more a matter of degree than of kind.

We also carry out this type of instruction while responding to individual reference questions, of course. What is most effective, however, is to let students hear such information first, and to explain its importance in the context of bibliographical instruction. Timing, specificity, and relevance are at least as important in stimulating students to explore the variety of arguments and data as they are for helping students acquire research skills. A central aim in bibliographical instruction, then, is to get students to incorporate a variety of points of view into their research, rather than ignore that variety and flatten out the interpretive character of the research. Faculty members' contributions during bibliographical sessions are also especially helpful in this effort.

Bibliographical instruction has yet another dimension that librarians can incorporate into their teaching. Students engaged in research must think about the selectivity of publishers' lists and libraries' collections, which tend to reflect and emphasize certain points of view more than others. This does raise interesting and important questions about the dominant modes of research and interpretation, and about how the availability of research materials shapes and restricts students' research in specific ways. (The librarian may be well advised to be cautious about opening this particular box and about how wide open is expedient.)

What all this means is that the librarian deliberately leads students to understand that researching an important issue is more complicated, interesting, and rewarding than merely searching out a putative "right answer." The librarian's work with students has to reinforce this stance, which is promoted by faculty members in their courses. $\mathcal{240320}$

Results

The type of bibliographical instruction outlined in this chapter is not easy. At the most immediate level, it is very time-consuming. During the middle of the semester, one of us may have as many as five classes per week, each one requiring the researching and writing of a guide, the gathering of material, and the presentation (which usually lasts an hour and a half). Each session requires five or six hours of preparation if the course is new (and many Hampshire courses do change every semester or year), and two or three hours even when most of the guide from a previous course can be used.

The need to show students the multifaceted nature of research means that each librarian must stay conversant, at least in a general way, with the substance and forums of major research currents and debates in her or his field of responsibility. This requires continual reading, staying in touch with the faculty, and attending faculty seminars and school meetings.

No one should have any illusions about the amount of effort this type of program entails, but the rewards are substantial. Students really do improve their knowledge of and familiarity with the world of scholarship. One obvious indicator is the sheer volume of library use among Hampshire students, who, on a per-student basis, consistently borrow library books and materials at a rate well over twice that of students at other institutions in the Five College Consortium. This fact reflects the nature of the Hampshire program, which requires so much independent research and in which few courses rely on textbooks, but we think it is reasonable to believe that it also reflects our effectiveness as bibliographical instructors.

The number and quality of the reference questions posed to librarians is another index of students' competence in using the library. Another aspect of the rewards is that bibliographical instruction establishes an initial relationship with students that encourages them to work closely with us, sometimes over several years, on the substance of their projects. Such direct involvement with teaching and learning, which includes helping students reframe their questions in order to encompass a variety of perspectives and use available research sources, is very important to us. As a consequence of these activities, we have the satisfaction of working in a library that is used extensively and well, and we are truly central to the educational program.

Helaine Selin, science librarian at Hampshire College since 1978, has an A.B. from the State University of New York, Binghamton, and an M.L.S. from the State University of New York, Albany. She has been a science librarian at the University of Georgia and the State University of New York, Purchase.

Index

A. F. Lucas, (ed.). *The Department Chairperson's Role in Enhancing College Teaching.*
New Directions for Teaching and Learning, no. 37. San Francisco, Jossey-Bass, Spring 1989.

ERRATA

p. i:

The editor's affiliation should read as follows: *Fairleigh Dickinson University.*

p. ii:

The Library of Congress Catalog Card Number should be LC 85-644763.